GRAVES
of Upstate New York

Chuck D'Imperio

GRAVES
of Upstate New York

A GUIDE TO 100 NOTABLE RESTING PLACES

SECOND EDITION

SYRACUSE UNIVERSITY PRESS

Copyright © 2018 by Syracuse University Press
Syracuse, New York 13244-5290

All Rights Reserved

Second Edition 2018

18 19 20 21 22 23   6 5 4 3 2 1

First edition published as *"Great Graves of Upstate New York!"*: *The Upstate
New York Final Resting Places of 70 True American Legends!* (2006).

∞ The paper used in this publication meets the minimum requirements
of the American National Standard for Information Sciences—Permanence
of Paper for Printed Library Materials, ANSI Z39.48–1992.

For a listing of books published and distributed by Syracuse University Press,
visit www.SyracuseUniversityPress.syr.edu.

ISBN: 978-0-8156-3575-8 (hardcover)
978-0-8156-1097-7 (paperback)
978-0-8156-5440-7 (e-book)

Library of Congress Cataloging-in-Publication Data

Available from publisher upon request.

Manufactured in the United States of America

*This book is dedicated to my beautiful,
talented, and brilliant granddaughter—*

REESE HONOUR CASSAVAUGH

*It is my greatest hope that as you grow up you will question,
you will be fascinated, you will be fascinating,
you will be compassionate,
and you will always, always . . . persist!*

CHUCK D'IMPERIO is a longtime, award-winning radio broadcaster, newspaper journalist, and author of nine Upstate New York books. He has been on the air at Townsquare Media in Oneonta, New York, since 1989. He writes a popular column for the *Oneonta Daily Star* newspaper, and he has written hundreds of articles for publication over the last quarter century. His Facebook blog, *A Taste of Upstate New York*, is one of the most followed of its kind with approximately one-hundred thousand readers. Chuck is a prolific author, with the focus of his books mostly on his native Upstate New York. Among his books currently in print are *Monumental New York*, *Unknown Museums of Upstate New York*, and *A Taste of Upstate New York* (all by Syracuse University Press). He is also the author of *Upstate Uncovered* (SUNY Press). Chuck is married to Trish, an educator, and they are the parents of Frances, Katie, Abby, and Joey. The author lives (of course) in Upstate New York.

CONTENTS

Part Six: HUDSON VALLEY/WESTCHESTER

Part Seven: CAPITAL DISTRICT AND SARATOGA REGION

INTRODUCTION

*I*f you saw Lucille Ball picking over some produce in a Hollywood grocery store, would you go over and ask her for a photograph? If you saw singer Kate Smith ensconced in a corner booth at the Lake Placid Howard Johnson's enjoying a stack of blueberry pancakes, would you go over and introduce yourself? If you saw boxer Floyd Patterson pumping gas next to you, would you go over and ask him to sign an autograph for you? I think the answer to all of these and more is a no.

What is it about celebrities? We follow their lives voraciously in the press and watch for their every move to be documented. We "love" them from afar. We enjoy them; sometimes we even worship them. But none of us would feel very at ease actually confronting them face to face for a personal greeting. We are too shy, too embarrassed, too in awe to be in their presence. I am the same way.

But to visit a celebrity's gravesite is something completely different, and that is what *Graves of Upstate New York* is all about. In this book I have chronicled the final resting places of one hundred famous and infamous names from our past. Each chapter gives explicit directions to the person's grave and also offers up a little information about the celebrity who is buried there.

Each gravesite is in Upstate New York, and I have been to all of them.

There is something comforting about visiting Lucille Ball or Kate Smith or Thomas E. Dewey's grave. Or George Armstrong Custer's or Rod Serling's or Susan B. Anthony's. Or many others. It is a private act, a personal one. To walk through the woods and come upon a gravestone that reads "William Morgan: Inventor of Volleyball," or even to find a memorial epitaph that reads "Congresswoman Shirley Chisholm: Unbought and

Unbossed" can be a humbling experience. To visit each of these grave sites is to take one hundred mini-pilgrimages down the footpaths of history.

Sometimes we are there to say thank you—for example, at the grave of one of the most awarded actresses of our time, Maureen Stapleton. Oh, the enjoyment that woman gave America over a fifty-year career. Sometimes we are there to be a part of history, albeit a tiny sliver of it. Like when visiting the grave of Sybil Ludington, the female Paul Revere. Or sometimes a visit to a grave allows one a private little smile as if to say, "Now that is quite a story." You will no doubt feel that way at the grave of Exterminator, one of the Kentucky Derby's most unlikely and most beloved champions. Yes, each of these celebrities is buried in Upstate New York, and they are all in this book.

Graves of Upstate New York is not an encyclopedic, biographical journal. It was not meant to be that. And besides, with a mere thousand words or so allotted for each of the one hundred chapters, there simply was no room for me to describe the subtle nuances of John Burroughs's lifetime love affair with nature, or to describe the dozens of personal statistics posted by heroes like Ernie Davis, Johnny Podres, or any of the other sports stars in these pages. How much more can I add to the story of Franklin D. Roosevelt's historic four terms, or to the life and legacy of Susan B. Anthony or Frederick Douglass? Not much in a thousand words or less. So for that reason I stuck to information on where they are buried in Upstate New York. Yes, the chapters mention some of the most familiar highlights of each person's life, but my goal is to get you up and out on the road to visit the famous people buried in Upstate's gorgeous and historic cemeteries.

As with all of my previous Upstate New York books, I offer a gentle reminder: For the sake of simple geography, I recognize Upstate as being anywhere in New York State that is up and out of New York City. I fully recognize that this defies the preference of many purists who like to segment our state into a never-ending series of regions, but for the simplicity of the subject (and the title of this book) I hope you will allow me to use the term Upstate New York generously and very loosely. Trust me, as a person born in Delaware County, who went to college in Albany County, and who now resides in Otsego County, I am fully aware of where Upstate New York really is.

So come and say hello to the famous residents who slumber eternally under Upstate's beautiful skies. You will meet four US presidents, the real Niagara Maid of the Mist, a Woman Called Moses, the Yankee Leaper, the Brewer Philanthropist, Joe the Barber, the Padre of the Poor, the Catskills' Innkeeper, the Strongest Man in Washington's Army, the Human Bomb, the Wickedest Woman in New York, and the most famous one-legged tap dancer in the world. And they are all right here in Upstate New York.

I hope you enjoy these one hundred totally fascinating and totally unforgettable Upstate stories.

Part One

WESTERN NEW YORK

1

SUSAN B. ANTHONY

1820–1906

"FAILURE IS IMPOSSIBLE"
BURIED IN ROCHESTER,
MONROE COUNTY

Susan Brownell Anthony was born February 15, 1820, in Adams, Massachusetts. She was the second of eight children born to a strict Quaker family. Her father, Daniel, believed in total dedication from his children, but not necessarily to reading and writing. His hand came down heavily on self-discipline, moral integrity, a principled lifestyle, and a zeal for justice and equality for all. Young Susan taught herself to read and write by the age of three and was homeschooled thereafter. Her private teacher was Miss Mary Perkins, and it was through Perkins that a young, growing Anthony would gain her confidence and independence. After all, Perkins was a rarity—a female teacher in a "man's profession." Anthony progressed through her education and became a teacher herself in several different schools before settling in the Rochester area.

Ms. Anthony met Elizabeth Cady Stanton in Seneca Falls, New York, in 1851. From this meeting came a decades-long association and bond in which the two women acted as the most prominent figures in the women's rights movement in the United States. In 1869, they helped organize the National Woman Suffrage Association in an effort to bring women the right to vote. During the 1872 presidential election, Anthony was actually arrested for trying to vote. She died fourteen years before the right for women to vote was secured in 1920. On August 18, 1920, the Susan B.

Anthony Amendment became the Nineteenth Amendment to the US Constitution.

Anthony died on March 13, 1906, at her home in Rochester. She was eighty-six.

Grave Location: Mount Hope Cemetery is filled with many familiar names of famous Americans. Anthony's grave is much visited, and signs will point you to her final resting place in Section C, Lot 93.

Author's Note: The great abolitionist Frederick Douglass is also buried in this cemetery (and featured in this book). Anthony and Douglass were contemporaries, friends, and neighbors. There is a wonderful double bronze statue of these two legendary Americans located near the Susan B. Anthony Home and Museum in Rochester. The depiction shows these two famous people doing something rather innocuous, sitting and sharing a cup of tea.

Factoid: Anthony's grave gained national recognition during the presidential election of 2016. With Hillary Clinton running for president, hundreds of supporters found their way to Anthony's grave site to place their "I Voted" stickers on Anthony's grave. So many people came to do this that television cameras were set up to broadcast this outpouring of support for both Clinton and Anthony.

For More Information: National Susan B. Anthony Museum and House, susanbanthonyhouse.org.

2

FATHER NELSON BAKER

1842–1936

PADRE OF THE POOR
BURIED IN LACKAWANNA,
ERIE COUNTY

There is no more incongruous sight in Upstate New York than what the unsuspecting visitor to 767 Ridge Road finds amid the blue-collar ordinariness of Lackawanna, New York: a church like no other rising gloriously over the suburban landscape. The sight is jolting. The majestic towering cathedral is a powerful symbol of faith, a monument to the memory of the life of a true servant of God. The church is the Basilica of Our Lady of Victory National Shrine, and the man it memorializes is Father Nelson Baker, the Padre of the Poor.

On a return trip from a papal visit in 1874, he stopped at the famous Shrine of Our Lady of Victory in Paris. This visit set into motion a dream of his to build a giant American shrine to the Blessed Mother that would rival any house of worship in the world. With the help of thousands of contributors worldwide, his dream came true in 1926. Father Baker's $3 million cathedral has since been judged to be one of the most beautiful churches in the United States. Guarded by four eighteen-foot angels, the building is awe-inspiring in its sweeping grandeur. Inside the great bronze doors are several priceless French stained-glass windows, dozens of imported African mahogany pews, life-sized marble statues of all the saints, an exact replica in size and detail of the Grotto of Lourdes plus an eight-ton statue of Our Lady of Victory (Blessed Virgin Mary).

In 1882, when Father Baker became the head of St. John's Protectory (a Buffalo orphanage), he was shocked to hear of baby bones being

Father Nelson Baker. With permission of Our Lady of Victory Institutions, Inc.

dredged up from the muddy bottom of the local section of the Erie Canal. He was determined to open the orphanage's doors to anyone who needed assistance, regardless of means or situation. He took in stray boys and gave them vocational training, and he founded an Infant Home that became the largest adoption center east of the Mississippi. He opened avenues of hope to hundreds of young girls when he established a Maternity Home for Unwed Mothers. He also provided learning centers for the handicapped, a segment of society quickly forgotten in the late 1800s. It was Father Baker's intention to leave no need unfilled, and soon his City of Charity was the largest of its kind in the United States.

The declaration of a basilica denotes a "place of special beauty and historical significance," and the only way a church can be identified as such is to have it so declared by official apostolic decree. Just two months after completion of his dream church, Father Baker witnessed its renaming by Pope Pius XI to the Basilica of Our Lady of Victory. It is only the second church to be deemed so in America.

Father Baker's Infant Home was always left unlocked at night, with an empty crib standing just inside the front door. Many desperate young mothers anonymously placed their newborns in that crib, entrusting the care of their infants to Father Baker's organization. It is estimated that more than 50,000 orphans passed through the doors of his Infant Home.

Father Nelson Baker died on July 29, 1936, at the age of ninety-five. Over a half million people attended the funeral services at the basilica, a service that was officiated over by seven hundred priests. Many in the crowd of mourners that day were "Baker Boys," orphans who had received a second chance at life due to the kindness of the Padre of the Poor.

In the summer of 1987, the Congregation for the Causes of the Saints approved the initiation of Father Baker's path to sainthood and forever bestowed upon him the title "Servant of God."

Grave Location: Father Baker was originally buried in Holy Cross Cemetery, which abuts his basilica. Here, among the graves of early Irish immigrants who dug the Erie Canal, built the railroads, worked the docks, and built the Great Lakes steamships, Baker rested for over six decades. Today, however, you will find his tomb inside the Our Lady of Victory Basilica in a special crypt.

Author's Note: More than twenty thousand people a year visit the basilica to pray at Father Baker's tomb. In 1999, in an effort to make this site more accessible to those who travelled far to pay their respects, basilica authorities decided to exhume his body and reinter him inside the basilica. Amazingly, the cemetery workers who dug up his coffin were stunned to find a small container on top of his original coffin. Upon opening the miniature casket on top, church officials found three mysterious vials of liquid. These sealed vials were taken to a laboratory for analysis, and it was discovered that they contained Father Baker's own blood. Blood in liquid form some six decades later. Certainly a mystery.

This finding no doubt accelerated the canonization process of one of the most popular Catholic priests of the twentieth century. Six elderly orphans who had lived in Baker's orphanage as children were summoned to carry the coffin of their mentor into the church and place it in its new resting place.

Father Baker's masterpiece, the Our Lady of Victory Shrine and Basilica, is one of Upstate New York's most stunning houses of worship.

The photograph accompanying this chapter is of a life-sized bronze statue of Father Baker that stands across the street, as if he is gazing at his church. Although the basilica is open to the public, I did not take a photograph of Baker's final resting place inside because of the solemnity of the site.

Factoid: Tours of this magnificent basilica are offered at 1:00 and 2:00 p.m. every Sunday. A museum dedicated to the life of Father Nelson Baker takes up the entire lower floor of the basilica.

For More Information: Our Lady of Victory National Shrine and Basilica, www.ourladyofvictory.org.

3

LUCILLE BALL

1911–1989

I LOVE LUCY
BURIED IN JAMESTOWN,
CHAUTAUQUA COUNTY

Lucille Ball was the undisputed Queen of Comedy. She was born in and raised around Celoron, New York, just outside of Jamestown. She lived for more than a half century in Hollywood, where she became an iconic figure on the entertainment scene. She died in 1989 and was buried in Forest Lawn ("Cemetery of the Stars") in Los Angeles. The call to return home was just too great, and she was reinterred in Lake View Cemetery in Jamestown in 2003. Today, she rests eternally with her beloved mother (Desiree, who died in 1977 at eighty-five) and her father (Henry, who died at age twenty-eight in 1915). On her gravestone, below her name, it reads, "You've Come Home."

It is pointless to try to list every great Lucy moment, for really, we all know each and every one of them—the stomping on the Italian grapes, dressing as Superman with actor George Reeves, trying to keep up with a maniacal candy conveyor belt, getting drunk while shilling a vitamin elixir, and on and on. So, rather than go over familiar information, I'll offer some interesting tidbits you might not know about Lucille Ball.

She made over one hundred films, from *The Bowery* (1933) to her acclaimed final performance in *Stone Pillow* (1985, at age seventy-four). Appropriately, one of her Hollywood Walk of Fame stars is for her movie work (it is located at 6436 Hollywood Boulevard). On TV she was one of the medium's most durable superstars, from *I Love Lucy* (1951), to *The*

Lucy-Desi Comedy Hour (1957), to *The Lucy Show* (1962) to *Here's Lucy* (1968), and finally to *Life with Lucy* (1986). So it is also appropriate that another of her Hollywood Walk of Fame stars is for her television work (it is located at 6104 Hollywood Boulevard).

Ball won a warehouse full of show business awards over her forty-year career. These include four Emmy Awards, plus the Kennedy Center Honors Award. She was inducted into the National Women's Hall of Fame, the National Comedy Hall of Fame, and the Television Hall of Fame.

She was famous for inviting her celebrity friends to appear on her popular TV shows, and they all eagerly accepted those invitations. Milton Berle and Tennessee Ernie Ford made five appearances each, Ann Sothern and Jack Benny six each, and Carol Burnett—perhaps Lucy's closest celebrity girlfriend—appeared seven times on Lucy's shows. Lucille Ball was the first woman to own her own studio (Desilu) and was a powerhouse to be reckoned with in television's infancy. When Lucy gave birth to her son, Desi Jr., a record 44 million viewers followed Mom's pregnancy right up to his arrival episode ("Lucy Goes to the Hospital," January 19, 1953).

Ball split from her husband and costar Desi Arnaz in 1960, and she later married comic Gary Morton, who survived her.

Lucille Ball remained active right up until the end. Her last public appearance came on March 29, 1989, when she and Bob Hope presented the Best Picture Oscar at the Sixty-Second Academy Awards ceremony. Lucy was a classic Hollywood trouper to the end. She died just four weeks later of a ruptured aorta.

Grave Location: Lucille Ball is buried in Lake View Cemetery in Jamestown. The cemetery is fully aware that throngs of visitors wish to visit Lucy's grave to say thank you for her many years of entertaining us. Tiny hearts are tattooed on the roadway leading from the main entrance to her final resting place in the Highland section. Visitors come by almost every day. Her headstone displays the iconic pink heart on the front, similar to the heart that opened her *I Love Lucy* show for many years. The back of her stone lists fellow family members who are interred in the plot. Her name is listed as Lucille Desiree Ball Morton. There is no mention of Desi Arnaz.

Author's Note: Jamestown is now famous as the host of the Lucille Ball Desi Arnaz Museum and Center for Comedy. At this interesting museum you can see many artifacts and memorabilia from Lucy's extensive show business career and several funny, unforgettable comedy clips from her shows. One of the most popular is her classic "Vitameatavegamin" commercial. A real head-turner is Lucy's monogrammed 1972 gold-plated Mercedes Benz 280SE. The museum holds several major Lucy-themed events each year, culminating in a giant Lucy festival that attracts thousands of visitors.

Factoid: When Lucy had her baby it was national news. Little Desi Jr. appeared on the very first cover of *TV Guide* magazine, April 3, 1953. Lucy would eventually rack up a record thirty-one cover appearances.

For More Information: Lucy-Desi Center for Comedy, www.lucy -desi.com.

4

CONGRESSWOMAN
SHIRLEY CHISHOLM

1924–2005
"UNBOUGHT AND UNBOSSED"
BURIED IN BUFFALO,
ERIE COUNTY

*S*hirley Chisholm was born in New York City but was raised from an early age by relatives in Barbados. At the age of ten she relocated back to New York City, where she attended public schools in Brooklyn. She was a bright and inquisitive student who excelled in her classes and caught her teachers' eye. She was encouraged to apply for scholarship tuition help to attend a university to become a teacher herself. She was accepted at Brooklyn College and was a graduate there (cum laude) in 1946. She then entered the teaching world by running day care centers and formulating programs for early childhood development.

Chisholm's initial foray into public life came in the 1950s, and she successfully ran for the New York State Assembly in 1964. She fought hard for children and those living in poverty and was interested in bettering the life and careers of New York's female teachers. Four years after being elected to the state assembly, Chisholm defeated the powerful civil rights icon James Farmer in a race for Congress. The size of her historic victory, where she garnered almost three quarters of the vote, catapulted the diminutive firebrand toward an illustrious career in Washington that lasted until 1982. She became the first African American woman to serve in the US Congress. A strident critic of the Vietnam War, she took to

the floor of the House of Representatives on many occasions pleading for an end to the conflict which, in her opinion, was diverting money from important causes in the War on Poverty at home, as well as costing too many American lives in a conflict that was ill-defined from the start. She also helped found the Congressional Black Caucus and the National Organization of Women. During the Nixon administration, she was labeled a "political opponent" of the president, as revealed in the Nixon tape recordings.

Representative Chisolm's forceful personality initially rubbed many of the old lions in the US Congress the wrong way. When she received her first congressional committee appointment to the Agricultural Committee, the congresswoman declared it to be an insult to her home district in New York City, which was decidedly nonagrarian. After she took her complaint to the leaders of the House, she was reluctantly appointed to the Veterans' Affairs Committee. Always a clever wordsmith, Chisholm took to the House floor to state, "At least there are a lot more veterans in my district than trees."

In 1972, Shirley Chisholm made history by becoming the first announced black female candidate for the US presidency. Her platform included women's issues, prison reform, issues that dealt with inner city problems and, of course, her antiwar stance against the Vietnam conflict. During her campaign, she was an articulate and exciting figure on the stump and generated a great deal of enthusiasm from her younger, mostly black and female, base. Her slogan became the familiar "Unbought and Unbossed."

After the presidential election of 1972, she went back to the US House of Representatives and served until her retirement a decade later. She returned to her first career of education by accepting a teaching position at Mt. Holyoke College in Massachusetts.

After divorcing her first husband, Chisholm married Arthur Hardwick, a former New York State politician with roots in the Buffalo area in 1977. She spent the remainder of her life keeping a hectic speaking schedule (more than 150 college lectures in twenty-five years) as well as enjoying and curating her five thousand book library at her home in Williamsville, New York.

She died on New Year's Day 2005. She was eighty.

Grave Location: Congresswoman Chisholm is buried in Forest Lawn Cemetery, located at 1411 Delaware Avenue in Buffalo. Her final resting place can be found in the large, enclosed Beechwood Mausoleum. Her crypt can be seen in the second row down from the top, Row 158, Tier F. Her epitaph reads: "Unbought and Unbossed. Hon. Shirley Chisholm-Hardwick. November 30, 1924–January 1, 2005."

Author's Note: There are several mausoleums holding hundreds of burials in Forest Lawn. They are open to the public during regular hours. The office at the main entrance will provide you with directions not only to the Beechwood Mausoleum but also to the many other famous burials in this historic cemetery. The photograph accompanying this chapter is of the exterior of the Beechwood Mausoleum. I did not take a photograph of the interior out of respect for the solemnity of the location.

Factoid: President Barack Obama bestowed the Medal of Freedom upon Representative Chisholm posthumously on November 24, 2015. He said, "There are people in our country's history who don't look left or right—they just look straight ahead. Shirley Chisholm was one of those people. Shirley had guts!"

For More Information: US House of Representatives History, Art and Archives, "Chisholm, Shirley Anita," history.house.gov/People/Listing/C /CHISHOLM,-Shirley-Anita-(C000371)/.

FREDERICK DOUGLASS

1818–1895

EMANCIPATION'S VOICE
BURIED IN ROCHESTER,
MONROE COUNTY

*W*ith his fierce leonine look, his glowering eyes, his impeccably tailored clothes, and his "from Hell and back" thundering voice, Frederick Douglass was considered by many to be the most important African American figure of the nineteenth century. Born into slavery, he rose to the highest pinnacles of fame and notoriety as the voice of the antislavery movement in America.

In 1838 Douglass was living in bondage in the city of Baltimore when he decided it was time for him to join his brothers in the North in their fight against slavery. Maryland, at the time, required every black man to carry identification papers describing him accurately and stating his situation, free or owned. Douglass disguised himself as a sailor and endured a frightening twenty-four-hour flight to freedom in New York City. He would later recall that there were several times along his harrowing journey that he knew he had been recognized, but friends had remained silent and let him pass. He felt as if "God himself had let him escape from the den of hungry lions."

Douglass was publisher of the two most important antislavery publications of the day, *The North Star* and *The Frederick Douglass Paper*, which brought all the latest abolition news to the free and slave alike. His life did hold a certain degree of mystery to it. A few contradictions caused him great concern. A passionate fighter for the freeing of slaves, Douglass refused to

support John Brown's raid on Harper's Ferry and in fact denounced it. As the son of a black mother and a white father, his detractors called him a fraud as a civil rights spokesman. In 1845, he authored *The Narrative Life of Frederick Douglass, American Slave* to dispel any suspicions. After the publication of this work, and on the heels of John Brown's fiasco, he traveled to Europe, where he was welcomed as a great champion of emancipation. While he was there, a year later, his friends purchased his permanent freedom for 150 British pounds.

Douglass was a confidant of several US presidents, and Ulysses S. Grant appointed him to the position of US marshal for the District of Columbia, then to assistant secretary of Santo Domingo, and then to general consul in Haiti. He wrote two more well-received books, *My Bondage* (1855) and *The Life and Times of Frederick Douglass* (1881).

A powerful and important personality to the very end of his life, Frederick Douglass was mourned on a national scale when he passed on February 20, 1895.

Grave Location: Douglass was buried with great pomp and ceremony at Mt. Hope Cemetery, located at 1133 Mt. Hope Avenue in Rochester. Inside the cemetery make your first right, Fifth Avenue, and go through the second intersection. Douglass's grave is on your right. His plot overlooks the roadside fence. A plaque tells of his historic significance. His and Susan B. Anthony's graves (chapter 1 in this book) are the most visited in this famous cemetery.

Author's Note: This cemetery is the final resting place of many notables, and the cemetery office will provide you with a map to their graves.

Factoid: An eight-foot-tall bronze statue of Douglass stands in Rochester's Highland Park. It was dedicated in 1899. It was the first public statue in the country to honor an African American citizen.

For More Information: National Park Service, "Frederick Douglass," www.nps.gov/frdo/learn/historyculture/frederickdouglass.htm.

JOSEPH ELLICOTT

1760–1826

*THE GREAT SURVEYOR
BURIED IN BATAVIA,
GENESEE COUNTY*

*I*n the late 1700s, long before western New York was settled and before the Erie Canal was even in the planning stages, a group of Dutch bankers and financiers owned the hundreds of thousands of acres of wilderness from the center part of the state to Lake Erie's shore. In business to turn a quick profit, the company, known as the Holland Land Company, began selling off parcels in 1800 to those brave enough to explore the wilds of this rugged land. Treaties had to be handled delicately with the large number of Seneca Indians who had lived in the region for many years. And finally, boundaries and division lines had to be drawn up to give this sprawling tract of over three million acres of mostly forests some semblance of organization.

Joseph Ellicott had already enjoyed a successful career as a surveyor in Pennsylvania, and when the Holland Land Company hired him and his team to survey and record the land, he was clearly the man for the job. No expense was spared in this incredible endeavor, and Ellicott was meticulous in his work. He lived in the woods for several years plotting boundaries, journaling his discoveries, and creating a diary of everything from river depths to wildlife observations. The Holland Land Company spent $700,000 to have Ellicott's survey completed, and following the completion of the Great Survey, Ellicott was named chief agent for the selling and transferring of deeds to thousands of acres of western New York land.

Ellicott was a clever businessman who knew it would take more than just dramatic stories of the Wild West to coerce landowners to invest in this uncivilized place. He came up with generous installment plans for the purchase of parcels and plotted out areas to be inhabited, taking into consideration forest wood, cultivable land, proximity to rivers and water power, and harvest potential.

Ellicott was also an early supporter of the Erie Canal, and, recognizing that land along a proposed canal route would be of high value, saw to it that his company donated more than 100,000 acres of land to New York State, bringing the completion of the canal ever closer. The canal opened in 1825, and successful canal towns sprouted up along the water route from the Finger Lakes region to Lake Erie.

The master planner founded the city of Batavia, his home for many years. Ellicott also founded the city of Buffalo, designing it with an innovative series of eight street grids that radiated out from the hub of the city, much like the canals of the European city of Amsterdam. In fact, he named the city New Amsterdam. Locals stubbornly continued to refer to it as Buffalo, since it was near Buffalo Creek. Another inspiration for the concept of the city of Buffalo was Pierre L'Enfant's street grid plan for the nation's capital, Washington, DC.

Ellicott was a brilliant, imposing, six-foot three-inch pioneer who was more comfortable in the solitary confines of a wooded forest than he was in the center of a social whirlwind. He never married, and he suffered mental problems late in his life. In 1824, he was institutionalized in a New York City asylum, where he resided until he committed suicide on August 19, 1826. He left an estate valued at over $600,000, which was a sizable fortune in those days.

Many experts today credit Joseph Ellicott with the successful transformation of western New York from a rugged frontier into a well-thought-out, successful land of villages and small cities that contributed to making the Empire State one of the greatest economic stories of the early nineteenth century.

Grave Location: Ellicott is buried in Batavia Cemetery, located at 65 Harvester Street in Batavia. His grave is near the southern border of the cemetery. An American flag flies next to his monument. The Ellicott family plot is surrounded by an ornate black wrought-iron fence and gate. A large bronze plaque on his memorial obelisk tells his story and his connection to Batavia, a city he founded. Joseph's brother, Benjamin, who was also a noted surveyor for the Holland Land Office and who was elected to the US Congress in 1817, is also buried in this plot.

Author's Note: The division of the millions of acres of western New York is one of Upstate's great stories. The Holland Land Office Museum in Batavia tells about the venture in fascinating detail. The museum, the last of the three original administration buildings of the Holland Land Office, is located on West Main Street in Batavia in a stone building that was erected in 1815. Fittingly, the structure was surveyed and built by Joseph Ellicott.

Factoid: It is hard to escape the footprint of Joseph Ellicott in this part of New York State. Roads, streets, lakes, office buildings, schools and other public places bear his name, and villages in both Chautauqua and

Cattaraugus Counties carry his name (Ellicott and Ellicottville). Ellicott City, Maryland, was the place where three of the Ellicott brothers—Joseph, Andrew, and John—came to set up their first flour mill in 1771.

For More Information: Holland Land Office Museum, www.holland landoffice.com.

7

WILLIAM FARGO

1818–1881

WELLS FARGO COMPANY
BURIED IN BUFFALO,
ERIE COUNTY

*T*he image is vivid—a dashing stagecoach hurtling along at breakneck speed barely outdistancing a pistol-blasting band of undesirables . . . the frightened passengers crouching low inside for protection . . . the gold-laden strongbox bouncing wildly on the roof of the coach . . . the driver straining and whipping and shouting his steeds onward . . . and the familiar, reassuring name emblazoned in red across the side of the carriage: WELLS FARGO. Such was the stuff that legends were made of!

William Fargo was born in tiny Pompey (Onondaga County) on May 20, 1818. From his earliest years he worked as a messenger. At thirteen, he was a rural mail delivery person making a daily thirty-mile circuit on horseback. Eventually he went into the grocery business. After several years progressing through the ranks of managing and owning grocery and freight companies, he returned to mail and package delivery at age twenty-five when he joined the Livingston, Wells & Company as a messenger.

In 1845, Fargo combined with Henry Wells to create the Western Express Company, which delivered mail and packages on routes strung far into the American West. The names Wells and Fargo became synonymous with safe, reliable mail delivery in the rough-and-tumble time of American western expansion. From Buffalo to St. Louis and Chicago and Kansas City and beyond, they employed railroads, canal boats, steamships, and pony riders to get the mail to its destination at unheard-of speeds. By

1850, the two men had created the premier overland delivery system in the country. Henry Wells was president. William Fargo was the secretary. By 1861, the new company, named American Express, was handling almost all of the US mail. They had established the first transcontinental delivery service in the country.

Ultimately the Wells Fargo Company had 700 offices and employed 1,200 men. The American Express company had 2,700 offices and employed 5,000 men. The two companies combined covered more than 40,000 route miles. When railroads became the transportation of choice in the nation, Fargo got involved and utilized them extensively for his business. He was either the chairman or a board director of the New York Central Railroad, Northern Pacific Railroad, and Buffalo & Philadelphia Railroad.

William Fargo was a gregarious, deal-making, back-slapping go-getter who later pursued a life in government. As cofounder of both the Wells Fargo and American Express companies, his fortune secured, he ran for mayor of Buffalo in 1861 and won. His reelection campaign two years later was also successful. As mayor during the Civil War, Fargo saw to it that salaries for any of his employees who joined the Union Army would continue on during their service in the military.

Fargo was still serving as president of the American Express Company when he died on August 3, 1881, at the age of sixty-four.

Grave Location: William Fargo is buried in Buffalo's Forest Lawn Cemetery, located at 1411 Delaware Avenue. His grave, in Section AA, is marked by a tall obelisk that is surrounded by the graves of his family members. He and his wife are buried in side-by-side sarcophagi.

Author's Note: Few outside of Upstate New York know that Fargo served as the twenty-seventh mayor of Buffalo, but he is remembered fondly in his city. He made many generous (and often anonymous) donations to Buffalo's charitable and arts organizations. For many years his mansion was the largest private residence in the city. It cost him $700,000 to build ($10 million in today's currency). It was an extravagant 22,000-square-foot showplace that had ballrooms, priceless antiques, gold door knobs, the city's first elevator, and even a barber shop that replicated the shop where Fargo once got his hair cut before he became wealthy. After Fargo's widow died in 1890, the house remained empty for a decade. Sadly, the mansion was torn down in 1901, just thirty years after its completion. (The story of Henry Wells is told in chapter 25.)

Factoid: The two companies that William Fargo had a hand in founding have proven to be durable, to say the least. Both are still in existence more than 150 years later. American Express was one of the founding thirty members of the Dow Jones industrial average index.

For More Information: Virtual Museum of the City of San Francisco, "William G. Fargo," www.sfmuseum.net/hist11/williamgfargo.html.

PRESIDENT MILLARD FILLMORE

1800–1874

*THIRTEENTH PRESIDENT
OF THE UNITED STATES
BURIED IN BUFFALO,
ERIE COUNTY*

*M*illard Fillmore was a towering political figure in western New York. Born in Locke (Cayuga County) at the dawning of the nineteenth century (January 7, 1800), he moved to Buffalo in his twenties and would be connected to the city for the rest of his life. He was elected to represent Buffalo in Congress twice (in 1833 and 1837) and was voted in as comptroller of New York State in 1847. Then, as Zachary Taylor's vice president, Fillmore ascended to the presidency upon Taylor's death on January 9, 1850.

After he left the White House, Fillmore returned to his beloved Buffalo, where he was revered as a pillar of society, an influential power broker, and a generous contributor to the well-being of his city. He served as the first chancellor of the University of Buffalo (now the largest school in the State University of New York system), was a founder of the Buffalo Historical Society, founded the Buffalo General Hospital (now Millard Fillmore Hospital), and was a deep-pockets contributor to many of the city's nonprofits and charitable organizations.

Upon his death on March 8, 1874, at the age of seventy-four, he was remembered as a great friend to the city and its residents.

Grave Location: President Fillmore is buried in Forest Lawn Cemetery, located at 1411 Delaware Avenue in Buffalo. Fillmore's grave is one of

the grandest in the cemetery. His plot covers a large area of Section F and is surrounded by a tall, decorative wrought-iron fence. Inside the fence is a tall obelisk (his grave marker), as well as a flagpole, several other graves, and some beautiful landscaping. Many famous Americans are buried in this cemetery, and maps to these historic graves can be obtained at the cemetery's main office.

Author's Note: Although to many people President Millard Fillmore is a mere footnote in presidential politics, he is revered in his adopted city of Buffalo. A larger-than-life statue of the president can be found in front of Buffalo City Hall. It was sculpted by Bryant Baker and is very impressive. The inscription on the statue reads: "Millard Fillmore. Lawyer. Educator. Philanthropist. Statesman." It is interesting that there is no mention on this statue of Fillmore's presidency. Fillmore's home in nearby East Aurora is a National Historic Landmark.

Factoid: The Fillmore plot at Forest Lawn contains many of his family members. Curiously, both of his wives are interred next to him. The first Mrs. Fillmore, Abigail, caught a cold while attending the inauguration of his successor, Franklin Pierce, and died three weeks later. Fillmore married his second wife, Caroline, five years after leaving the White House. She passed away in 1881.

For More Information: Aurora Historical Society, "Millard Fillmore Presidential Site," www.aurorahistoricalsociety.com/pages/millard-fillmore -presidential-site/.

9

SAMUEL HOPKINS

1743–1818

US PATENT #1
BURIED IN PITTSFORD,
MONROE COUNTY

*S*ounds pretty boring, doesn't it? "The process and procedures in the improvement in the making of potash and Pearl ash by a New Apparatus." Yup, boring. But Samuel Hopkins, a Revolutionary War veteran and prolific inventor, came up with this idea and filed for the first ever United States patent in 1790.

Potash was a valuable commodity in the late 1700s, and Hopkins acted to protect his intellectual property rights in an era when there was no such thing as a legally binding patent. The newly signed Patent Act of 1790 established a protocol for securing these rights, and Hopkins, a Philadelphia Quaker, successfully applied for and received the very first patent on July 31, 1790.

Hopkins made considerable money in developing a method to refine and produce potash, sometimes called "black gold" for its important and multitude of uses (it was used in the making of glass, fertilizer, soap, clothing, and more). Today, millions of patents later, each successful patent comes with a standard US government-issued certificate bearing a cold and formal patent number on it. In Hopkins's day, the patents were described as works of art. Hopkins's own US Patent #1 is an official document written with a quill pen on sepia-toned parchment paper. To add to its rare and unique cachet, his document is hand-signed by President George Washington, Secretary of State Thomas Jefferson, and US

Attorney General Edmund Randolph. The original document is in the archives of the Chicago History Museum.

To add to his resume, Hopkins also received the first Canadian patent a year later for the same potash manufacturing idea.

He died in 1818.

Grave Location: Pittsford, a suburb of Rochester, has much history involving the development of the area, including the Erie Canal, which runs through the village. Hopkins is buried in the Pioneer Burying Ground on South Main Street, a small cemetery located at the intersection of three busy roads. The Hopkins family plot is easily located. Samuel's grave is officially in Section M, Lot 12, but there are no clear section markers in the cemetery. The best way to find his grave is to locate the large Hopkins family monument and then walk five rows back, away from the sidewalk. A careful inspection of his stone shows that the original name and date carving has been severely faded by time, but someone (historical society, family members, Quakers?) recarved his name and birth and death dates for easy viewing.

Author's Note: As mentioned, this is a busy intersection so you may miss the cemetery on your first pass. There is no historical marker telling of the cemetery's most famous resident, but there is a historical marker in front of the cemetery. It reads: "District 1. First School House in Monroe County Erected Here in 1794."

Factoid: Although there most certainly is no question as to Hopkins's final whereabouts, there was much controversy and confusion about where he lived. Much of his biographical information was lost in a fire at the US Patent Office in 1836 (his patent survived and was discovered years later). Confusingly, his birthplace was said to be Pittsford, Vermont. That city even erected a historical marker commemorating him at the place where he was supposed to have lived. Many thought that he lived in Pittsford, New York, for some time. And also in Philadelphia. In fact, at one time all three communities boasted historical markers claiming Hopkins as a native son. A historical investigation in 2013 declared Philadelphia to be his true home, and the other two markers have since come down.

For More Information: Explore PA History, "Samuel Hopkins Historical Marker," explorepahistory.com/hmarker.php?markerId=1-A-395.

10

CHARLES W. HOWARD

1896–1966

SANTA CLAUS
BURIED IN ALBION,
ORLEANS COUNTY

*C*hapter 87 in this book features Virginia O'Hanlon Douglas, the little girl who in 1897 famously asked her father, "Is there a Santa Claus?" Her story, her father's direction, and the editorial reply she received from the *New York Sun* newspaper have made for one of Upstate's most endearing holiday legends. If little Virginia had come along a half century or so later, she would have had to look no farther than to Albion, New York, to get her answer. To many, Charley Howard was indeed Santa Claus.

Howard had been enamored with the Christmas icon since childhood and lived out his dream as he became an adult. He portrayed Santa in various places around his home in Albion. He was "discovered" by singer Kate Smith, who had him on as a guest on her popular radio program in 1936.

A year later, Howard opened his Santa Claus training school in Albion. His goal was to ensure consistent and reliable encounters between the man with the beard and his many young admirers. The school was initially located in the living room of Howard's home. Graduates received a "Bachelor of Santa Claus." He later constructed a small amusement park, dubbed Christmas Park, in Albion, which was a popular holiday destination for many years. It featured animated holiday figures, animals (including reindeer), a train ride, Christmas lights, and a visit from Santa himself (played by Charley). Nearly 100,000 visitors would seek out Christmas Park between Thanksgiving and Christmas every year.

Howard's love affair with Santa Claus gained him national fame. He was the featured Santa in the Macy's Thanksgiving Day parade from 1948 to 1965. He made personal appearances during the holiday season around the country. He was the mystery guest on *What's My Line?* and was even on the *Tonight Show.* He was interviewed by the *Saturday Evening Post, Life* magazine, and the *New York Times.* He also owned a business that made "proper" Santa Claus suits, which he sold to department stores.

Serious health problems forced Howard to retire from his school, and his Christmas Park eventually went bankrupt and closed in 1965. The school was later picked up by a couple who continued in his name in Midland, Michigan, where it still exists today. About 125 students visit the school each year to hone their craft in making perfect "ho-ho-hos" and to learn how to properly balance a fidgety child on their knee.

Charles W. Howard died May 1, 1966, at the age of seventy.

Grave Location: Charles Howard is buried in Mount Albion Cemetery in Albion, just a short distance from where his school once was.

His grave can be found at the intersection of the Hop, Dellwood, and Oak cemetery sections. A large display exhibit (permanent) tells of this Albion legend with text and photographs of Howard as Santa Claus at many events. The plaque quotes him as saying, "To play the part of Santa Claus is a privilege, not a job."

Author's Note: As with many other graves in this book, Howard's grave is not forgotten. On the day of my visit, I found the landscaping to be well tended—fresh flowers had been planted around his gravestone, and several Christmas-themed trinkets were seen in the grass, obviously having been left by recent visitors.

Factoid: Howard initially priced the tuition for his school at fifteen dollars. It was not an immediate success. Friends told him that people thought the price was too cheap to get an education such as the one he was promising. He then raised the price of tuition to fifty dollars a year, and his classes immediately sold out.

For More Information: Charles W. Howard Santa Claus School, www.santaclausschool.com.

11

JUSTICE ROBERT H. JACKSON

1892–1954

JUDGEMENT AT NUREMBERG
BURIED IN FREWSBURG,
CHAUTAUQUA COUNTY

$\mathcal{R}$obert Jackson was born in Pennsylvania and raised on a farm in the Jamestown area. After high school, he attended Albany Law School, where he opted out after two years and was given only a certificate rather than a graduation diploma in 1912. He returned to Jamestown, passed the bar, and began practicing with a local legal firm. Although Jackson's heart was in western New York—a place he loved and would return to often over his lifetime—this small town boy would travel the world and reach heights in his profession that few could even imagine.

From Jamestown, Jackson gained national attention as one of the state's leading attorneys and soon was drawn into the political arena. A Democrat, he became friends with Franklin Delano Roosevelt and soon found himself as a powerbroker in the national Democratic Party. After prosecuting several high profile cases, he was named US Solicitor General in 1938, which led to his eventual appointment (by Roosevelt) to the post of US attorney general in 1940. A year later he joined the US Supreme Court, filling a seat left vacant upon the retirement of Chief Justice Charles Evans Hughes. Hughes's replacement, Justice Harlan Stone, left a seat vacant, allowing Jackson to join the court.

Justice Jackson is most famous for his appointment by President Truman as the lead prosecutor against the Nazi defendants at the Nuremberg Military Tribunal in Germany. Truman was moved by Jackson's insistence

that the German High Command be brought before the world to face their crimes and accusers and then be sentenced appropriately. He thought that was the only real American way to find justice. Some have suggested that other allies, such as Winston Churchill and Josef Stalin, had desired to simply take the German officers out into a field and shoot them. Truman agreed with the American jurist.

Jackson served in the Nuremburg post from 1945 to 1946, successfully securing long prison terms and death sentences for many of the most infamous Nazi war criminals. A soaring orator, he gave several speeches at the Nuremberg trials that some call among the greatest American speeches of the twentieth century. At the close of the war tribunal, he returned to the United States and rejoined the US Supreme Court, where he remained until his sudden death from a heart attack on October 9, 1952. He was just sixty-two years old.

Grave Location: Justice Jackson is buried in the small town of Frewsburg, New York. Enter Maple Grove Cemetery through the two main stone pillars and follow the signs to his grave. It is in Section 3, Lot 232. There are plantings, memorial flowers, American flags, and two benches at his grave site. His epitaph recalls his accomplishments: "Justice of the Supreme Court, Attorney General of the United States, Solicitor General of the United States, America's Chief Counsel at International Military Tribunal Nuremberg. 'He kept the ancient landmarks, and built the new.'"

Author's Note: It is clear to me that this cemetery's most famous notable is not forgotten in this region of the state. On the random day I was researching this book there were fresh flowers planted at his site, and a large bouquet from an area military organization was situated on a stand near one of the benches. It is obvious from the way this grave is tended that the locals hold Jackson in high regard.

Factoid: Robert Jackson is the last US Supreme Court justice to reach the high bench without receiving a law degree. He is also the only person in history to hold all of the highest legal offices in the land (those mentioned on his gravestone). In 2016, a life-sized bronze statue of Jackson was moved and rededicated to a Jamestown square named in his honor. Supreme Court Justice Sandra Day O'Connor gave the keynote address.

For More Information: Robert H. Jackson Center, www.roberthjack son.org.

12

RICK JAMES

1948–2004

SUPER FREAK SENSATION
BURIED IN BUFFALO,
ERIE COUNTY

*J*ames A. Johnson's life reads like a movie script. Born into an unstable family of ten, he drifted around his native Buffalo, dropped out of high school, had early experiences (before age twelve) with both sex and drugs, joined the Navy at fifteen years of age, moved to Canada to avoid going to Vietnam, found fellowship and musical camaraderie in Canada with local musicians such as Joni Mitchell and Neil Young, gave himself up to the FBI, did time in the brig for going AWOL, and eventually emerged to go on to Motown where he met Stevie Wonder (who told him to change his name to Rick James) and Marvin Gaye. Like they say in Hollywood, you can't make this stuff up.

James became a superstar of the first order. He was a leading proponent of funk music (some even suggest he and Prince were the cofounders of the musical movement), and his hard driving songs, which filled the dance floors of discos and concert halls around the country, soared to the top of the charts. His live performances were edgy and dynamic. Clad in skin tight leather pants, a shirt open down to his belt buckle (if he wore a shirt at all), and knee-high silver platform boots that made him a half foot taller than he really was, he sensually strutted and teased up and down the stage apron, his long hair flying around his head like a black whip. Rick James put on a concert performance that some attendees have suggested was a seminal moment in their own personal musical journey. James's

fusion music, blending everything from rock to soul to R&B, caught the ears of a wide young audience and the eye of major labels and high-powered managers.

A Rick James discography reveals dozens of albums and single releases. His biggest album was *Street Songs* (1981), which sold seven million copies. He also scored four number one singles.

As the singer's career took off, he became a frequent guest at a long line of prestigious award shows as a performer, a presenter, and a winner. He won a songwriting Grammy Award in 1991 for MC Hammer's "U Can't Touch This" and was voted favorite R&B and Soul singer by the American Music Awards in 1982. While James's albums and singles were selling by the millions in the 1980s, he once again descended into the hopeless spiral of drug abuse. He suffered through a decades-long addiction to cocaine and was in and out of emergency rooms on a frequent basis. He also had several well-publicized run-ins with the law, including one arrest that got him a three-year sentence to Folsom County Prison.

The singer died of heart problems on August 6, 2004, at his Hollywood home. An autopsy revealed a medicine cabinet's worth of different drugs, prescribed and otherwise, in his system at the time of his death. Including cocaine. He was fifty-six.

Grave Location: Rick James is buried at Forest Lawn Cemetery, located at 1411 Delaware Avenue in Buffalo. The sections of this well-tended cemetery are very plainly identified, and there is a map at the main gate of the famous dead interred here. James's grave is in Section 10. It is unmistakable from the others. A two-ton ebony granite stone carries a large etching of the singer. His epitaph reads: "I've had it all. I've done it all. I've seen it all. It's all about love. God is love." Along the bottom of the stone is his birth name: James Ambrose Johnson Jr.

Author's Note: Rick James's funeral was a very public event, held in Los Angeles. More than one thousand mourners, including celebrities and fans, filed past his open coffin to pay their respects. There were several musical and video tributes played to the audience. Three days later, more than six thousand people lined the streets of his native Buffalo as his remains were carried into Forest Lawn Cemetery.

Factoid: The singer's gravestone strained the limits of the size allowed at Forest Lawn. Cemetery rules say that no stone could weigh more than two tons, which his does. The polished granite marker is four feet nine inches high, with a four-foot-wide base. He is buried alone in a four-plot site. The etching of James on the front of his gravestone is from the cover of his 1981 hit album *Street Songs*, which included his signature song, "Super Freak."

For More Information: Facebook, "Rick James," www.facebook.com /RickJames. Years after his death, this page receives posts daily from its nearly 500,000 followers.

13

WILLIAM G. MORGAN

1870–1942

INVENTOR OF VOLLEYBALL
BURIED IN LOCKPORT,
NIAGARA COUNTY

*I*t actually all started with basketball for William Morgan.

As a youngster, he attended the Mt. Herman Preparatory School in Northfield, Massachusetts. It was there that he started a long friendship with James A. Naismith. Naismith encouraged young Morgan to continue with his education and his skill in athletics by joining the Young Men's Christian Association located in Springfield, which was later named Springville College. Morgan was a talented athlete and was a standout on the college's football team under the tutelage of the legendary Alonzo Stagg. Morgan stayed with the YMCA after graduation and ended up becoming the physical director at the YMCA in Maine and then, finally, in Holyoke, Massachusetts.

Morgan was tasked with coming up with new, entertaining sporting games for his large clientele. Basketball was all the rage at the time (his mentor, Naismith, was known as the Father of Basketball), but Morgan wanted something a little less stressful for the older, middle-aged business-men who attended his classes. Basketball was simply out of the question.

Surveying the physical landscape, Morgan came up with a simple game that required no running or heavy equipment (other than a net and a ball), placed no limit on team size, and would be a game all ages could play and enjoy. The first initial obstacle he had to overcome was finding the right size ball to use in the game. Existing balls (such as a

basketball) were too heavy and unwieldy. He turned to the A.G. Spalding Sports Equipment Company in nearby Chicopee, which came up with the perfect ball for the solution. Morgan set the net height at six feet six inches, just out of reach for the average size male at the time. He set out a simple list of rules about serving, spiking, rotating, and scoring, and he introduced the game at his YMCA in Holyoke. He originally called the game "mintonette," but it quickly became volleyball because of the frenzy of back and forth volleys employed in every game.

Springfield College holds the original draft of Morgan's rules for the game of volley ball (then using two words in the name). As his hand-typed rules state, the game consisted of nine innings, the line splitting the two teams was called the dribbling line, the express object of the game was to "serve the ball into the opponent's court" (as in tennis), and the ball "must be batted at least ten feet." Batting, dribbling, serving to an opponent's court, and nine innings. Morgan appeared to use the already established sports terminology in his new invention.

The game was an immediate success.

Morgan died on December 28, 1942, in his home town of Lockport. The city of Holyoke, Massachusetts, authorized the funding for a Volleyball Hall of Fame in 1971, and Morgan, by now widely recognized as the inventor of the game, was its first inductee in 1985.

Grave Location: Morgan is buried in Lockport's Glenwood Cemetery. Enter the cemetery through the large, ornate stone entranceway and veer to your right. At the next left, Morgan's grave can be found on a small hill on your right. His plot is approximately eight rows up from the road. His gravestone identifies him as the "Inventor of Volleyball."

Author's Note: When seeking out Morgan's grave, be careful to go to the correct cemetery. There are two, side by side. You will want Glenwood Cemetery and not St. Patrick's.

Factoid: There is a small plaza along Lockport's Main Street that has paver stones engraved with the names of a surprising number of famous Lockportians. Among them are supermodel Kim Alexis, author Joyce Carol Oates, Barry Goldwater's vice presidential running mate William E. Miller, and, of course, William G. Morgan.

For More Information: International Volleyball Hall of Fame, "William G. Morgan," www.volleyhall.org/william-g-morgan.html.

14

SAM PATCH

1799–1829

THE YANKEE LEAPER
BURIED IN ROCHESTER,
MONROE COUNTY

$\mathcal{S}$am Patch is one of the greatest "unknown" legends in Upstate New York.

Famed as a daredevil jumper (the Evel Knievel of his day), Patch would jump off just about any precipice around if the publicity was plentiful, the check was for the right amount of money, and the crowd was big enough. He made his first jump in September 1827 from the heights of the Passaic Palisades. This seventy-foot leap was unheard of, and news of the feat quickly made Sam Patch one of the more curious celebrities of his era. Next, he jumped off a one-hundred-foot platform hanging over Niagara Falls, the first ever to do such a stunt and live to tell about it. No challenge was too great for this daredevil, as he could be found jumping off cliffs, rock ledges, and more. He even once jumped off a ninety-foot-tall ship's mast into the Hudson River. As was usually the case, Patch would pass the hat among the growing crowd of onlookers to raise funds for the next stop on what he called his "jumping tour."

One of his greatest feats was jumping the raging whitewater of the Genesee River in Rochester. On November 6, 1829, he leaped over the eighty-three-foot waterfalls and into the foaming river below with his pet bear in his arms! When they both emerged from the water safely, he was hailed as the greatest jumper in history. One week later, he attempted the same jump in front of a huge crowd (this time without his bear) and failed.

The large throng of more than ten thousand onlookers stood in stunned silence as they waited for Patch to surface. His body was discovered on March 17, 1830, several miles downriver. Medical records showed that Patch had broken both shoulder blades in the plunge, prohibiting him from swimming safely to shore. Perhaps he should have taken into consideration that the date of his fateful, and final, jump was Friday, November 13, 1829. A bad luck day for sure.

Newspaper accounts of the day reported Sam Patch's final words, addressed to the large crowd on hand: "Napoleon was a great man and a great general. He conquered armies and he conquered nations. Wellington was a great man and a great general. He conquered armies and he conquered Napoleon. But he could not jump the Genesee Falls. That is left for me to do. I can do it and I will."

Grave Location: Patch is buried in the Charlotte Cemetery, located at 28 River Street in Rochester (Charlotte is a northern neighborhood of Rochester). You will know you are at the cemetery when you come to the

Charlotte Fire Department, which is right across the street. His grave is in Section D, Row 1, Lot 10, and can easily be seen from the street.

Author's Note: Sam Patch was one of the first inductees into the Daredevil Hall of Fame, which is located in Niagara Falls, Ontario, Canada. Another inductee is Annie Edson Taylor, the subject of chapter 15.

Factoid: Patch's remains were buried in the Charlotte Cemetery in a crude grave. Only a worn, wooden plank marked his final resting place. The epitaph scrawled on this piece of wood read: "Here Lies Sam Patch. Such is Fame." Soon after his burial, the wooden plank was stolen by vandals, and he remained in an unmarked grave for decades. More than a century later, students from the Charlotte High School organized a fundraiser for a gravestone, which was dedicated on March 17, 1948, and still marks his plot.

For More Information: Niagara IMAX Theatre, "Niagara Daredevil Exhibit," imaxniagara.com/daredevil-exhibit/.

ANNIE EDSON TAYLOR

1838–1921

NIAGARA'S MAID OF THE MIST
BURIED IN NIAGARA FALLS,
NIAGARA COUNTY

*T*our boats chugging through the whitewater of the Niagara Falls basin bear the name of the mythical Maid of the Mist. But make no *myth*take about it, Annie Edson Taylor was the first Maid of the Mist. She was the first person to go over Niagara Falls in a barrel and live to tell about it.

On October 24, 1901, the sixty-something widowed schoolteacher crawled into a rickety old pickle barrel and launched herself over the 158-foot Horseshoe Falls at Niagara in a desperate attempt to grasp fame's brass ring. And she did it! Strapped into place inside the homemade vessel by leather straps to keep her immobile, a bicycle pump for air tucked under her arm, and a one-hundred-pound blacksmith's anvil between her legs to keep the barrel upright, Taylor plunged into the whirlpool below the falls and disappeared for a heart-stopping seventeen minutes. The crowd that had gathered went silent as they waited for either her barrel or her body to pop up from the foam and wash up on shore.

A cheer went up when the battered pickle barrel with the words "Queen of the Mist" hand-painted on the side shot up out of the water and drifted to shore. Friends wrestled the barrel to land and smashed it open with a sledgehammer. Inside they found the tiny lady unconscious and bleeding from a head gash but very much alive. In a moment, she came to and emerged from the barrel still wearing her best dress and high heels. The wide-eyed throng gave out with a series of lusty hurrahs. News

cameras captured the moment when she stepped on dry land. Her first public comment was, "Nobody ought ever do that again!"

Headlines screamed her miraculous ride over the falls on the front pages of newspapers around the world. In a rush to make good on her vow to profit from this publicity stunt, she appeared to great excitement nine days later at the nearby Pan American Exposition on its closing day. Declared "the highlight of the entire show," Taylor sat regally in a high-backed chair, still a bit unsteady from her rollicking ride to fame. With nary a word or a handshake she sat stoically and quietly as more than three thousand spectators paid a nickel to pass by and see her in person. With no business manager or public relations guru to guide her, she began a helter-skelter nationwide schedule of appearances that was ill-conceived and poorly scheduled. She spoke in front of large crowds for little or no pay, she wrote a ten page booklet, *Over the Falls*, which failed to sell well, and she spent any money she received quickly and foolishly. Within a year, other jumpers and daredevils took her place in the public spotlight and interest in her story waned. She was soon broke and forgotten.

When Annie Edson Taylor died on April 10, 1921, she was blind and a pauper living in the Welfare Ward at the Niagara County Home in Lockport, New York.

Grave Location: Annie's grave can be found in the Stranger's Rest section of Oakwood Cemetery, located at 763 Portage Road in Niagara Falls, New York. Her grave marker reads: "First to go over the Horseshoe Falls in a barrel and live." There are maps at the cemetery's front office directing visitors to the famous people interred there.

Author's Note: Directly next to Annie's grave is that of Carlisle D. Graham. His marker reads: "First to go through the Whirlpool Rapids in a barrel and live. July 11, 1886."

Factoid: Because of Annie's fame and the number of well-known burials at Oakwood, the cemetery has been nominated for a selection on the National Registry of Historic Places. The barrel in which Annie rode to fame is reported to be the one on display at the Heroes and Daredevils exhibit at the IMAX Theatre in Niagara Falls, Canada. An exact replica of the barrel is located at the New York State Museum in Albany.

For More Information: Oakwood Cemetery, Niagara Falls, "Annie the Brave," myoakwoodcemetery.com/annie-edson-taylor/.

16

GLENN SCOBEY "POP" WARNER

1871–1954

GODFATHER OF AMERICAN YOUTH FOOTBALL
BURIED IN SPRINGVILLE,
ERIE COUNTY

*W*hile growing up in rural Erie County, Glenn Warner had never played the game of football. He excelled at baseball, but football was something mysterious to him and his young friends in the late 1800s. He recalled later that nobody had even ever heard of the game, and when they finally decided to learn about it and play it in the fields around Springville, they used a cow's bladder as a football. So it is a curious route that this young boy made from those early days to ultimately becoming one of the sport's greatest proponents and innovators.

Warner was encouraged to try out for football at Cornell University, where he was studying law. Because of his large frame (he weighed over two hundred pounds), he excelled as a guard and was named captain of the team in 1894. Later, as a coach, he began developing new plays and on-field strategies that caught the eye of several scouts for various teams. He later coached at Iowa State University, the University of Georgia, and then briefly back at Cornell. In 1899, he was named head football coach at the Carlisle Indian Industrial School in Pennsylvania, where he ended up coaching Jim Thorpe. Over a period of more than three decades he also was a successful football coach at Pittsburgh, Stanford, Temple, and San Jose. At retirement he had a career football record of 319–106–32, making him one of the winningest coaches in college football history.

During his long career as a football coach, he was credited with introducing several new plays to the game, including the screen pass. He was also the first coach to employ a single and double wing formation and to use a team huddle. He was instrumental in the development of safety enhancements to football uniforms, such as improved knee and thigh pads.

In 1934, an organization of youth football teams was looking for a spiritual and inspirational leader to attract greater numbers of young boys to play the game. They looked to Glenn "Pop" Warner as a leader, and what was known as the Junior Football League was renamed the Pop Warner Conference in his honor. Since he was one of the most popular sports figures of the time, memberships grew in this fledgling organization until nearly two hundred teams were signed up all across the nation. Teams played in structured leagues, both in rural and urban areas. By the late 1940s, these "midget football" teams (as they were called then) were playing for championships titles. With players fifteen years or younger, the first championship game, dubbed the Santa Claus Bowl, was played in freezing temperatures before a crowd of two thousand paying spectators. This first-ever Pop Warner Super Bowl pitted the two top teams of the year: the Crickets, sponsored by a swanky Philadelphia restaurant, played against Frank Sinatra's Cyclones. Philadelphia won, 6–0, and the game was covered by the national sporting press. This insured the organization's success for the future. A recent survey of the organization showed that there are currently 5,000 Pop Warner Football Teams worldwide, with more than 400,000 boys and girls participating.

Glenn "Pop" Warner died September 7, 1954, at the age of eighty-three.

Grave Location: Glenn Warner is buried in Maplewood Cemetery, located at 46 Rachel Lane in Springville. His large family plot, under a granite marker that reads "Warner/Scobey," can be found in Section 7 at the intersection of cemetery roads 2, 7, and 17.

Author's Note: Like many other graves I visited in researching this book, Warner's grave site showed evidence of memorabilia and trinkets left by visitors. These included a child's football, an American flag, and a small, plastic Cornell megaphone.

Factoid: Glenn Warner got his nickname early on in his football playing days. His teammates called him Pop because he was the oldest player on his Cornell University team.

For More Information: Pop Warner Little Scholars, www.popwarner .com.

Part Two

GREATER FINGER LAKES REGION

17

JUSTUS D. BARNES

1862–1946

FIRST MOVIE VILLAIN
BURIED IN WEEDSPORT,
CAYUGA COUNTY

*J*ustus Barnes was a silent film actor who appeared in more than seven hundred movies between 1903 and 1917. Despite all of these films, it is his debut movie role that earned him a niche in Hollywood lore and a chapter in this book.

Barnes was an actor in the 1903 classic *The Great Train Robbery*. Although it was officially recognized as a short film (it ran only twelve minutes in length), it was nonetheless groundbreaking and set the mark for filmmaking for the near future. The movie, directed by Edwin S. Porter, used many filming techniques for the very first time. Perhaps the most significant new application was that of cross cutting a scene. The film employed this tricky maneuver with great success, allowing audiences to watch two simultaneous spheres of action in a single scene, which created an intimate relationship between the audience and the film. It allowed the viewer to feel as if they were part of the action. Because it used this technique and was also one of the first instances of on-location shooting, the film has been called America's first western action movie.

The film tells the story of a train robbery with all the usual silent movie subplots. Bandits rob a telegraph office, people are tied up, men are knocked out, women arrive on the scene to rescue men, a train is hijacked, passengers are kidnapped, people are shot, and a posse chases down and

ultimately catches the bad guys. A shootout ensues and good prevails over evil. Pretty ambitious action for a twelve minute movie!

Barnes was referred to as Outlaw Leader (even though the actors were uncredited), and it is in the final scene of the movie where the Upstate New Yorker finds immortality. Following a wild gunfight in the woods, we last see Barnes's character staring down the camera in a dramatic close-up, lingering and sinister. The actor is dressed in a broad-brimmed cowboy hat with a plaid scarf tied around his neck. His walrus mustache droops below his prominent nose (Barnes was clean shaven; the mustache was glued on for the scene). Slowly the train robber raises his arm, Colt pistol in hand, and fires six shots directly at the audience. The realism is startling. Newspaper reports of the day noted that several audience members screamed at seeing this scene, fearing that an actual bullet might emerge from the screen and strike them. It was a daring and startling ending to a historic film.

On the success of this movie, Barnes found steady work until he retired in 1917. He then retired to Weedsport, where he became a milkman and a cigar store owner. He died on February 6, 1946, at the age of eighty-three.

Grave Location: The Weedsport Rural Cemetery is located on East Brutus Street, about a half mile from the downtown business district. It is a midsize cemetery consisting of many older tombstones set amid a rolling landscape. The cemetery has marked each section clearly, which is very helpful because Justus Barnes is buried under one of the smallest headstones in the cemetery. It is located in Section 8, third row back from the roadway. Look for the tall, ornate grave marked "Brockway." Barnes's small stone is next to it.

Author's Note: Although he was without a doubt a person of some fame, not much is known about Barnes's life after he retired from films. He never married, and it is suspected that he did not have much (or even any) money. The large Brockway grave marker next to his smaller one is the burial place of a rooming house owner who rented a room to Barnes for the last years of his life. It is presumed she paid for the actor's plot and stone.

Factoid: In 1998, the US Post Office honored the historic *Great Train Robbery* with its own commemorative postage stamp. Of all of the scenes and graphics they could have used for the image on the stamp, they chose the iconic scene of Justus D. Barnes firing his pistol directly at the audience (or the stamp buyer).

For More Information: Internet Movie Database, "Justus D. Barnes," www.imdb.com/name/nm0055661/.

18

SERGEANT DANIEL BISSELL

1754–1824

*FIRST PURPLE HEART
BURIED IN RICHMOND,
ONTARIO COUNTY*

*T*he US Army officially listed Daniel Bissell as a deserter. General Washington ordered this so as to mask Bissell's real identity and purpose. Bissell was Washington's "master spy."

In 1781, young Bissell walked away from the American Army and fled to New York City. There, for the next thirteen months, he played the role of a discontented deserter preparing to join up with the British Army. He was so convincing in this part that he was able to ascertain vital information about the enemy and their troop strengths and deployment. He observed sensitive British maps and listened in on key strategy sessions between enemy officers. At the completion of his being held captive, he began his long walk back to his company to report to General Washington on what he saw.

Along his route back to his headquarters, he became seriously ill, was found, and was taken to a British hospital where he hovered for weeks between life and death. During this time, his fever caused him to babble incoherently for days on end. Seemingly out of his mind from delirium, Bissell had no way of knowing that he had blurted out the information that he had gathered during his clandestine mission behind enemy lines. The British doctor either took his rantings as the ravings of a madman or chose to sympathetically ignore what he heard. In any case, after a month of recuperation, Bissell was once again able to escape and returned to Washington's camp where he gave detailed reports on what he saw.

For his bravery and meritorious conduct, he was awarded the newly commissioned Award of Merit (the forerunner to today's Purple Heart) in 1783, one of only three so honored by General Washington.

Daniel Bissell died on August 21, 1824, at the age of sixty-nine.

Grave Location: Allens Hill is one of the smallest communities I visited in search of the graves in this book. It is just basically a four-corner crossroads north of Honeoye in the Finger Lakes region. Travel exactly three and a half miles north of Honeoye High School on Allens Hill Road, and then turn left at Belcher Road. The cemetery is on your right. Bissell's grave is easy to find in this very small cemetery. It is marked with flags and veterans' organizations adornments. His epitaph reads: "He had the confidence of Washington from whom he received a badge of merit."

Author's Note: The National Purple Heart Hall of Honor and Museum, located in New Windsor, New York, is trying to compile a database of as many of the recipients of this oldest military medal as possible.

Factoid: It should be noted that General Washington gave out just three Badges of Merit on the same day in 1783. They were awarded to Elijah Churchill, William Brown, and Daniel Bissell. All three soldiers were from Connecticut, and Bissell was the only one who lived in and was ultimately buried in New York State. Only two of the three original medals are still with us: Brown's is on display at the American Independence Museum in Exeter, New Hampshire; and Churchill's is on display at the Purple Heart Hall of Honor in New Windsor. Unfortunately, Bissell's treasured medal was lost when his house burned down in July 1813.

For More Information: National Purple Heart Hall of Honor, www .thepurpleheart.com.

19

EZRA CORNELL

1807–1874

"HIGH ABOVE CAYUGA'S WATERS . . ."
BURIED IN ITHACA,
TOMPKINS COUNTY

*A*mid the rolling foothills of western New York, at the edge of the wine region and high above the waters of Cayuga Lake, stands a sprawling monument to a great man of vision and generosity—an internationally honored university that bears his name. That man is Ezra Cornell.

Cornell was born in Westchester County, New York (near today's Bronx), grew up in rural Upstate New York in DeRuyter, and lived in Ithaca from 1828 until his death in 1874. As a near lifelong resident of Upstate New York, he saw many opportunities become available to him, and he grabbed every one of them. He was a successful farmer, business-man, and financier, although much of his fame and fortune came well after his fiftieth birthday.

After securing a comfortable niche for himself in the upper echelons of Ithaca society, he turned his energies toward inventing and his interest in the new field of telegraphy. Cornell invented the single most impor-tant way to erect and string up telegraph poles and wires. This invention helped Samuel F. B. Morse successfully lay the first telegraph line from Washington, DC, to Baltimore, and it made Cornell very wealthy man. It was Cornell's wires that carried Morse's famous first telegraph message on May 24, 1844: "What hath God wrought?" Cornell immersed himself in the frenetic development of telegraph lines throughout the expanding countryside—New York, Washington, Quebec, Baltimore, Kansas City,

Chicago, and all points west soon saw the familiar lines of his telegraph systems. Joining his largest competitor, Hiram Sibley of the New York and Mississippi Valley Printing Telegraph Company, Cornell founded and led the newly formed Western Union Company in 1855. For fifteen years he was the largest stockholder of the company and earned millions from his investment.

Once he reached a stage where money was no longer the great driving factor in his life, Cornell devoted his passion and his vast fortune to the development of a seat of higher education to be located in his beloved Ithaca. He gave $500,000 and a large tract of land to be used for the site of the university that would bear his name. Cornell University opened in 1868.

He was always extremely proud, in a patriarchal way, of his university. In his autumnal years he lived on campus and became a familiar sight wandering the halls and lawns of the school, mingling with the students.

From the founding of the Western Union Company to the establishment of a world-renowned university, Ezra Cornell's influence in the nineteenth century was vital to our country's growth. His legacy lived on through his children, and his offspring included son Alonzo Cornell, who was elected governor of New York in 1880.

Cornell died in 1874, and in accordance with his wishes, he was buried on the campus of the school he so loved.

Grave Location: Sage Chapel is Cornell University's stunning, non-denominational house of worship. It is a place of quiet majesty and peaceful serenity in the midst of a busy campus. Founder Ezra is buried with his wife, Mary Ann, in side-by-side sarcophagi that display remarkable marble images of the couple so exact you can count the pleats on his pants!

Author's Note: Ithaca is a thriving community of more than 30,000 people. In large part because of Cornell University, the city has a distinct international air. It is located at the southern tip of Cayuga Lake, one of the largest of Upstate's famous Finger Lakes. Because it is known for its many dramatic gorges and hiking paths, the city's clever slogan is "Ithaca is Gorges!"

The photograph accompanying this chapter is of the exterior of Sage Chapel. I did not take a photograph of the interior out of respect for the solemnity of the location.

Factoid: Andrew Dickson White, Cornell's partner and cofounder of the university, is also buried in Sage Chapel, although not in a sarcophagi. White was the college's first president. His wife, Helen, was the first woman in the United States to earn a PhD.

Sage Chapel is also the home of the famous Cornell University Glee Club and Chorus. Author E. B. White (class of 1921) was a member of this famous choir. In the loft is a plaque to his memory that carries a passage of White's immortal book *Charlotte's Web* ("Life in the barn was very good, night and day . . .").

For More Information: Cornell University, www.cornell.edu.

20

GLENN HAMMOND CURTISS

1878–1930

PILOT'S LICENSE #1
BURIED IN HAMMONDSPORT,
STEUBEN COUNTY

*A*side from perhaps the Wright brothers, probably no other American contributed more to the development of aviation in America than Glenn H. Curtiss of Hammondsport, New York.

His career paralleled that of the Wright brothers, and their paths would cross many times (sometimes with unhappy results). Like Orville and Wilbur, Curtiss began by building motorcycle engines. In 1907, he raced his cycle at speeds over 135 miles per hour—an astonishing speed for the time and a feat that got him dubbed the "fastest man on Earth."

In tiny Hammondsport—today a small Finger Lakes community, but then a hub of aviation activity—Curtiss flew the first witnessed flight of one kilometer in the country on July 4, 1908.

Curtiss was a most energetic advocate of the use of aviation in the military. During World War I, his Curtiss Aeroplane Company was the largest manufacturer of aircraft in the nation. In 1919, a Navy-Curtiss Flying Boat, commanded by Albert C. Reid, made the very first flight across the Atlantic Ocean. Curtiss chalked up several other firsts, including becoming the first naval instructor of air pilots. In 1910, he won $10,000 in cash in a contest sponsored by the *New York World* newspaper, which was looking for the fastest flight time from Albany to New York City. Curtiss did it in a then-amazing two hours and fifty-one minutes.

One of the most famous meetups between Curtiss and the Wright brothers resulted in a long-lasting feud between the aviation pioneers. In

1908, Curtiss had already built his first airplane, the *June Bug.* It was controlled by a new innovation called ailerons (wing flaps). Perhaps with their noses slightly bent, the Wright brothers filed a patent infringement lawsuit against Curtiss for using what they claimed was their own flight control mechanism. The court ruled in favor of the brothers.

On June 8, 1911, Glenn Curtiss was awarded U.S. Pilot's License #1. Because this very first assignment of pilot licenses was awarded alphabetically, the Wright Brothers were awarded pilot's licenses #5 and #6 on the very same day. Curtiss was at the height of his fame when he made the cover of *Time* magazine on October 13, 1924.

Curtiss died while undergoing an appendectomy at a Buffalo hospital on July 23, 1930. He was fifty-two years old.

Grave Location: Curtiss is buried in the Pleasant Valley Cemetery on Route 54, just two miles south of the village of Hammondsport. His large gray monument features his last name chiseled in large letters across the front. Although Pleasant Valley Cemetery uses Route 54 as its address, it is much easier to find Curtiss's final resting place if you enter the cemetery from the back, off South Valley Road. Here, at the back entrance to the cemetery, you will find a plaque telling of Curtiss's achievements, and his grave is located straight ahead as you enter from the rear.

Author's Note: A wonderful museum dedicated to the life and work of the Father of Naval Aviation is also located on Route 54 just a mile from the cemetery. The Glenn H. Curtiss Museum holds many of his planes, bicycles, motorcycles, photographs, family memorabilia and personal items. You can't miss the museum. At the entrance on Route 54 sits a large C-46 World War II transport plane.

Factoid: In his later years, Curtiss and his partner, James Bright, became the largest land speculators in southeastern Florida. They intended to capitalize on the aviator's name by starting a flying school there. Curtiss eventually became the founder of what are today three vibrant Florida cities—Hialeah, Opa-Locka, and Miami Springs.

For More Information: Glenn H. Curtiss Museum, www.glennhcurtiss museum.org.

21

Captain Myles Keogh

1840–1876
IRISH AMERICAN MILITARY HERO
BURIED IN AUBURN,
CAYUGA COUNTY

*T*wo of the chapters in this book are dedicated to soldiers who fought and died during the Battle of Little Bighorn, "Custer's Last Stand." One of them was the dashing George Armstrong Custer himself (chapter 69), who is buried in the storied cemetery at West Point Military Academy in the Hudson Valley. The other is Myles Keogh.

Keogh was born in County Carlow, Ireland, and as a child was among the waves of Irish immigrants to the United States. By the time he was assigned to Custer's Seventh Cavalry, he had been a soldier almost his entire adult life, including serving as an officer during the entire three-day Battle of Gettysburg. Keogh and all those he served with Custer at Little Bighorn died on June 25, 1876. The story of Custer's Last Stand has been told in schools for generations. But there are a couple of mysteries surrounding the legend and the death of Myles Keogh that fateful day on the plains of the Montana Territory.

When the battle had ended and the battlefield lay strewn with bodies, the US Army medics and attendants came out to the scene of the massacre to retrieve the bodies of the fallen. Almost all of the American soldiers, including Lieutenant Colonel Custer, had been butchered, their bodies mutilated and their heads scalped. Clearly it was a scene of savage bloodletting.

Amazingly, Keogh's body was found to be untouched. He died with a full head of hair and without so much as a scratch on his body, other than

the mortal wound. No one knows why, but speculation is that the Native Americans were confused and intrigued by the very light skin on the Irishman, that they were wary of the religious medallions he wore around his neck, or that he remained untouched in tribute to the great courage he showed being one of the last men to die. The truth will never be known.

Another enduring story about Keogh and Little Big Horn revolves around his horse, Comanche. This horse was the only participant on the American side, man or animal, to live through the battle. Comanche was badly wounded during the skirmish but was nurtured back to health by Cavalry medics. The horse, who then became a symbol for the US Calvary of great courage and bravery in the face of daunting odds, made many public appearances around the country, usually leading a parade, and the public grew very fond of the horse and his heroic story. It is pure speculation as to why the Indians left the wounded horse alone on the battlefield, the only survivor of Little Bighorn.

Myles Keogh was thirty-six years old at the time of his death.

Grave Location: Fort Hill Cemetery in Auburn, New York, is one of Upstate's most historic burying grounds. Myles Keogh is buried near the highest point in the cemetery, in the Mount Hope section. His grave is an elaborate monument covered with military symbolism, located in a peaceful, circular area under a canopy of old trees. Next to Keogh is the grave of Maj. Gen. Emory Upton, a legendary Civil War officer. Other military officers can be found in this section.

Author's Note: Shortly before he died, Keogh wrote a letter to a friend instructing that upon his death he be "packed up and shipped to Auburn" to be buried with his military friends. He never married and had no children. His funeral in Auburn was one of the largest military funerals held in that city up to that time.

Factoid: While Keogh rests eternally in Upstate New York, his famous horse rests "partially" in a museum in Kansas. Comanche died on November 7, 1891, at the age of twenty-nine. His internal remains were buried in one place and the rest of him was stuffed to go on display. Visitors can see the taxidermied remains of this proud horse at the Dyche Museum of Natural History on the campus of the University of Kansas, Lawrence. The horse is shown wearing his Seventh Cavalry army blanket.

For More Information: National Park Service, Little Bighorn Battlefield, "Capt. Myles Keogh," www.nps.gov/libi/learn/historyculture/capt -myles-keogh.htm.

22

GOVERNOR JOHN MILLER

1843–1908

*FIRST GOVERNOR OF NORTH DAKOTA
BURIED IN DRYDEN,
TOMPKINS COUNTY*

*T*his will be perhaps the shortest chapter in this book. There is not a lot to write about John Miller's career, but I wanted to include him because his grave is most unusual. He is buried in an elaborate mausoleum in Green Hills Cemetery in Dryden, New York. But it is not the mausoleum that makes this unique. It is the flag flying next to it. While we would obviously not be surprised to see an American flag flying by his or anybody else's grave, this is not an American flag. It is the official state flag of North Dakota.

That has to be a first for any researcher of Upstate New York graves.

John Miller was born in Dryden in 1843 but found whatever fame and fortune he acquired in the unmapped area of North Dakota. He moved to that territory at the age of thirty-five and made one of the largest land purchases there to that time. He turned the nearly 20,000 acres of newly acquired scrub brush into a profitable farming conglomerate. With the stretch of railroads spreading westward, he added more and more property and more and more farm operations to his name. He became extremely wealthy and interested in local politics.

Arthur Millette was the territorial governor of North Dakota, and when statehood was achieved John Miller ran for the governor's seat. Miller won, becoming the first governor of the recognized state of North Dakota on November 20, 1889. His term in office lasted just two years,

ending in 1891. Although he is to be credited for leading a state in its infancy and helping to set the structure of a new state government, his accomplishments were few, except for one brief "profile in courage."

During Miller's administration, something called the Louisiana Lottery was all the rage. It was the first national lottery, and many states were cashing in on huge payouts, lucrative bribes, and "deals with the devil" associations. The Louisiana Lottery wanted to get into North Dakota in a serious way, but Governor Miller refused. The lottery came with significant baggage and a bad reputation, but it was loaded with cash. The company offered to change the name to the North Dakota Lottery to give the nascent state some national credentials. It was also reported that Miller was offered a personal bribe of $10,000 to not veto the bill allowing the lottery into the state. He stood fast, and shortly after North Dakota said no the Louisiana Lottery began to implode under the weight of its own corruption.

Following this act of political courage, John Miller left politics and returned to farming in the Red River Valley with his business partner,

Herbert Chaffee, where they had amassed tens of thousands of acres of farmland and had built many mills and company towns.

He died on October 26, 1908, at the age of sixty-four.

Grave Location: The governor's family mausoleum is located in Section 2 of Green Hills Cemetery on Highland Road in Dryden. The North Dakota flag, which is replaced by a new one sent from the state every year, flies proudly next to it. A bronze plaque affixed to the mausoleum tells of the Dryden native's fame in the wild, wild west.

Author's Note: The date 1910 is on the capstone of the mausoleum. That is the year it was built. After a century, it was in need of great repair and donations were sought. Contributions to the effort were sent from many prominent North Dakotans, including the two sitting US senators at the time, Kent Conrad and John Hoeven. The restored mausoleum is now one of the finest in the cemetery.

Factoid: John Miller's longtime business partner, Herbert F. Chaffee, was a first-class passenger on the doomed luxury liner RMS *Titanic*. His body was never found.

For More Information: National Governors Association, "Governor John Miller," www.nga.org/cms/john-miller.

23

Rod Serling

1924–1975

GATEKEEPER OF THE TWILIGHT ZONE
BURIED IN INTERLAKEN,
SENECA COUNTY

A recent entertainment magazine honored the "Immortals of Television," naming twelve of the guiding lights and brightest stars of early TV. The impact left by these show-business giants is undeniable—Lucille Ball, Milton Berle, Jackie Gleason, Walter Cronkite, Ed Sullivan, and others. Each name brings to mind a vivid trademark, a definitive characteristic that instantly conjures up the golden years of early TV—Lucy stuffing her mouth with chocolates trying to keep up with a runaway conveyor belt, Uncle Miltie raising cross-dressing to an art form, Gleason's Ralph Kramden and his "to the moon, Alice," Cronkite's "and that's the way it is . . . ," and so much more.

By comparison, it is then quite interesting to note that among these three-dimensional, larger-than-life characters, another immortal was recognized as one of the medium's most iconic figures. He was not outrageous or bombastic, nor was he a clown or even an actor. He was a quiet, unassuming writer who created a show that remains, decades after it first aired, one of the seminal television shows of all time. His name was Rod Serling, and the show was *The Twilight Zone.*

Rod Serling's magical gift to television was an ingenious, macabre imagination, which he translated so brilliantly to the American public through his scripts and teleplays. So vivid were the fruits of his imagination that these shows remain fresh and intriguing more than a half century after they first aired.

After going to school in the Binghamton area, Serling attended Antioch College, where he wrote and sold his first television script. It didn't take long for his unique talents to be recognized and sought after by the entertainment centers in New York and California. He quickly found steady work as a scriptwriter. He was honored early on for one of his first pieces, *Patterns* (1955), a searing look at boardroom-level desperation in corporate America. In the 1960s he wrote several classic movie scripts, including *Requiem for a Heavyweight* (1963), *Seven Days in May* (1964), *Assault on a Queen* (1966), and *Planet of the Apes* (1967). All were warmly received by both critics and audiences alike.

Despite his success in the movie industry, there can be no doubt that his real memorial is the television series *The Twilight Zone* (and later *Night Gallery*). Each episode took the viewer down a twisting path of incredible tension, subtle humor, bizarre visual effects, and wildly flip-flopping endings. Shot in the standard black and white of that era, *The Twilight Zone* still mesmerizes audiences with its on-the-edge storylines and haunting messages.

Serling liked to use movie stars from Hollywood's past as featured performers in his episodes of the two programs. It is in these particular shows that he produced some of his most memorable vignettes. Who can ever forget Ed Wynn as the desperate timekeeper trying to "keep time" with his clocks? Or a blind Joan Crawford who regains her sight during a power blackout? Or Burgess Meredith as the timid bank employee who is finally alone with his beloved books after surviving a nuclear bomb blast? You could almost hear the nation as it offered up a collective groan when he broke his glasses.

One of the most famous *Twilight Zone* episodes was called "The Invaders." It broke all new ground in this genre of sci-fi shows. It aired on January 21, 1961. The star was Agnes Moorehead, who played a lonely old crone whose ramshackle house is invaded by tiny space aliens. With virtually no dialogue, a frenetic pace of action, stark sets and lighting, and Moorehead's intense acting technique, this tale of defending one's home from unseen outsiders made for one of the most unforgettable and harrowing viewing nights of the season.

Rod Serling was born on Christmas Day 1924. He died following heart surgery on June 28, 1975, at the age of just fifty.

Grave Location: Rod Serling is buried in Lakeview Cemetery in Interlaken, New York, just north of Ithaca on the west side of Cayuga Lake. His grave can be found near the back (lake side) of the cemetery in Section 2, Lot G, Plot 1044.

Author's Note: While searching for Serling's grave, I was looking for a monument or large stone with his name and his achievements listed on it. Instead, he is buried beneath a simple, government-issued military gravestone. The epitaph reads only: "Rodman E. Serling. TEC5, US Army World War II." It is evident that fans and friends visit this grave frequently. On the day I was there, his grave marker was covered with trinkets, painted stones, *Twilight Zone* memorabilia, and tokens of admiration.

Factoid: Serling is remembered in Binghamton with a New York State historical marker in front of Binghamton High School telling of the fame of the school's most well-known graduate. His real home at 67 Bennett Avenue was used in filming of a *Night Gallery* episode, "They're

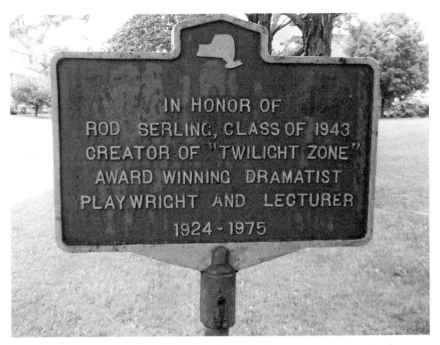

This historical marker stands in front of Rod Serling's alma mater, Binghamton High School.

Tearing Down Tim Riley's Bar." Also, in an episode of *The Twilight Zone* that aired on October 30, 1959, Serling featured one of the carousels he used to play on in Recreation Park in Binghamton. That carousel is still there, and a painting on the carousel shows Serling riding it. There is also a plaque nearby that reads: "Rod Serling. Creator of *The Twilight Zone*. Walking Distance."

For More Information: Television Academy, "Rod Serling," www .emmys.com/bios/rod-serling/.

24

HARRIET TUBMAN

1822–1913

A WOMAN CALLED MOSES
BURIED IN AUBURN,
CAYUGA COUNTY

*F*or most of us, the whole concept of slavery seems so immoral and inde-
cent that we find it hard to believe that it occurred in our country at all.
But it did happen, and it became the benchmark of a turning point in
American history, standing out as the most controversial issue during a
time of great fear and divisiveness in America. Out of those terrible times
came the courageous figures we all learned about in high school, secretive
figures who were entrusted with the care and safety of groups of frightened
slaves fleeing the shackles of bondage in the South to a new beginning in
the North. They were unsung, and for the most part, unknown heroes we
came to know as "conductors." They journeyed along their fabled route
to freedom known as the Underground Railroad. None was more storied,
more heroic, or more colorful than Harriet Tubman.

Tubman was a daring and fearless escort to hundreds of escaping
slaves, and she won the respect of men and women alike (and friend and
foe alike) for her cunning and inventiveness in completing her flights to
the North. She ultimately made nineteen individual trips along this dangerous route, guiding more than three hundred slaves to freedom.

The Compromise of 1850, which included the Fugitive Slave Act, seg-
mented the nation into free and slave states. The Fugitive Slave provision
required citizens to aid in the search, arrest, and return of fugitive slaves
caught trying to flee the South. This provision accelerated the abolitionist

movement and gave rise to the Underground Railroad, especially during the period from 1850 to 1860. The act preserved the unity of the nation in the short run, but it sowed the seeds of racism and insurrection and led to the Civil War.

At one time Harriet Tubman had a bounty on her head, dead or alive, of more than $40,000. She was sought far and wide by whole armies of men. She bragged that she never failed to complete a mission. Coldly unafraid, she would often threaten the nervous or fainthearted fugitives with a loaded pistol, ensuring the successful competition of their flight.

Harriet Tubman's actions were an inspiration to people in all walks of life. She served her country unselfishly for years, both as a guide to fleeing slaves and as both a nurse and a spy/scout for the Union Army. Her autumnal years were spent in Upstate New York, where she welcomed visitors regularly and never tired of retelling the thrilling stories of her days as one of America's most vocal and active opponents of slavery. When she died at the age of ninety-two, on March 10, 1913, she was hailed nationally as an "American original."

Grave Location: Tubman's grave is in Fort Hill Cemetery, located at 19 Fort Street in Auburn. Her simple gravestone can be found under a towering Norwegian spruce tree in the West Lawn section of the cemetery. It is much visited, and there are usually mementos, flags, cards, and other acknowledgements of people stopping by to pay their respects. Her epitaph reads: "To the memory of Harriet Tubman Davis, Heroine of the Underground Railroad, Nurse and Scout in the Civil War. Servant of God. Well Done!"

Author's Note: There are many famous graves in this historic cemetery. The office staff is very helpful in giving grave locations and directions if you are able to visit during business hours.

Factoid: Perhaps Harriet Tubman's greatest supporter and advocate was William H. Seward (also buried here), a US secretary of state, US senator, and governor of New York State. He was Tubman's chief patron, and in 1859 he sold her a seven-acre plot of land near the outskirts of Auburn, which she used for her home and as a home for the aged. It would ultimately become a museum in her honor, which it remains today.

For More Information: Harriet Tubman Historical Society, www .harriet-tubman.org.

25

HENRY WELLS

1805–1878

WELLS FARGO COMPANY
BURIED IN AURORA,
CAYUGA COUNTY

*H*enry Wells and William Fargo were wedded to each other through business and financial entanglements most of their lives. They were cofounders of Wells Fargo and American Express, and both became millionaires many times over. Fargo was the ebullient social gadfly. Henry Wells could not have been more different.

Henry Wells was a shy, some would say meek, "numbers man" who would remain in the more three-dimensional Fargo's shadow throughout their partnerships. Wells was plagued with a stammering speech impediment that caused him to be less forceful in his public persona than Fargo. He was contemplative and enjoyed his privacy. He was an arts patron and enjoyed travel and the opera. Born in Vermont, he came from "good Yankee stock," and one of his earliest ancestors is famous for holding every major elected office in the state of Connecticut, including governor.

Wells was involved with messenger delivery, transportation services, railroads, and banks. He was president of American Express from 1850 to 1868 and served on the board at Wells Fargo for many years. In retirement, he moved to Aurora, New York, on the eastern shore of Cayuga Lake, where he built a mansion and served as the president of the First National Bank of Aurora.

He dedicated much of his fortune to the founding of Wells Seminary in Aurora, which later became Wells College, one of the first women's

colleges in the nation. One of the main buildings on campus is Glen Park, Wells's elegant residence which the college acquired in 1906. Recognizing the serious ramifications of his speech impediment throughout his life, he also donated large sums of money to schools that addressed speech problems.

Henry Wells died while visiting Glasgow, Scotland, on December 10, 1878. His body was brought home to Aurora, where he is buried in the local cemetery.

Grave Location: Wells is buried in the old cemetery off Main Street in Aurora. Exit Cherry Avenue (across from the town post office), and you will see Oak Glen Cemetery. Walk straight back about halfway through the cemetery and you will find Wells's tall obelisk. Fittingly, you will pass Wells College on your way to this cemetery.

Author's Note: There is no office or main gate at Oak Glen Cemetery. And it appears as if there are few, if any, new burials taking place here. Wells's monument is unmistakable in the center of the burial grounds. If you visit the final resting places of both Mr. Wells and Mr. Fargo, you will be struck by the similar design of their monuments. (The story of William Fargo is told in chapter 7 of this book.)

Factoid: Among the many famous women to graduate from Wells College is Frances Folsom Cleveland. She was the first First Lady of the United States to graduate from college and served on the Wells College Board of Trustees for nearly forty years. After her husband, President Grover Cleveland, died, she married Thomas Preston, a professor of archeology and art history at Wells, and moved with him to Aurora. Cleveland Hall on the Wells campus is named in her honor.

For More Information: Wells College History, www.wells.edu/about /wells-college-history/.

Part Three

ADIRONDACKS AND NORTH COUNTRY

26

JOHN BROWN

1800–1859

"JOHN BROWN'S BODY LIES
A-MOULDERING IN THE GRAVE . . ."
BURIED IN NORTH ELBA,
ESSEX COUNTY

John Brown was an unmitigated failure when it came to business. He tried his hand at everything, it seemed, and almost always failed. From sheep raising to land surveying to tanning animal skins, he was always running from debt. He did set one personal goal in his life, a goal of missionary proportions. The abolition of slavery. And this goal cost him his life and the lives of several of his sons.

It was said that John Brown's hatred of slavery began when he was just five years old. He witnessed a black slave, just a child himself and a close friend of his, being beaten unmercifully by his master. Brown tried to intercede on his young friend's behalf and received a terrible thrashing of his own. That incident would spark his life's burning passion. He would go on to become one of the preeminent abolitionist activists of his time.

In the 1840s, wealthy antislavery organizer Gerrit Smith offered plots of land high in the remote Adirondack region of Upstate New York to free black slaves who wished to settle on the land on farms he had purchased. In 1849, Brown, being chased by his creditors, settled his family in North Elba (just outside of Lake Placid) on land he purchased from Smith for a dollar an acre. His reputation had clearly preceded him, and he was regarded as a man of great leadership qualities in the all-black community. Author Richard Dana, who met Brown during this time, dubbed him the

Statue of John Brown and a young boy, located next to Brown's grave. Statue by Joseph Pollia, 1935. Courtesy of the John Brown Farm State Historic Site.

King of the Negroes. From his new remote outpost, Brown began expanding his antislavery activities throughout the region and the state. By the late 1850s, he was openly engaged in the direct confrontation of proslavery forces.

He and his many children (he had twenty offspring by two wives) formed a "core army" that directed the forced freeing of slaves. Brown's righteous cause met its moment of destiny when the Kansas-Nebraska Act of 1854 was instituted, causing the anti- and proslavery forces to engage in open warfare in the new, desolate territories of the American West.

Brown moved his family to Kansas and settled in Osawatomie. There he established himself as an abolitionist leader in the tiny town and began referring to himself as "Old Osawatomie Brown." His pitched battles with proslavery militias were fierce and bloody. In the end, one of Brown's sons was slain, and his Kansas town was burned to the ground.

This deadly turn of events caused a noticeable unbalancing of Brown's demeanor. Many thought the tragic events at Osawatomie had caused him to become unhinged, even deranged. In fact his mother, his first wife, and two of his sons were actually believed to be outright insane. His zealous behavior became more dangerous and unpredictable.

He tried to raise an "Army of Emancipation" but found blacks, by and large, unwilling to take the risks. Frederick Douglass and Gerrit Smith, both longtime friends and supporters of Brown, encouraged his efforts, but many others in the movement thought that more could be gained by peaceful, legislative means. Brown became more daring and more foolhardy, attacking farms and settlements with his small band of marauders, freeing slaves and killing slave owners. Many innocent people were killed by mistake. Eventually even the US government considered him a rogue outlaw and put a warrant out for his arrest.

In a final attempt to put some life in his faltering movement, Brown and a small band of his men set their sights on a small, sleepy town northwest of Washington, DC. Here, at Harper's Ferry, West Virginia, the US Army kept a large stockpile of munitions, weaponry badly needed by Brown's band. With a group of twenty-one armed men, including five freed slaves, they assaulted the arsenal and captured it. Brown's group delayed their own escape for unknown reasons, and the US Army, under the command of Col. Robert E. Lee, had plenty of time to surround the captured buildings and wait for a surrender. It would be a surrender that never came.

Brown and his men went out with guns blazing, and when the smoke cleared at Harper's Ferry that day, October 19, 1859, ten of Brown's men and seven US troops were dead. Two of the dead were Brown's sons. The leader was arrested and placed in chains and taken to a federal prison in Charlestown, Virginia. After being treated for wounds he received during the gun battle, Brown went on trial for murder and treason. He was convicted.

Brown was given the death sentence and was hanged on December 2, 1859, in front of a large gathering of federal troops. He had ridden to the gallows sitting on his own coffin in the back of a hay wagon. Other participants of the raid were also convicted and hanged that same day.

Brown had directed that his body be removed to North Elba for burial. A large entourage of family and friends escorted his remains to the Adirondacks, where he was buried on his farm six days after his death.

Grave Location: John Brown's grave and farm are located on John Brown Road, just off Route 73, on the southern outskirts of Lake Placid. There are many signs to lead you to this famous place. His grave site, covered in glass and located near the farmhouse, consists of boulders and monuments and an imposing larger-than-life statue of John Brown with his arm draped around the shoulders of a young African American child.

Author's Note: There are many signs to lead visitors to the Brown farm and grave site, which has been a member of the New York State Parks Association since 1995. In fact, Brown's grave, as well as that of singer Kate Smith (chapter 34), are two of the most visited tourist sites in the Lake Placid area.

Brown's farm has been restored to 1860-era condition and offers many historical signs, exhibits, and photographs. In 1999, at the rededication of this site, then New York Parks Commissioner Bernadette Castro spoke of Brown: "The life of John Brown helped shape the history of our nation. It is fitting to memorialize his lifelong commitment to the abolition of slavery, and that of his sons and comrades, in this humble setting that he called home."

Amazingly, in attendance that day in 1999 were Mrs. Douglas Sutliffe, a great-grandniece of Brown supporter Aaron Stevens (hanged alongside of Brown), and Mrs. Ann Chetsky, great-grandniece of Oliver Brown, who was killed at the raid led by his father. Both Stevens and Oliver Brown are also buried at this site in North Elba.

Factoid: John Brown's grave site is in close proximity to the Lake Placid Olympic Jumping Complex. The towering training slopes can be seen overhead near the Brown Farm. Tours are offered at the complex.

For More Information: New York State Parks, Recreation, and Historic Preservation, "John Brown Farm State Historic Site," nysparks.com /historic-sites/29/details.aspx.

27

BRODERICK CRAWFORD

1911–1986

HIGHWAY PATROL
BURIED IN JOHNSTOWN,
FULTON COUNTY

*W*illiam Broderick Crawford was born to parents who were vaudevillians and never stayed in one place for very long. He traveled with them on "the circuit" from childhood on and caught the acting bug at a young age. Although he was a good student (accepted at Harvard), he left a shortened term in school to go to New York to work and train as an actor. He was a large, hulking man who seemed destined to portray thugs, policemen, and menacing personalities. An early reviewer said he had "a face like a catcher's mitt." He made his mark early on Broadway playing Lenny in *Of Mice and Men*, a role for which he received stellar reviews from the critics. From that launching pad he found steady work on the stage, in radio, in films and, later, on television.

After appearing in numerous films, he scored his career breakthrough with a mercurial performance as Southern politician Willie Stark in *All the King's Men*. His searing portrayal of a corrupt political boss was the talk of the 1949 film season. At Oscar time, Crawford walked away with the Academy Award for Best Actor, beating out Kirk Douglas, Gregory Peck, John Wayne, and Richard Todd. The following year he played the male lead in another Hollywood blockbuster—and a rare light comedy for the actor—*Born Yesterday*, costarring with Judy Holliday and William Holden. The film was nominated for the Best Picture Academy Award, although it did not win.

Broderick Crawford was now a major movie star who found as much work as he wanted. But by 1955 the new age of television was calling, and he signed to play a police officer in the popular series *Highway Patrol*. If movies hadn't made him a household name, this popular show, which ran for three seasons, did. It also made him a wealthy man, with reports suggesting that he made several million dollars for his run of the series. He left the show for other movie roles in 1959, but by then his star was on the wane.

To a generation of baby boomers, Crawford's portrayal of no-nonsense Captain Dan Matthews of the California Highway Patrol is a sentimental bridge to the black and white TV days of their youth. He appeared in 156 half-hour episodes of the drama. The actor's three-dimensional acting style—huffing, puffing, hulking, scowling, and barking out orders—made a big impression on kids, especially young boys, who dreamed of one day growing up and shouting "Ten-four, ten-four!" into a police walkie-talkie after chasing down a bad guy on a lonely California highway.

Crawford, who was married three times, suffered bad health in his last years, brought on by heavy smoking, alcohol abuse, and years of being seriously overweight. After a series of strokes he died on April 26, 1986, at the age of seventy-four.

Grave Location: Broderick Crawford is buried with his parents in Ferndale Cemetery in Johnstown. To reach his grave, enter the main gate of the cemetery off North Perry Street and make an immediate right. As the road winds to the left, follow it until you can make a sharp left. Section B will be in front of you. The actor is buried in the western part of this section.

Author's Note: Broderick Crawford and his parents, Helen and Lester, all have identical gravestones.

Factoid: Broderick Crawford's father, Lester, was a popular vaudeville performer. His mother, Helen Broderick, was much more successful. She was a talented comedic actress with a spot-on deadpan delivery who performed with the Ziegfeld Follies as well as in dozens of movies. She costarred several times with Fred Astaire, including in *Top Hat* (1935) and *Swing Time* (1936).

For More Information: Los Angeles Times Hollywood Star Walk, "Broderick Crawford," projects.latimes.com/hollywood/star-walk/broderick -crawford/.

28

JOHN W. "BUD" FOWLER

1858–1913

BEFORE JACKIE ROBINSON . . .
FIRST BLACK IN BASEBALL
BURIED IN FRANKFORT,
HERKIMER COUNTY

*N*early seventy years before Jackie Robinson broke the "visible" color line in baseball, Bud Fowler broke the "invisible" one.

At the dawning of the organized baseball era, it was a white man's game. Few men of color even dared to think about facing the gauntlet of racial scorn they would certainly endure by joining a baseball league in late-1800s America. John Fowler was the *first* documented black man to don a baseball uniform for a recognized organized baseball team. He was a talented and aggressive player who put some serious numbers up on his statistic sheet. Another serious number he reached was twenty. That is the number of teams he played for in just ten years. As a black man in a white man's sport, Fowler was a man on the move.

Born John Jackson in 1858 to an escaped slave, no one really knows why he adopted the name John Fowler. He started playing for the Keokuk, Iowa, team in 1885. There were many blacks in minor league baseball from the start (around 1877), but Bud Fowler was the first (and the best) to make the big time. He stood only five foot seven and was a wiry spitfire of a man. He threw and batted right handed. In seven of his ten years of active playing, he batted over .300. Although he played at every position on the field, and did so with excellence, he was the league's standout second baseman and was one of the sport's most feared base runners. His exploits on the baseball diamond stirred the insecurities of white Southern audiences,

and team after team traded him for "safety reasons." At the turn of the century, when "whites only" became the official rule of the game, Fowler played for and managed many black teams in the Negro Leagues.

In 1894, he founded the famous Page Fence Giants. This all-black team was sponsored by the Page Woven Wire Fence Company of Adrian, Michigan. They travelled America playing before large crowds and were a commercial success. With this success came the trappings of fame. They traveled in a comfortable, custom-made railroad car equipped with a commercial kitchen and plush sleeping quarters. Cooks, servants, and porters catered to their every need.

Bud Fowler became the first black baseball celebrity. He never lived to see Jackie Robinson smash through professional baseball's color barrier in 1947. Fowler died on February 26, 1913, at his sister's home in Frankfort, at the age of only fifty-four.

Grave Location: Although he was the first notable black baseball player, Fowler rested in anonymity for decades in an unmarked grave in

Frankfort's Oak View Cemetery. To bring attention to this forgotten sports legend, the Society for American Baseball Research bought and paid for a modest stone to mark his final resting place in 1987. It reads simply: "Bud Fowler. Black Baseball Pioneer." Frankfort is six miles east of Utica. Exit Route 5s at Higby Road and make a left where Higby turns into Cemetery Road. The cemetery is located near the sprawling Frankfort Fairgrounds. Enter the cemetery at the northern gate and proceed half way down the road. Just past the large mausoleum, on your right, is Fowler's grave. It can easily be seen from the road.

Author's Note: Cooperstown, and the National Baseball Hall of Fame, have honored Fowler in several ways. At famed Doubleday Field in the village, there is a plaque commemorating his achievements. The road to the field was dubbed Fowler Way on April 20, 2013, as the village held a Bud Fowler Day in his honor.

Factoid: Note a series of New York State historical markers located in front of a large mansion next to Oak View Cemetery. These markers tell the story of Carl and Carlotta Meyers, whose house is known as the Balloon House. Carlotta was the first American woman to fly solo in a hot air balloon and was known as the Lady Aeronaut. Their home and farm was their base of operations and is where they housed their many balloons, equipment, and other inventions.

For More Information: Society for American Baseball Research, "Bud Fowler," sabr.org/bioproj/person/200e2bbd/.

29

NASA Astronaut
Gregory B. Jarvis

1944–1986

SPACE SHUTTLE CHALLENGER
CENOTAPH IN MOHAWK,
HERKIMER COUNTY

Gregory Bruce Jarvis was born in Michigan but was raised in Upstate New York. He graduated from Mohawk Central High School in 1962 and earned a bachelor's degree from SUNY Buffalo and later a master's degree from Northeastern University in Boston. After retiring from the military (1969–73), he worked for several space-related firms before joining NASA.

Jarvis was a payload specialist when he boarded the Space Shuttle *Challenger* for his first flight in space. He and the entire crew were killed almost instantly when the craft exploded over the Atlantic Ocean at 11:30 a.m. on January 28, 1986.

Astronaut Jarvis loved physical activities, especially cycling, skiing, and playing squash. He played classical guitar to relax. He was survived by his wife, Marcia.

Jarvis was posthumously awarded the Congressional Space Medal of Honor. Remembrances to hometown boy Greg Jarvis can be found throughout Mohawk, and the local high school was renamed in his honor.

Grave Location: The remains of most of the *Challenger's* crew members were discovered in the wreckage on the ocean floor some six weeks after the disaster. Jarvis's remains were cremated and his ashes spread over the Pacific Ocean. A gravestone in Mohawk Cemetery honors him with an

inscription and his official, full-color NASA photograph. The cemetery is on Route 28 just as you enter the village from the south. Make the first left-hand turn into the cemetery and proceed three-quarters of the way to the back. Stop here, and Jarvis's monument is in the center section on the right.

Author's Note: Space Shuttle *Challenger* crew members are buried as follows. In some instances, no remains were found and grave markers act as a memorial only.

S. Christa McAuliffe (First Teacher in Space), Calvary Cemetery, Concord, New Hampshire

Ronald McNair, Rest Lawn Cemetery, Lake City, South Carolina

Judith Resnik, Arlington National Cemetery

Dick Scobee, Arlington National Cemetery

Michael J. Smith, Arlington National Cemetery

Ellison Onizuka, National Memorial Cemetery of the Pacific, Honolulu, Hawaii

Factoid: The University of Buffalo has named their engineering building after Gregory Jarvis, who received his degree there.

For More Information: Sea and Sky, "Challenger Memorial," www .seasky.org/space-exploration/challenger-gregory-jarvis.html.

30

SIR WILLIAM JOHNSON

1715–1774

"HE WHO DOES MUCH BUSINESS"
BURIED IN JOHNSTOWN,
FULTON COUNTY

*H*is Mohawk Indian name was Warraghyagey, which means "he who does much business." William Johnson certainly lived up to his name. As a most trusted friend of the Mohawk tribe for decades, he rose to the position of Superintendent of Indian Affairs in 1756 and was largely responsible for guiding the tribe's destiny through both peace and war.

Johnson came to America to oversee the vast land holdings of his English uncle, Sir Peter Warren. Johnson himself would use his lucrative fur-trading profits to become one of the wealthiest and largest landowners in New York State. At one time, he personally held title to over three hundred square miles of fertile farming land along the Mohawk Valley. The inhabitants of the region, including a sizeable number of Indians, became his tenants and his subjects.

Johnson was no ordinary land baron. He was deeply committed to the nurturing of the land and to the well-being of his people. He became particularly friendly with, and trusted by, the Mohawks. He joined them in a battle against the French in the French and Indian Wars of 1754. He vigorously educated himself on the customs and rituals of their forefathers and earned their respect as a spokesman for their causes. He took on a concubine, Molly Brant, who was the sister of the powerful Mohawk war chief, Joseph Brant. He sired many descendants whose extended families would make up a large segment of his constituents.

Sir William was the most influential figure in Indian affairs in the mid-1700s. So strong was his impact on the life of the Mohawk Nation that even after his death he was revered as a leader, and his policies were adhered to as if he were still alive.

Johnson died on July 11, 1774, and was buried in the community that he designed and planned and which was named after him.

Grave Location: Johnson's grave is in a most public of places. Large plaques and memorials to him line Johnstown's Main Street leading to his grave in the side yard of St. John's Episcopal Church at 1 North Market Street. A man of some ego, Sir William would probably not argue with the inscription on his headstone: "Grave of Sir William Johnson. 1775–1774. His Indian Name Warraghyagey. 'He Who Does Much Business' Founder of Johnstown Supt. of Indian Affairs Major General British Army Colonel of the Six Nations Builder of an Empire."

Author's Note: Johnson's baronial estate, Johnson Hall, is a centerpiece of any Johnstown historic tour.

Factoid: While visiting Johnson's grave, if you turn around and look across the busy thoroughfare you will notice what is today the Fleet Bank building. There you will find a brass plaque announcing that this building was the birthplace of one of the founders of the women's rights movement in America, Elizabeth Cady Stanton.

For More Information: Montgomery County Historical Society, "Old Fort Johnson," www.oldfortjohnson.org.

31

BRIGADIER GENERAL ZEBULON PIKE

1779–1807

*PIKE'S PEAK
BURIED IN SACKETS HARBOR,
JEFFERSON COUNTY*

Zebulon Pike was born in New Jersey, explored the far West, fought wars in Canada, was arrested by Spain, and is buried in Upstate New York.

Pike entered the army in 1793 and rose to the rank of second lieutenant. In 1805, he led a twenty-man party on a two-thousand-mile exploration journey seeking the headwaters of the Mississippi River (then uncharted). A year later, he led another expedition surveying the far-reaching borders of the newly acquired Louisiana Purchase territory. It was on this trip that he first spied the mountain peak in Colorado that would ultimately bear his name. Despite reports to the contrary, there is no record of Pike ever successfully scaling Pike's Peak.

Heading south on this expedition, Pike and his troops were arrested after straying into Spanish territory (now New Mexico). His party was taken hundreds of miles south of the region into an area hitherto unseen by European Americans. His journals and reporting of what he saw illuminated the potential trading bonanza with the Spanish and brought about a great land rush to the region of Texas and the Southwest. On seeing the vast desert area of the far west, however, he wrote that it had little to offer in terms of resources or climate. He likened this remote area to the African deserts, and because of this land investors stayed away in droves.

Throughout his later military career he was primarily assigned to the large military complex on the New York/Canadian border in Sackets Harbor. From here he led forays into Canada during the War of 1812 and was promoted to brigadier general.

On April 27, 1813, Pike led an army of 1,700 men across Lake Ontario to attack the city of York (now Toronto). The defenders threw everything they had at Pike and his men, and the battle was fierce. The British, anticipating the possibility of defeat, had cunningly laid a trap for the American. They planted a huge minefield near their fort and filled it with explosives and large boulders. They attempted to lure the Americans into this area to set off the explosions. Unfortunately, and unaccountably, the minefield exploded prematurely to devastating effect. Forty-two British and fifty-two Americans were killed in the blast. A boulder struck Brig. Gen. Pike so severely that his spine was nearly severed. Lying on the battlefield as the tide turned in the Americans' favor, legend has it that he called for the British colors to be struck and the American flag to be raised in victory.

The British flag was brought to him and put under his head to comfort him in his final moments.

He died on the battlefield. He was thirty-four years old.

Grave Location: Zebulon Pike is buried in the Old Military Cemetery in Sackets Harbor. It is now referred to as the Madison Barracks Post Cemetery. The cemetery is very small, and Pike's grave is near the back. A large cast iron mortar cannon marks his grave. His epitaph reads: "In memory of Gen. Z. M. Pike. Killed at York Upper Canada, 27 April 1813."

Author's Note: The Madison Barracks campus consists of nearly one hundred stone buildings that were used to house and train as many as six hundred troops. The majestic gray limestone edifices line up like, well, soldiers at attention all around a large manicured parade grounds, and each building today carries the name of a famous soldier who either led the troops or trained there. The feeling of the complex is akin to a smaller version of West Point.

Plaques on the various walls of barracks where soldiers lived jump out at you like vivid images from a history book: "Ripley, General Ebenezer. War of 1812, Sackets Harbor." "Forsythe, Col. Benjamin. Commander of Rifle Regiment at Battle of Ogdensburg." "Brown, General Jacob. War of 1812 Commander of U.S. Army until 1828." One unit declares itself "Grant's Quarters." A young soldier, Lt. Ulysses S. Grant, and his wife, Julia, were stationed in these very barracks. Another large boulder reads "Birthplace of General Mark Clark." Clark, a World War I, World War II, and Korean War hero, was the youngest soldier ever to be promoted to general. He was born at Madison Barracks on May 1, 1896. Former New York City Mayor Fiorello LaGuardia as well as President Martin Van Buren also served at Sackets Harbor.

Factoid: An ornate wrought-iron fence from England's Buckingham Palace surrounds the small military cemetery in reconciliation to the British burning Washington, DC, and the White House in 1812.

For More Information: American Forts, "Sackets Harbor Battlefield State Historic Site," www.northamericanforts.com/East/New_York/Sackets _Harbor/Sackets_Harbor.html.

32

JOHNNY PODRES

1932–2008

BROOKLYN DODGER HERO
BURIED IN MORIAH CENTER,
ESSEX COUNTY

*J*ohnny Podres was a mainstay of the Brooklyn Dodgers baseball team. He made his debut with the team on April 7, 1953, and pitched his last game for them in 1966 before being traded off to the Detroit Tigers and then finally to the San Diego Padres. But with star turns on the mound and a likable, welcoming presence in the sports press, he had legions of fans with the Dodgers in Brooklyn.

Podres posted some significant career numbers along the way, including being named an All-Star four times and the National League ERA leader in 1957. He ultimately would end up wearing four World Series rings from the years 1955, 1959, 1963, and 1965. He threw twenty-four shutouts in his fifteen-year career.

The peak of Podres's fame came in the World Series of 1955. It was in this series against the Dodgers' bitter crosstown rivals, the New York Yankees, that Podres earned his entry into the halls of Dodger greatness. The Dodgers had won seven pennants in their league before, but the title had remained elusive. Podres was a key member of a Brooklyn team that included such legends as Roy Campanella, Don Newcombe, Pee Wee Reese, Duke Snider, and the great Jackie Robinson. The Yankees would field Phil Rizzuto, Yogi Berra, Don Larsen, Whitey Ford, Elston Howard, and the legendary Mickey Mantle. It was a battle that tore New York City baseball fans in half.

Podres was on the mound in the deciding Game 7 of the series as the Dodgers clung to a tenuous two-run lead. One by one the Yankee greats came up against the Dodgers pitcher, and one by one they went down. With the help of some memorable fielding, particularly a dramatic save of a Yogi Berra extra base hit by Dodger outfielder Sandy Amoros in the sixth inning, Podres took the Yankees down in order in the ninth inning for the long-awaited win. The team erupted as the Dodgers celebrated on the field, including burly catcher Roy Campanella running full speed to the mound to triumphantly lift the grinning Podres. The home team fans at Yankee Stadium were stunned.

And that is how Johnny Podres reached Dodger immortality.

He was a true son of Upstate New York. He was born in the tiny Adirondack mining village of Witherbee and returned to the area (Moriah) after his retirement from baseball. During the last years of his life, Podres was a frequent visitor to the stores, coffee shops, and playing fields of his hometown. He drove what many called the most recognizable car in town, a green Cadillac with the custom license plates that read MVP 55.

Johnny Podres is remembered in Cooperstown with this popular action statue on the grounds of the National Baseball Hall of Fame and Museum. Courtesy of the National Baseball Hall of Fame and Museum, Cooperstown, NY.

The Brooklyn Dodger legend died on January 13, 2008. He was seventy-five.

Grave Location: Podres is buried in the small Saints Peter and Paul Cemetery in Moriah. His gravestone features an image of him in a Dodger uniform throwing a pitch. Under the image it reads "MVP 55" and along the bottom of his stone it reads "I did what I had to do, and I did it well."

Author's Note: The hometown baseball hero is well-remembered in this small town he called home. There is a welcome sign in his honor on Route 9N coming into Moriah that features his baseball card photograph, and the Moriah Central School athletic field is named in his honor.

Factoid: One of the greatest public monuments in Cooperstown (a village with a plethora of public monuments) can be found directly outside the walls of the National Baseball Hall of Fame and Museum. It is a double bronze statue tableau depicting Podres throwing to his catcher Roy Campanella. The statues are life-size, and the distance between the two figures is exactly sixty feet and six inches, the standard major league baseball regulation distance between the pitcher's mound and home plate.

For More Information: Baseball Reference, "Johnny Podres," www.baseball-reference.com/players/p/podrejo01.shtml.

33

FREDERIC REMINGTON

1861–1901

MASTER PAINTER OF THE OLD WEST
BURIED IN CANTON,
ST. LAWRENCE COUNTY

$\mathcal{F}$rederic Remington was already an established and well known painter and sculptor by the time the Spanish-American War began in 1898. Remington became a war correspondent for William Randolph Hearst, who sent him to Cuba to document the trials and tribulations of the military, both in combat and while experiencing the mundane activities of camp life. Remington's colorful dispatches were met by an eager audience of readers of Hearst's *New York Journal*. While near Santiago, Cuba, he witnessed future president Theodore Roosevelt leading his group of Rough Riders up San Juan Hill in a dramatic frontal attack on the enemy. Remington's depiction of this exciting event became his most famous painting as well as one of the great iconic images of Roosevelt as a courageous and daring leader. The painting shows Roosevelt riding his horse into a field of enemy fire while some of his men lie dead in the grass and others are reacting to the moment of being shot. Both Remington and Roosevelt were forever linked to this great American painting, which was titled *Charge of the Rough Riders at San Juan Hill*.

Remington created hundreds of paintings, mostly depicting cattle roping, bronco busting, and campfire-sitting cowboys. The American Indian was frequently the subject of his work as were the animals of the American West, particularly the buffalo. Among his most famous works are *A Dash for the Timber* (1889), *The Blanket Signal* (1898), *Fight at the Waterhole*

(1903), *The Cowboy* (1902) and *The Scout* (1907). Several of his paintings were issued as US postage stamps, and his original works are prized possessions of many of America's most prestigious art galleries. He was a most prolific artist, having created and signed over three thousand works of art in his short lifetime.

Remington was also a pioneer in American sculpture. His works, showing the movement and connection between man and horse, are vibrant and muscular. Perhaps his most recognizable piece is *The Broncho Buster*, done in 1895. An original cast of this statue has resided in the White House Oval Office since the days of the Carter administration. He created a total of twenty-two bronze statues.

A native of remote Canton in rural Upstate New York, Remington became an international celebrity through his paintings, sculptures, novels, and articles published in some of America's most popular newspapers and magazines of the day. He was a wealthy man who lived for many years in New Rochelle, New York. Shortly before his death he designed and oversaw the construction of a mansion in Ridgefield, Connecticut, but he died shortly after it was completed. Following the painter's death, his widow, Edith, moved to Ogdensburg, New York, where she lived the remainder of her life. That home is now a museum to Remington's work.

Grave Location: The artist is buried in Evergreen Cemetery in Canton. Enter the main gate off Route 11 and stay to your right. The large Remington monument is on your left in Section B.

Author's Note: Another fascinating grave in this cemetery belongs to that of Milton H. Freeman. He was the chief engineer of the construction of the Holland Tunnel in New York City. His epitaph reads: "He lives on in the mighty works that he wrought." He is buried in Section G, plot B.

Factoid: The Frederic Remington Art Museum is one of Ogdensburg's tourist attractions. The exhibits rotate on a fairly frequent schedule, and at any time you can find many of Remington's greatest works on display. The museum also has a wonderful gift shop where many posters, prints, sculptures, and books pertaining to the artist are available for sale.

For More Information: Frederic Remington Art Museum, www.fredericremington.org.

34

KATE SMITH

1907–1986

"GOD BLESS AMERICA"
BURIED IN LAKE PLACID,
ESSEX COUNTY

The parents of little Kathryn Smith were duly alarmed when she still had not spoken a word by her fourth birthday. Specialists were sought out and treatments were considered. Finally, halfway through her fourth year, little Kate started to talk—and didn't stop for seventy-five years!

Endowed with a disarming naturalness and a much-envied singing voice, Kate Smith would become one of the most famous women in the world, with tens of millions of fans and admirers. Through singing, Smith found her way into America's history books. On her twenty-first birthday, May 1, 1931, she made her debut on national radio. Her legendary career would span half of the twentieth century and set standards for professionalism and excellence rarely seen today.

After beginning her career as a featured Broadway singer and dancer, where her three-hundred-pound frame would not only shake the theater rafters but would also bring her a torrent of nasty and hateful remarks from critics, Smith sought refuge in the nascent and semi-anonymous medium of radio. Her newfound manager and friend, Ted Collins, sensitively guided Smith's career into radio, and they formed a corporation together all on the simple formality of a handshake. It went on to become one of the most successful mergers in entertainment history, earning both of them untold millions of dollars.

Ted fashioned Kate Smith into the greatest star of the earliest days of radio (where she could be heard rather than seen) and managed the

singer to an $18,000 per week salary by the age of twenty-three. Yes, a week!

Smith's songs sold in the millions all across the heartland of Depression America. She was a veritable music engine. She introduced more than six hundred songs, with many of them becoming the standards of the day. During her lifetime she is credited with recording more than three thousand songs, more than any other entertainer. She became an overnight legend when she introduced Irving Berlin's immortal "God Bless America" on Armistice Day, 1938. It quickly became our nation's unofficial national anthem.

With the dawning of television, and her popularity at its peak, Smith became one of the new medium's superstars starting in 1950. She would remain a welcome and frequent television guest star for the next three decades.

For several years in the 1970s, Kate Smith was the "good luck" symbol of the Philadelphia Flyers NHL team. Her stirring rendition of "God Bless America" was played before home games, and the ice hockey team ran up a memorable winning streak when it was played. She traveled to the city to sing "her song" live before several crucial hockey games.

Kate Smith died on June 17, 1986, at the age of seventy-nine.

Grave Location: Smith is buried in St. Agnes Cemetery in Lake Placid. She was a summer resident of this small Adirondack community for over forty years. As you enter the main gate of the cemetery, keep going up a small rise and you will see her mausoleum (the only mausoleum in the cemetery) on the far left. The capstone reads: "Kathryn E. Smith."

Author's Note: Kate Smith was considered to be a neighbor by the residents of Lake Placid over her many years living here. She owned a summer home and boathouse on Buck Island in the middle of the lake. She would cheerily come down to the dock and wave at the tour boats that passed by her place. She was a regular churchgoer at St. Agnes Roman Catholic Cemetery, and there is a large color portrait of her in the sanctuary to honor her memory. The village also placed a plaque in her memory on Main Street that tells of her fame and of her connection with Lake Placid.

Factoid: When Smith died, her will stipulated that much of her estate be left to her church in return for being buried in a large, pink marble mausoleum at St. Agnes Cemetery. The only problem was that the cemetery did not allow mausoleums. An unseemly legal case ensued, and more than a year after her passing the singer was finally buried in the tomb she had desired.

If you look through the glass door of Kate's tomb, you will see gold script over her last remains. The words were Franklin D. Roosevelt's way of introducing Kate to the King and Queen of England when they visited the United States: "This is Kate Smith. This is America."

For More Information: National Radio Hall of Fame, "Kate Smith," www.radiohof.org/kate_smith.htm.

35

MARY EDWARDS WALKER

1832–1919

ONLY FEMALE MEDAL OF HONOR RECIPIENT
BURIED IN OSWEGO,
OSWEGO COUNTY

*M*ary Walker was born in Oswego in 1832. Her parents were stern non-believers who preached that their children should not adhere to the normal practices of life when the urge to be different presented itself to them. Walker's parents were also active abolitionists in Oswego County, where there were more than a dozen known Underground Railroad stations. The family home was a lively center for political discussions and debate. Mary's father believed that his many daughters would be encumbered by wearing tight-fitting "women's clothes," which he said would hamper their movement and free spirits. In her early years, young Mary swore off wearing female clothing and would dress in "masculine" style for the rest of her life.

When Walker got married in 1864, she daringly wore a man's suit at the ceremony and refused to take her new husband's last name, which was scandalous for the time. She also omitted the word "obey" in their wedding vows. Once, she was even arrested for impersonating a man. She was a brilliant student and entered college, coming out of Syracuse Medical College in 1855 as its first female graduate and only the second female graduate of any medical school in America (six years behind Elizabeth Blackwell).

During the Civil War, Mary Walker was appointed Assistant Surgeon of the Union Army. She tended to the battlefield wounds of her charges

while exposing herself to hostile fire on numerous occasions. One time, she was captured by the Confederates and held prisoner. Four months later, she and sixteen Union doctors were part of a prisoner exchange involving twenty-four Confederate surgeons. The South had pegged Mary Walker as a spy and had placed a large bounty on her head for her capture.

For her wartime heroics, Dr. Walker was awarded the Congressional Medal of Honor. She wore it proudly every day of her life. In 1917, when the US Board of Military Medal Awards decided to rescind the medal from nearly one thousand recipients who were not classified as "traditionally combat in nature," Walker was ordered to return her medal. She refused and fought the government on this issue until her death. In 1977, under orders from President Jimmy Carter, the US military restored Mary's Medal of Honor with apologies.

To this day, out of the more than two million women veterans of our armed forces, Dr. Walker is the *only* female recipient of this prestigious honor.

Grave Location: Mary Walker is buried in the Town of Oswego Rural Cemetery, located on Cemetery Road about a mile from Route 104. Enter the main gate of the cemetery and stop at the second set of steps on your right (Fruit Valley section). On the right you will see the military gravestone of Dr. Walker. Her marker carries the insignia of the Medal of Honor.

Author's Note: Although Mary Walker is not well-known to the general public, she is remembered with fondness in her native Oswego. The wellness center at the State University of New York at Oswego is named the Walker Health Center in her honor. A life-sized statue of Dr. Walker stands in front of the Oswego City Hall.

Factoid: Dr. Walker was buried wearing a man's jacket and trousers. Some in Oswego say she was even buried wearing her beloved Medal of Honor.

For More Information: Congressional Medal of Honor Society, "Walker, Dr. Mary E.," www.cmohs.org/recipient-detail/1428/walker-dr -mary-e.php.

Part Four

CENTRAL NEW YORK

36

EMMETT ASHFORD

1914–1980

SUPERSTAR UMPIRE
BURIED IN COOPERSTOWN,
OTSEGO COUNTY

$\mathcal{B}$efore Emmett Ashford came along, baseball umpires were anonymous men in black covered in heavy padding, their faces hidden behind a wire cage face mask. They called balls and strikes and kept a civil order during a baseball game. On some occasions they were called upon to intercede in a fracas, throw out an unruly player, and even play weatherman to call or not call a game on account of rain. Almost nobody knew the names of these men.

When Ashford arrived in the game, umping his first Major League contest on April 11, 1966, he created a seismic shift heard from Boston to Los Angeles. He was flamboyant, dramatic, and colorful, and no play was too mundane to dodge his shtick. A called out was a ballet of leg turns, karate chops, and elbow thrusts. When a runner on base was safe, Ashford signaled this with a pageant of spread arms and legs, and a flourish of hand gestures. He wore flashy jewelry and dressed as nattily as the million-dollar players he was calling out and safe. He brought style to a styleless profession and was embraced by the fans in ballparks in both leagues.

He was also historic. Emmett Ashford was the first African American umpire in Major League Baseball.

Ashford was a post office clerk for fifteen years before he began umpiring minor league baseball games at age thirty-six. Next came the majors.

Some believe that there were several reasons for Ashford not entering the majors until middle age. Many thought race played a part, and others

offered that his flashy style on the field was a distraction to the game and in fact hindered play. He proved them wrong when it soon became apparent that fans would inquire, "Is Emmett umpiring today?" before buying a ticket. He was a sensation, in as much as any umpire in America's pastime could be. He officiated at several important games, including all five games of the 1970 World Series. Because Ashford was so popular and because he got such a late start in his umpiring career, Bowie Kuhn relaxed the mandatory retirement age for umpires, allowing Ashford to stay one year past the legal retirement age of fifty-five.

After retiring, he stayed in baseball as a special consultant in Commissioner Bowie Kuhn's public relations department. Ashford was extremely popular with Americans of all walks of life, and he soon found himself being booked for interviews in magazines, on the talk circuit, and even for some television appearances. While still in the minors, on November 17, 1955, he made his first national public appearance on the game show *You Bet Your Life* with Groucho Marx. The two bantered breezily about Ashford's umpire duties. He was also on an edition of *What's My Line?* On this program, host John Charles Daly asked Ashford to show off his antics when he called a strike. As most baseball fans already knew, the ump called a strike three with particular flair, making the word three sound as if it had multiple syllables. Ashford, in a rare bout of shyness, got up from the desk and pantomimed his gyrations in calling "Strike three!" but he was too embarrassed to do the actual yelling. Mr. Daly, the host, provided the vocals.

Emmett Ashford died of a heart attack in Marina del Rey, California, on March 1, 1980, at age sixty-five. At his funeral, Commissioner Kuhn eulogized him as a "magnanimous, uncomplaining, lively personality" who was a true pioneer. Although he was never inducted into the National Baseball Hall of Fame, his remains were sent there, and the hall purchased a plot in Lakeview Cemetery for his burial.

Grave Location: Emmett Ashford's grave is very easy to find. Drive up the east side of Otsego Lake in Cooperstown, and just a quarter mile from Main Street you will come to Lakewood Cemetery, with sections on both sides of the road (Route 31). Enter the first cemetery driveway on your left and stop immediately after leaving the road. Ashford's grave is the first one on the left. His gravestone carries these words: "He believed an umpire should have integrity, perseverance, and dedication. As an American League umpire 1965–1970 he added drama to baseball with his zestful, flamboyant style."

Author's Note: A baseball fan named Charlie Vascellaro created a small shrine in front of the umpire's grave, placing several artifacts in a Plexiglas cube in 2016. The items include tributes to several pioneering African American baseball stars, including baseball cards featuring Jackie Robinson and Frank Robinson plus a standard Major League baseball stamped with the signature of former National League president Bill White.

Factoid: Although Emmett Ashford is considered one of the greatest umpires of all time—and a historic figure for breaking the color line—he has never been seriously considered for enshrinement into the National Baseball Hall of Fame because of the short span of time he spent umpiring. There are ten umpires in the Hall with an average career span of almost twenty-eight years. Ashford's major league career lasted just five

Emmett Ashford brought excitement and drama to the formerly staid role played by baseball umpires. He was known for his extravagant base calls, his outspoken personality and his stylish sense of fashion. Courtesy of the National Baseball Hall of Fame and Museum, Cooperstown, NY.

years. He has not been without honors, however. In 2016, all umpires wore uniforms with "EA" on their sleeves honoring Ashford's ground-breaking first appearance in the majors in 1966.

For More Information: Society for American Baseball Research, "Emmett Ashford," sabr.org/bioproj/person/40af3222/.

37

JOSEPH BARBARA

1905–1959

JOE THE BARBER
BURIED IN JOHNSON CITY,
BROOME COUNTY

*D*uring the late 1950s, organized crime was perceived as *un*organized by most Americans. They had heard of unions of "families" controlled by bosses that had brought Old World heavy-handed discipline to the world of crime, but still, the magnitude of the La Cosa Nostra (literally "our thing"), or the mafia, was unimagined. That is until Joe the Barber decided to throw a barbecue.

Joseph Barbara came from Sicily in 1920 as a teenager. In the post-Prohibition era, he secured a major beer and soft drink distributorship in the New York's Southern Tier. Here, in Binghamton, he became a popular, yet relatively small-time, player in the crime families of the East. In 1957, he hosted a large gathering of mafiosi at his centrally located Apalachin, New York, home, which was on the border of New York and Pennsylvania. He had been afflicted with heart problems over the years and thought this event—a barbeque party at his home—would reduce any stresses he might suffer while attending a family sit-down somewhere else on the East Coast.

On November 14, 1957, New York State police Sgt. Edgar Croswell and Inv. Vincent Vasisko stumbled upon the Mob gathering while working on a totally unrelated case. They followed a long parade of shiny black automobiles to Barbara's rural estate and staked it out. Sensing they had come upon something big, they started writing down license plate numbers of the cars passing by and initiated a raid on the home.

At the first sign of trouble, the crime bosses headed for the woods. Later, Croswell and Vasisko would regale the press with stories of a bunch of overweight grown men running through the backwoods in thousand-dollar Italian suits and black felt fedoras. These men could be seen tossing larges wads of cash as well as handguns into the thicket as they fled the authorities. Needless to say, all fifty-eight mobsters were caught. At the local police barracks just down the road from the house, more than $300,000 in cash was emptied from the soiled and torn pockets of the out-of-breath crooks.

The lineup of names attending the crime summit surprised even the feds. Almost every major crime boss in the East was there including Carlo Gambino, Joe Profaci, Joseph Magaddino, Russ Bufalino, Vito Genovese, Joseph Bonanno, and Paul Castellano. No crime had actually occurred, and ultimately no jail time was served as most participants declared that they were simply attending a casual barbecue at the home of a sick friend. Still, the press came alive with stories of the length and breadth of the crime syndication in the country, and there could no longer be a denial of the Mafia in America. This discovery embarrassed the head of the FBI, J. Edgar Hoover, and he attacked the Mob with a fury. The Apalachin Raid would go down as the beginning of the end for all of the players who were caught eating some of the three hundred steaks barbecued at Joe the Barber's place that beautiful autumn day.

Crime boss Joseph Barbara died of a heart attack at the age of fifty-five on June, 17, 1959.

Grave Location: Barbara is buried at Calvary Cemetery in Johnson City. Leave Route 17 at the exit to the sprawling Oakdale Mall and make your first right onto Harry L. Drive. Just a few hundred feet down the road is the cemetery on your left. Enter at the first gate, and travel up and into the cemetery. Go through four major intersections and stop. Most of the graves are marked with relatively low-rising stones. Barbara's grave, however, is noted by one of the tallest monuments in this section and is easily recognized. A large, dark cross behind a white marble Christ figure marks his grave. The gold letters along the base read: "BARBARA." His family is buried with him here in the northernmost plot of Section 14.

Author's Note: Items from Joseph Barbara's country estate were auctioned off in August 2002. Hundreds attended hoping to go home with a bit of Mob history. One of those on hand that day was Joseph Barbara's grandson. Items went from $18,000 for a large hand-carved poker table down to $80 for a small end table (purchased by former New York sports and news radio broadcaster Jeff Bishop). The home sold for $300,000 to Mrs. Susan Deakin of Connecticut, and yes, the barbecue pit went with the house!

Factoid: The Apalachin Raid has been depicted in several crime-themed movies, from a serious treatment in *Inside the Mafia* (1959), starring Cameron Mitchell, to the big-budget Hollywood comedy *Analyze This* (1999), starring Billy Crystal and Robert DeNiro.

The five major crime family heads that attended the "Mob-a-que" are deceased. Paul Castellano (d. 1985) is buried in Moravian Cemetery, New Dorp, New York; Joseph Profaci (d. 1967), Vito Genovese (d. 1969) and Carlo Gambino (d. 1976) are all buried in St. John's Cemetery (often called the Mob Boot Hill) in Middle Village, New York; and Joseph Bonanno (who lived the longest and died in 2002) is buried in Holy Hope Cemetery, Tucson, Arizona.

For More Information: The Apalachin Mafia Convention, www.greaterowego.com/communitypress/1997/11-97/MAFIA.htm.

38

FRANCIS BELLAMY

1855–1931

"I PLEDGE ALLEGIANCE . . ."
BURIED IN ROME,
ONEIDA COUNTY

$\mathcal{T}$he New York State historical marker near the cemetery entrance tells of its most famous occupant: "The Grave of Francis Bellamy, Author of the Pledge of Allegiance." Rome Cemetery has seen its fair share of famous names since its incorporation in 1851, but none has brought more fame than Mr. Bellamy.

The son of a pastor, he was a writer for a magazine called *The Youth's Companion*. The publisher of the magazine, Daniel S. Ford, was a passionate patriot who believed that every school in the country should fly the American flag. Of course, many schools worked on a shoestring budget and couldn't afford a flag, so Ford began an aggressive campaign to sell flags out of his magazine. In 1892, with more than 25,000 public schools now having purchased a flag from his magazine, he tasked Bellamy with coming up with a "Salute to America" to sell even more flags. Since that year was the four-hundredth anniversary of Columbus Day, Bellamy used that occasion for his tribute to America.

The pledge was to be used by students attending our nation's public schools and later to be recited at public gatherings. Bellamy came up with arguably the most familiar twenty-three words in our history, words that have been recited by students and adults alike for well over a century—"I pledge allegiance to my flag and to the republic for which it stands; one nation indivisible, with liberty and justice for all." Bellamy addressed the

National School Superintendents convention that year, and they whole-heartedly endorsed his patriot endeavor. Soon, the pledge was being said by students in virtually every classroom in the nation.

Three minor changes were made through the years. Although Bel-lamy professed to believe in the strict separation of church and state, the phrase "under God" was suggested by President Dwight Eisenhower in the 1950s.

Grave Location: Bellamy is buried in Rome Cemetery, located at 1500 Jervis Avenue. His plot is the most prominent in the cemetery (Sec-tion D, to the right of the entrance), and a plaque bearing testimony to his fame is affixed to his monument. A towering flagpole at this site guides visitors to his grave.

Author's Note: The first burial at Rome Cemetery took place in 1853. The cemetery was originally only twenty-five acres in size. Over the years, more and more land was added, and today the cemetery sprawls over nearly 150 acres. Most of Rome's founding families are buried here.

The words to Francis Bellamy's original Pledge of Allegiance are written on his gravestone.

Factoid: Once Bellamy's pledge was accepted, he really concentrated on making it a pageant of patriotism. He designed an official program setting up a protocol for how his pledge was to be "performed" each day in schools. Bellamy also devised a "pledge salute," which he instructed had to be used during the recital. The "Bellamy salute" was an outstretched arm with palms down. This led to some uncomfortable feelings as World War II approached and images of Nazi supporters using the very same salute were seen by all. It was at this time that the outstretched arm salute was replaced with the hand-over-heart gesture.

The United States Flag Code of Conduct (Chapter One, Title Four) reads:

> The Pledge of Allegiance to the Flag: "I pledge allegiance to the Flag of the United States of America, and to the Republic for which it stands, one Nation under God, indivisible, with liberty and justice for all"

should be rendered by standing at attention facing the flag with the right hand over the heart. When not in uniform, men should remove any nonreligious headdress with their right hand and hold it at the left shoulder, the hand being over the heart. Persons in uniform should remain silent, face the flag, and render the military salute. Members of the Armed Forces not in uniform and veterans may render the military salute in the manner provided for persons in uniform.

For More Information: Smithsonian, "The Man Who Wrote the Pledge of Allegiance," www.smithsonianmag.com/history/the-man-who -wrote-the-pledge-of-allegiance-93907224/.

39

GRACE BROWN

1886–1906

AN AMERICAN TRAGEDY
BURIED IN SOUTH OTSELIC,
CHENANGO COUNTY

*G*race Brown was a beautiful young country girl working in a drab garment factory in Cortland, New York. The boss's nephew, Chester Gillette, was smitten with the diminutive lass, known to all of her friends as Billy, and he pursued her with tenderness and sincerity. They took long, lingering walks together, sharing their dreams of the future. In a short time, however, Chester started to feel the clawing constraints of emotional entanglement and tried to end their relationship. Grace would have none of that and begged him to stay with her. Chester relented, the romance continued (although the passion was gone on his part), and they went on seeing each other, living in the same small town and in fact working in the same factory.

Their lives would change dramatically in the spring of 1906, when Grace announced she was pregnant.

Chester wanted out of the relationship immediately and plotted the grisly denouement of their love affair. Under the guise of taking a vacation together, he took Grace on a train outing to the remote lake region of the Adirondack Mountains. On Thursday, July 11, 1906, he rented a rowboat and they left their hotel (Hotel Glenmore, Big Moose Lake) for a leisurely trip around the lake. By nightfall, Grace Brown was dead and Chester Gillette had vanished.

On the following day, a search party discovered the drowned girl's body, and within a few days Gillette was caught, arrested, and imprisoned

for her murder. Such was the beginning of the most celebrated murder case in New York in the early twentieth century.

Hundreds of onlookers stood in the rain to see the murder suspect arrive at the local Herkimer County jail in handcuffs. Tours of the lockup were added to afford the public a view of the suspect's cell. New York City newspapers sent their best reporters Upstate to cover the scandalous story. Rumors were fanned and embellished. And through it all, Chester Gillette stoically proclaimed his innocence.

Passions ran deep against the accused murderer. Headlines screamed his every move, and spectators scorned his lack of remorse. The *New York Morning Telegraph* sent its most famous reporter, Bat Masterson, to cover the trial. Courtroom drama went unchecked. One highpoint was when the prosecutor brought into court a cloth-covered bottle containing (he said) the fetus taken from Grace's body to prove her pregnancy. He never revealed it.

To the surprise of no one, Gillette was found guilty of murder and sentenced to death in the electric chair. His mother, Louise, waged an emotional and highly publicized clemency campaign on his behalf to no avail. He was electrocuted at Auburn State Prison on March 30, 1908.

Grave Location: Grace Brown is buried in Valley View Cemetery in tiny South Otselic, New York. You will find the grave on Route 26 directly across from the village fire department. Enter off Gorge Avenue and follow the main road into the cemetery. Halfway to the end, on your right near the road, is Grace's grave. Her stone reads: "Grace M. Brown. 1186–1906. At Rest."

Author's Note: Grace Brown's murder remained in the news for many years. In 1926, Theodore Dreiser wrote his now classic novel, *An American Tragedy*, about the case and it was a huge bestseller. His fictionalized account of the murder featured the character Clyde Griffiths in place of the real Chester Gillette, and Roberta "Bobbie" Alden in place of the real Grace "Billy" Brown. In 1931, Paramount Pictures produced a film based on Dreiser's account starring Sylvia Sidney. In 1951, the movie was retitled as *A Place in the Sun*, with the victim's role now being played by actress Shelley Winters. The 1951 movie was one of the year's big hits and rekindled serious interest in the Adirondack murder.

Factoid: After his electrocution, Gillette's body was buried in an unmarked grave in Auburn's Soule Cemetery. This is the same cemetery where Leon Czolgosz, the assassin of President William McKinley, is buried. His final resting place is also unmarked.

For More Information: Herkimer County Historical Society (Gillette's trial was held in the courthouse located across the street), www.rootsweb.ancestry.com/~nyhchs/gillette.html.

40

SAMUEL LANGHORNE CLEMENS

1835–1910

MARK TWAIN
BURIED IN ELMIRA,
CHEMUNG COUNTY

*O*f all of the incongruities in this book, none is more striking to me than the circumstances of Mark Twain's final resting place. Why on earth would this great chronicler of the Mississippi, this voyager to the four corners of the world, this bon vivant and social animal, this friend of presidents and millionaires, be buried in of all places in the Southern Tier community of Elmira? Actually it is quite simple. His wife's family was from Elmira, so he rests eternally with them. Still, it is a great surprise to come upon a tall monument in a shady area of this cemetery with the name Mark Twain on it.

As a young man, Clemens lived all along the fertile banks of the mighty Mississippi in small towns like Hannibal, Missouri. From ages four to eighteen he lived a life of ease and wonderment, caught up in the fascinating hustle and bustle of riverfront America. When he was twelve his father died, and he had to quit school and go to work as a journeyman printer to help support his mother and siblings. He eventually found himself along a peripatetic path that led him to St. Louis, Philadelphia, New Orleans, and then back to the Midwest. In his early twenties he took an apprenticeship aboard a riverboat heading north from New Orleans on the Mississippi. He stayed on this job until the Civil War closed the river. He called his years as a boat captain his "university" and would always say that from that time on his "mistress was that old river."

A natural writer and storyteller, Clemens left the river at the start of the Civil War and followed his wanderlust. He wrote for papers and journals as he travelled throughout the West, and in Virginia, where he was hired as a newspaperman, he took his pen name, Mark Twain. Even this nom de plume was an homage to his time spent on the river. Mark twain is a river call for a depth of two fathoms.

Twain published his first book, *The Celebrated Jumping Frog of Calaveras County*, in 1867, and it was an immediate success. Other much-loved works soon followed. He drew upon his past and his familiar surroundings to fill out his books. In *The Adventures of Tom Sawyer*, for example, the judge was modeled after his father, Aunt Polly was a tribute to his mother, Big Jim was a real neighbor slave named Uncle Dan, and Tom Sawyer himself was a reflection of the youthful writer. Having gained a great amount of success as an author, Twain started his own publishing firm in 1884, the Charles L. Webster Company, naming it after a favorite nephew. His initial publication, a mass printing of *Adventures of Huckleberry Finn*, sold more than thirty thousand copies.

As a writer, Twain was brilliant. As a businessman, not so much. After the Civil War he contracted with several of the war's legendary military leaders to publish their biographies, a venture that failed as a war-weary nation turned its attention to the future. His company had to file for bankruptcy protection on February 1, 1886.

Twain was a lover of gadgets and inventions. He held three US patents of his own—for an adjustable shirt strap, for a memory-building game, and for a glueless scrapbook. None made him rich, and after losing more than $100,000 on these items, he stuck to writing for the rest of his life.

He was one of America's most celebrated literati. He embarked on a lecture tour around the world and appeared in front of standing-room-only crowds everywhere. He hobnobbed with Rockefellers and Carnegies and received honors from Yale and Harvard. During his prime, he owned mansions in the Hudson Valley, Connecticut, and London. He also had a three-story home in Greenwich Village. Quarry Farm was the name of Twain's beloved sprawling estate in Elmira.

He died peacefully at his home in Connecticut on April 21, 1910. He was seventy-four.

The writer James Whitcomb Riley (*Little Orphan Annie*) eulogized Twain thusly: "The world has lost not only a genius, but a man of striking character, of influence, and of boundless resources. He knew the human heart and he was sincere. He knew children, and this knowledge made him tender."

Grave Location: Woodlawn Cemetery in Elmira has many famous people interred within. Visitors come seeking out Mark Twain's grave on an almost daily basis. The cemetery has wisely place directional signs to his plot in Section G. Twain is buried with his family, and his monument is remarkable. It is a tall pillar with a bronze cameo sculpture of the author gracing the top. A multipanel historical plaque shares information of his life, his time in Elmira, and photographs of him throughout his career.

Author's Note: Mark Twain is well-remembered in his wife's hometown. A pair of statues of the couple can be seen on the campus of Elmira College, her alma mater. Twain's original writing cottage was also moved to the campus and is staffed by "Twain Ambassadors" who can share the story of his life with the many visitors who come along. A small Twain museum is located inside a campus building.

Factoid: There are too many interesting tidbits in the life of Samuel Langhorne Clemens to fit in this short space. Some of our favorite facts are these: He loved his cats so much that visitors to his study in Elmira will notice little "cat doors" along the walls so they could enter and exit without bothering the writer. He smoked as many as twenty cigars a day for over a half century. Twain signed on as publisher for President Ulysses S. Grant's memoirs and visited the former president on a weekly basis during the final six weeks of Grant's life at a mountaintop home near Saratoga Springs. The last check he wrote was for $6,000 to fund a library near his home in Redding, Connecticut. And on and on it goes. Mark Twain led a full, American life.

For More Information: Welcome to Mark Twain Country, "Where Twain Remains," www.marktwaincountry.com/mark-twain/where-twain -remains/.

41

JAMES FENIMORE COOPER

1789–1851

LEATHERSTOCKING TALES
BURIED IN COOPERSTOWN,
OTSEGO COUNTY

*J*ames Fenimore Cooper has been called America's first popular writer. He was raised the eleventh of twelve children in a town built by his father and named for his family. In 1821, he found widespread fame with the publication of only his second novel, *The Spy*. His legacy in the annals of early American literature is without question. His exciting tales of Indians and frontiersmen were huge bestsellers at the time, and today—some two centuries later—the author's works are required reading for many young high school students. *The Deerslayer, The Last of the Mohicans, The Pathfinder*, and *The Pioneers* are as vivid today as when they were first written. Together the books comprise Cooper's epic *Leatherstocking Tales*. Many movies have been made of his books over the years, most notably *The Last of the Mohicans*, which has had several Hollywood treatments.

A man raised in the gentry, Cooper lived the last several years of his life in his family mansion in Cooperstown and died on September 14, 1851.

Grave Location: Cooper is buried in the family plot in the small churchyard cemetery at Christ Church in Cooperstown. This church was founded by his father, the legendary Judge William Cooper, in 1819. The Cooper plot is surrounded by a black iron fence and holds over two centuries of Cooper family history within. Cooper's parents, children, and wife are all buried next to each other. Members of the Cooper family

continue to live in the Cooperstown area, and the family burial section is still active. As recently as the 1980s Coopers were still being buried here at Christ Church.

Author's Note: Judge William Cooper founded the village of Cooperstown. Christ Episcopal Church is a small New England–style church that is one of the most beautiful in Upstate New York. Brilliant, original Tiffany stained-glass windows reflect a prism of colors throughout the small church. Historic altar-pieces and ornate hand-carved woodwork make it truly a historic place. The nave and the tower are original parts of the church, and the baptismal font was present at the church's founding. In 1840, stone additions were erected under the supervision of the judge's son James. The writer had just returned from Europe and dramatically changed the design of the Romanesque church to reflect the more modern Gothic design that was then all the rage in Europe. Visitors can still see the markings of this design change in the exterior outline of the church's windows.

The church cemetery holds many interesting graves besides those of the Cooper family. Near the front (by the road) are the graves of many of the slaves and indentured servants who toiled for the rich and famous of the village over the years. One of the most interesting is a grave that reads: "Joe Tom. Slave." Another, that of Joe Tom's daughter, reads: "Age of death probably 100."

Factoid: James Fenimore Cooper was one of early America's most famous men. When the writer died, eulogies read at his funeral included those by Washington Irving, Daniel Webster, and William Cullen Bryant. Also, directly across the street from the entrance to the cemetery is a small white residence that once was the home of Supreme Court Justice Samuel Nelson (1792–1873). Justice Nelson is buried in Cooperstown's Lakewood Cemetery.

For More Information: Christ Episcopal Church, www.christchurch cooperstown.org.

42

ERNIE DAVIS

1939–1963

PRIDE OF THE ORANGEMEN
BURIED IN ELMIRA,
CHEMUNG COUNTY

Ernie Davis's potential was so great, his star so bright, and his story so inspirational that an NFL team retired his playing jersey before he ever played a single professional football game. His story is one of the greatest sports stories of them all.

An incredible natural athlete, Ernie Davis came thundering out of the playing fields of Elmira, New York, and shot his way to the top almost instantly. A multi-record holder in school, the "Elmira Express" was courted by virtually every major college in the East before and after his high school graduation. Disciplined by a strong-willed mother (he never remembered his father, who died in a car accident when he was a small child), he finally took her advice when decision time was upon him. She strongly advised him to accept a generous offer to play football at Syracuse University. His mom liked the idea of him being so close to home, and the college's offer was alluring. The deciding moment came when a dramatic visit took place at Ernie's Elmira home. SU had dispatched the boy's hero, Jim Brown, to go and "get the kid signed." Davis enrolled in 1958 and played his first varsity game as an Orangeman in 1959.

A veritable engine of a man, he had a tenacity and sure-footedness that enabled him to set school records in several areas, all in his *first year on the squad!* Some of those records stood for many years, and some still stand today. His total yards gained (3,414), points scored (220), average per-play

yardage (6.8), and total number of touchdowns (35) even surpassed records set and held by his idol Jim Brown during his tenure at the school.

The six foot two, 225-pound powerhouse was a popular student on campus and was described by his classmates as being gentle and courteous. Because he was black, and a campus celebrity, a certain amount of inherent racial backlash was expected, and he wore his mantle with dignity. As a student, he achieved only modest success academically, but he ended up becoming the most popular ambassador for this sprawling northeastern university.

Davis's glory days on the field at Syracuse University were filled with many memorable highlights. Perhaps the two most dramatic moments were the 1960 victory over the University of Texas at the Cotton Bowl (where he ignored racial slurs from the fans, scored two touchdowns, and was voted the game's MVP) and the Liberty Bowl of 1961. In this game (against Miami), Davis energized his team with a spectacular 140 yards rushing total and carried his Orangemen to victory.

In 1961, he entered the history books forever when he was named the first African American Heisman Trophy winner. The award, given annually to the nation's best collegiate football player, was the high point of Davis's career.

After his college graduation, every major American team worth its wallet (and some Canadian teams) offered the new graduate the moon. He chose to follow his heart and his hero once more, so he signed with Jim Brown's Cleveland Browns for $80,000 per year. He was the top draft choice in the nation, and the world of sports was clearly his oyster.

In July of 1963, while practicing for an exhibition game against the Packers, Davis fell ill with what was thought to be mononucleosis. The team physician ordered him to strict bed rest. Slowly, medical setback after setback crept in as his doctors desperately tried to figure out why the sports star was not recovering. Finally, left with no other choice, his team had to place him on the disabled list for what would have been his debut professional football season. He would never don a football uniform again.

He and his family never really grasped what was ailing him, and Davis kept the hope of returning to football alive for months. Finally, after a diagnosis of leukemia as his illness entered its final stages, the young man passed away. He died quietly in his sleep at the age of twenty-three on May 18, 1963, at Lakeside Hospital in Cleveland.

The sports world, thinking he had been recovering, was in shock. Ernie's Syracuse coach, Ben Schwartzwalder, who had called him "the perfect athlete and the perfect gentleman," postponed all practice sessions at Syracuse University in his honor. Art Modell, the president of the Cleveland Browns, flew to Elmira to console Davis's mother. His hometown declared an official three-day mourning period. The sports star's funeral was the largest ever held in Elmira and drew the national spotlight to this Southern Tier community. His body lay in state at Neighborhood House, a community center where had had played sports as a child. Thousands of citizens passed by his open casket to pay tribute to their hometown legend. Pallbearers were members of his old high school football team. Honorary pallbearers included the *entire* twenty-six-member roster of the Cleveland Browns. Jim Brown, the hero that Davis never got to play alongside, led the delegation. Twenty-five thousand mourners jammed the funeral service at Davis's church, where a message of condolence from President John F. Kennedy was read, calling him "a young man of great character and inspiration." Davis's mother collapsed and was carried from the service. An eighty-car procession carried his body the mile and a half to his final resting place.

He was posthumously inducted into the College Football Hall of Fame in 1979.

Grave Location: Woodlawn Cemetery, located at 1200 Walnut Street, is Elmira's largest and most historic cemetery. It holds the remains of thousands of veterans, local residents, and many famous people. Ernie's grave is in the Evergreen section, near the center of the cemetery, near the Babyland section. A blue and white sign directs visitors to his grave. The words "Heisman Trophy 1961" appear on the front of his monument.

Author's Note: With so many notables buried here, Woodlawn Cemetery is to be commended for providing easily read directions to prominent graves. These include Mark Twain and famed movie director Hal Roach. Adjacent to the cemetery is Woodlawn National Cemetery; among those buried in this military cemetery are approximately three thousand Confederate prisoners of war who died in Elmira's infamous prison camp. Many of the Confederate dead were buried facing south.

Factoid: The famed Carrier Dome, on the campus of Syracuse University, hosts a room in Ernie Davis's memory, and the football playing field at the dome is named the Ernie Davis Legends Field. There are two life-sized statues of the sports hero in Upstate New York. One is just outside the Carrier Dome, and the other is in front of his old high school in Elmira, now named Ernie Davis Middle School. On September 12, 2008, a large crowd attended the premiere of the Hollywood movie *The Express* about Ernie Davis's life. The debut was held at the Landmark Theatre in Syracuse.

For More Information: ESPN Classic Biography, "Davis Won Heisman, respect," www.espn.com/classic/biography/s/davis_ernie.html.

43

EXTERMINATOR

1915–1945

OLD BONES
BURIED IN BINGHAMTON,
BROOME COUNTY

*W*illis Sharpe Kilmer was a raconteur, a colorful bon vivant and an extravagant renaissance man. He made huge sums of money in publishing (*he founded the Binghamton Press Company*) and in medicine (he created and sold the most popular home remedy medicinal product of its day, Swamp Root). He was also a major real estate investor in the growing turn-of-the-century Southern Tier of New York. This chapter, however, focuses on another of Kilmer's passions. Horse racing. He owned one of the premier racehorse stables in the state, and one of his horses—Exterminator—is among racing's winningest steed. His story rivals any in horse racing lore, including the well-told tale of Man-O-War.

But it is only by quirk of fate that we even know of this horse at all.

Kilmer's marquee horse was Sun Briar. This magnificent horse was groomed to be a Kentucky Derby contender and was the pride of the stable, which Kilmer called Sun Briar Court. Kilmer spared no expense at his horse farm, equipping it with state-of-the-art, steam-heated stables and real transplanted Kentucky bluegrass pastures.

The only problem was that his prized horse was an erratic runner and an unpredictable finisher. To remedy this, Kilmer paid $9,000 to the W. G. Knight Farm in Kentucky for a workout partner named Exterminator. This horse, who had never run a race before, was an excellent and challenging companion to Sun Briar and nudged him along to ever increasing

workout speeds. As Sun Briar performed more successfully with each training run, Exterminator stayed right behind him hoof to hoof. Kilmer proclaimed Sun Briar to be his entry for the forty-fourth running of the Kentucky Derby in 1918 and bragged to the world that he had a surefire winner. Disaster struck just weeks before the big race, however, when Sun Briar pulled up with a leg injury and was scratched from the Derby. Still holding a slot in the race, Kilmer was convinced to enter Exterminator instead.

On the day of the big race, Kilmer's horse, a complete unknown and the longest of longshots (30–1) swept the field and won the crown. A sentimental crowd favorite from that day on, Exterminator went on to win fully half of all the races he entered. He ran one hundred races, won fifty, and came in the money eighty-four times. While running his one hundredth race, he pulled up lame and was retired to pasture.

Exterminator, known in the press and by fans as Old Bones, was a gentle old soul of a horse who hated to be alone. Kilmer found this out when his trainer realized that the horse wouldn't eat if Sun Briar or another stablemate wasn't around. Kilmer remedied this by buying a small Shetland pony and penning him up with the huge champion. The pony, named Peanuts, and Exterminator were inseparable. They slept together in the same stable, appeared at parties at Kilmer's estate together, and romped through the bluegrass fields of the horse farm together.

Exterminator's final public appearance came just months before his death when he made a publicity run around Belmont Race Track to raise money for the war effort. His last parade down the familiar final stretch that he had seen so many times before was met with a standing ovation by the sellout crowd. His faithful sidekick Peanuts was at his side the whole way. His appearance this day helped raise $25 million in War Bonds.

Exterminator died in 1945 at the age of thirty.

Grave Location: Exterminator is buried at Whispering Pines Pet Cemetery, located at 3850 Gardner Road, just past Binghamton's Ross Park Zoo (from downtown Binghamton, follow the many signs toward the zoo). You can see the large headstone from the road. It features a chiseled portrait of a horse's head. Sun Briar (d. 1943) is also buried in this plot, and many believe, although it is unknown, that Peanuts is buried here also.

Author's Note: Exterminator was inducted into the National Museum of Racing and Hall of Fame in Saratoga Springs in 1957.

Factoid: Exterminator was very popular with racing fans and with small children. Groups of youngster would go and visit the horse in Binghamton and bring him a carrot cake for his birthday. A popular children's book, *Old Bones, Wonder Horse,* by Mildred Mastin Pace, has been in print since 1955.

For More Information: National Museum of Racing and Hall of Fame, "Exterminator," www.racingmuseum.org/hall-of-fame/exterminator/.

44

SHERMAN FAIRCHILD

1896–1971

FATHER OF AVIATION PHOTOGRAPHY
BURIED IN ONEONTA,
OTSEGO COUNTY

*A*lthough it could be argued that Sherman Mills Fairchild was born with the proverbial silver spoon in his mouth, he carved a career, independent from his powerful and wealthy father, to lead the invention of and innovation to aviation technology. This was no small feat, as airplane photographs were important tools to be used during World War I and, in the private sector, in mapmaking in general.

Fairchild was born in the rural Upstate city of Oneonta. His father was one of the community's influential elders. George Fairchild was a founder and the first president of International Business Machines Company (IBM), and he encouraged his son to follow his footsteps in the company. Sherman had different ideas, however.

He developed cameras specifically for use in airplanes, and when that met with some technological hurdles, he created *airplanes* specifically to be used with his cameras. He also invented the first closed cockpit airplane, ending the days of the dashing aces darting about the skies in biplanes wearing goggles with long scarves trailing behind them. Fairchild invented an aerial camera with the shutter contained inside the lens, giving it a sturdy stability. It was a huge success. One of Fairchild's cameras went aloft with an early balloonist to photograph, for the first time, the curvature of the earth. His aviation designs were groundbreaking and led him to cofound Pan Am and American Airlines.

Sherman Fairchild was a golden boy of his era. Fabulously wealthy (he did take financial gifts from his father over the years), he had mansions, expensive cars, and the finest clothes, and he was a socialite nonpareil. His mansion on East Sixty-Fifth Street in Manhattan was one of the city's most expensive. He was matinee-idol handsome, an avid sportsman, a renowned chef, and a bon vivant of the highest order who cut a dashing figure in either his tennis whites or a tailed tuxedo at a swanky soiree. He never married.

In 1955, Sherman Fairchild organized the family foundation which bears his name. To this day it has awarded hundreds of millions of dollars to art galleries, universities, medical centers, and other philanthropic endeavors.

When he died on March 28, 1971, Fairchild's *New York Times* obituary observed that he was the "largest single shareholder in IBM" at his passing. A look at his financial holdings at the time of his death revealed that he owned more than fifty companies that bore his name, from the massive Fairchild Industries to the smaller Fairchild Credit Corporation.

After a large funeral in New York City, his remains were brought back to his Upstate home where he was buried in a large family plot at Glenwood Cemetery in Oneonta.

Grave Location: Glenwood Cemetery is located on Main Street in the east end of Oneonta. Drive through the main gates and proceed all the way to the top of the cemetery. Look for the southern end of Section 11. There you will find the Fairchild family plot. It has a low slung wall surrounding the many markers representing the Fairchild family. The view from this point in the cemetery is stunning.

Author's Note: The Fairchild's family home, located in the downtown business district of Oneonta, is listed on the National Register of Historic Places. It is one of Oneonta's most magnificent mansions and has hosted the Oneonta Masonic Lodge since 1929.

Factoid: Among Sherman Fairchild's family members buried in Glenwood Cemetery is his father, George Winthrop Fairchild, who was a six-term US congressman and in 1896 helped to found IBM.

For More Information: National Aviation Hall of Fame, "Fairchild, Sherman Mills" (inducted in 1979), www.nationalaviation.org/our-enshrinees/fairchild-sherman-mills/.

45

SETH FLINT

1846–1941

BUGLER AT APPOMATTOX
BURIED IN WORCESTER,
OTSEGO COUNTY

*W*hen Seth Flint died at the age of ninety-four on March 18, 1941, he was Otsego County's last surviving veteran of the Civil War. And while many other veterans of the war could regale the generations that followed with tales of courage and bravado on the battlefield, Flint had another, different story to tell. He was an eyewitness to history serving as General Ulysses S. Grant's escort bugler during the war.

On the fateful day of surrender in the village of Appomattox Courthouse, Virginia, it was Flint who was given the order to signify the solemn event with a bugle call. Flint, for many years the last witness to this historic day, had been interviewed over the years for his impression of the events and how they unfolded. As he aged, more and more publications sought him out for interviews, from local newspapers to the *Saturday Evening Post*.

He gave a gripping account of General Robert E. Lee arriving, tall and stern atop his white horse Traveler, in full uniform with medals and sashes displayed across his officer's tunic and a sword belted around his waist. Grant, in contrast, arrived in muddy boots and a dusty Union Army uniform of indistinct nature. The official surrender took place inside a private residence. Following that surrender and the departure of his rival, General Grant ordered his bugler to sound "Taps" as the sun went down. The eighteen-year-old Flint blew the mournful tune so that it wafted

across the roads and into the territory held by the former enemy soldiers. Upon completion of his song, another bugle sound came echoing back through the mist toward Grant and the Union officers assembled for the surrender ceremony. It was "Taps" being played by a Confederate bugler.

Seth Flint saw much during the Civil War and was present at eighteen different battles, including Antietam, Gettysburg, and Fredericksburg.

Grave Location: Flint is buried in Maple Grove Cemetery in Worcester. Enter the main gate, and you will see a sign and map to the many historic graves in this beautiful Upstate New York cemetery. Flint is in Section 2. Go straight through the entrance and stop at the first leftward curve. His grave is in the center of this section. His stone reads: "Seth M. Flint. Escort Bugler to Lt. Gen. Grant. Company F, 5th Regiment of U.S.C. Died March 18, 1941, Age 94 Years."

Author's Note: Today, Flint's famous bugle is in the possession of the Worcester Historical Society, where it is brought out and displayed on ceremonial occasions. For such a small item it carries a great significance and is certainly one of the rarest military items from the Civil War era.

Factoid: Seth Flint wanted desperately to join the Union Army, but his parents told him under no circumstances would this happen. And besides, he was only sixteen years old. On a moonless June 11, 1862, young Seth slipped out his bedroom window and darted off into the hillside. He had been unable to retrieve his shoes, which were near his parents' bedroom, so he walked barefoot all the way from his home in Berne, New York, to the recruiting station in Albany—a distance of twenty-five miles. He lied about his age and enlisted under a false name, Charles M. Seaver.

For More Information: Worcester, New York, "History of Worcester," www.worcesterny.org/history.

46

HERBERT FRANKLIN

1866–1956

*CENTRAL NEW YORK'S HENRY FORD
BURIED IN SYRACUSE,
ONONDAGA COUNTY*

*H*erbert Franklin was an inveterate inventor, a tinkerer of moving pieces, and a dreamer with a vivid imagination. He spent his whole life in Upstate New York, having been born in Lisle, which is a small community south of Cortland, and later moving to Coxsackie on the Hudson River. Finally, he moved to Syracuse, where he began his automobile company. Along the way he worked in machine shops, newspaper publishing, real estate, and sleigh making, and also tried his hand in local government. He organized the Coxsackie Board of Trade, which helped to create a robust economy near this Hudson River community by enticing businesses to locate here.

Even as a young man, he had an interest in molding and casting iron. He secured one of the first patents for die casting (a term he invented) and founded his own company. It was the first commercial die casting company in New York, and he is considered to be the Godfather of Die Casting.

But, back to the Henry Ford comparison.

Franklin, along with an engineer friend named John Wilkinson, began to experiment with automobile engines and designs in the late 1800s. Cars were becoming more and more popular, and inventors of all stripes were looking to make daring, stylish improvements to them. Franklin and Wilkinson formed the H. H. Franklin Manufacturing Company in Syracuse in 1900. In 1902, the first Franklin car rolled onto the streets

of Syracuse. It was a large luxury car with an innovative four-cylinder engine, the first for any automobile in America. It was lighter than most other American-made cars and because of that was considered to be one of the most "user friendly" cars on the road. It sold new for $1,100 and was a great hit with city dwellers. The first car had taken two months to build, and orders were placed for many more. The company made a dozen more vehicles in its first year, and a quick expansion was needed.

Franklin's company was in business for twenty-eight years. The car was a high-end model type and comparatively expensive. With the onset of the Great Depression, business declined and the company eventually went bankrupt. At its peak, the H. H. Franklin Automobile Company was one of the largest firms in Syracuse. It is estimated that more than 35,000 Franklin automobiles were made and sold during the company's operation.

Herbert Franklin became a wealthy man with the invention of his Franklin automobile. He never married, lived in a grand Syracuse mansion, and was a socialite who belonged to many of the high profile fraternal and social organizations of the city. Franklin Square in downtown Syracuse, the site of his automobile manufacturing business, is named in his honor.

Herbert Franklin died on July 7, 1956, at the age of eighty-nine.

Grave Location: Herbert H. Franklin is buried in an impressive plot in Oakwood Cemetery, located at 940 Comstock Avenue in Syracuse. To get to his grave, enter the cemetery gates, go past the main office, and head to Section 66 (sections are plainly marked). The family plot is found in Lot 50 and features a very tall monument with the name FRANKLIN on the base. The auto maker and several family members are buried around the monument.

Author's Note: Oakwood is one of Syracuse's largest and oldest cemeteries. It opened in 1859 and consists of 180 acres of land adjacent to Syracuse University.

Factoid: The Franklin retains its popularity with auto enthusiasts and car collectors. One of the largest collections of Franklin automobiles can be found at the Northeast Classic Car Museum in Norwich (Chenango County).

For More Information: H. H. Franklin Club, Inc., www.franklincar .org.

47

RENÉ GOUPIL, JOHN LALANDE, AND ISAAC JOGUES

EARLY 1600s

NORTH AMERICAN MARTYRS
BURIED IN AURIESVILLE,
MONTGOMERY COUNTY

*T*his chapter is about America's first canonized saints. Three Jesuit missionaries—René Goupil, Isaac Jogues, and John LaLande—set about the virgin territory of Central New York in the early 1600s to evangelize and convert the many Native American tribes along the Mohawk Valley. Ultimately they paid the supreme sacrifice for their beliefs here in the shadow of the foothills of the Adirondacks.

Ossernenon was the home of the nomadic Mohawk Society known as the Turtle Clan. Faced with recurring disease, this community would move often to avoid being decimated by illness. With a population of about six hundred, Ossernenon was located on a high bluff overlooking the Mohawk River, about nine miles from present day Auriesville. It was here that the clan found lasting communal stability.

The Jesuits had come from New France (Canada) around 1625, and in 1642 they sent a small missionary group to Ossernenon to "bring forth the word of the Lord" to the Mohawks. Leading the small party was a young priest named Father Isaac Jogues. He knew the Native Americans harbored a deep suspicion toward the "black robes," but he was compelled to preach. En route to Ossernenon in a canoe filled with medicine and staples, his party was attacked by a group of Native Americans, and Jogues

was taken to their village. The young priest was harassed by the entire community upon his arrival.

A young assistant to Jogues, Brother René Goupil, was the only other survivor of the original party. Goupil was also tortured in Ossernenon, being made to run a Mohawk gauntlet where he was pummeled with sharp sticks. Despite their serious wounds, both Jogues and Goupil were kept alive as a "trading value." The two were forced to do manual work in the fields and were afforded just enough food to keep them alive. After many weeks, during which no opportunity arose to trade for the valuable black robes, the Mohawks killed them both.

Goupil was the first to die. He was murdered on September 29, 1642, the Feast Day of Saint Michael. His body was left in the open. Late at night, Father Jogues slipped out of his hut and recovered the remains of his friend. He pulled the body of the young priest to a nearby stream and buried it in the shallow water under a heavy mound of rocks. He quickly and quietly committed Brother Goupil's soul to God and then sneaked back to his hut.

Isaac Jogues was kept alive for another four years. During that time he was actually ransomed by Dutch traders from Albany, and he returned to France for a brief period. Despite his deprivations and the death of his friend, Jogues returned to the area of the Mohawk Valley to once again preach to the Native Americans that had once held him hostage. He brought with him a young Jesuit lay missionary named Jean (John) de LaLande. It was LaLande's intent to use his skills as a woodsman and carpenter to assist in rehabilitation of the village. The return of these Jesuits was again met with suspicion and fear, and soon both were held hostage at Ossernenon. The Native Americans believed the Jesuits carried evil spirits into their village and were agitated at their arrival. Both men were soon put to death.

Isaac Jogues was tomahawked to death on October 18, 1646, and Brother LaLande was killed the next day. Their dismembered remains were reportedly thrown into the nearby Mohawk River.

Although there is no real final resting place for you to see at Auriesville, the place is of utmost importance to Catholics and those seeking spiritual awareness. Some have even called this site, known as the Shrine of Our Lady of Martyrs, the birthplace of American Catholicism. The sites of the deaths of the three are marked with crosses, statuary commemorations, and religious relics. Today Auriesville is considered to be a shrine and a most holy place where these three men found the end of their journey and where they are commemorated as North American Martyrs.

All three were canonized on June 29, 1930, by Pope Pius XI at the Vatican City in Rome. The pope's declaration states that "these Servants of God were, by nature, meek and timid, but by constant self-humiliation and the continuous practice of prayer they so strengthened their spirit . . . and in facing dangers and torments, gave truly marvelous examples of Christian fortitude."

Grave Locations: With no real certainty as to the place of each man's death, their spirits are honored here in a place called the Ravine. It was here that Father Jogues stole away with his dead friend's body and placed it in a creek. He had intended to come back at a later date and recover it for a permanent burial. Floods, however, made that impossible. René

Goupil's skull and several bones were found and buried many years later. The Ravine is a solemn, holy place of quiet reflection. It represents the lives, deaths, and memory of the three martyrs.

Author's Note: There are many holy places at Auriesville. Walking paths lead visitors to glens, grottos, vistas, and places to pray in private. There is a football-field–sized rosary (the world's largest) made out of large white rocks that is said to be the place where the first rosary was prayed in America. A gigantic round church—the Coliseum Church, also known as the Church of the 72 Doors—is the central place of worship here, and it can hold thousands of people at one time. A four-hundred-year-old carved image of the Virgin Mary is considered one of the oldest religious icons in the North America.

Factoid: Visitors to the Ravine and the Church of the 72 Doors will find all amenities to make a visit pleasurable. There are clean rest rooms, an extensive gift shop selling many unique religious items, a cafeteria, and a large parking lot with many handicapped accessible sites plus parking for the many motor coaches that visit here from around the country.

For More Information: Shrine of Our Lady of Martyrs, www.auries villeshrine.com.

48

GEORGE F. JOHNSON

1857–1948

SHOEMAKER TO THE WORLD
BURIED IN ENDICOTT,
BROOME COUNTY

"As long as children are born barefoot, E-J will sell shoes!"

George F. Johnson, cofounder and head of the Endicott-Johnson Shoe Company (E-J) was a sage thinker, a compassionate innovator and a real man of the people. He led E-J from its start as a smokestack factory in Binghamton, New York, to "E-J, The Concept." He developed Upstate's rural Southern Tier into his own little petri dish of "welfare capitalism" and earned a degree of unabashed adoration from his employees that is still felt along the banks of the Susquehanna River more than seven decades after his death. At the time of his passing, Endicott-Johnson was the second largest shoe manufacturer *in the world*.

When George F, as he was called, arrived in Binghamton in 1881 to join Henry Endicott as part owner of the Lester Brothers Boot Company, his vision of where he wanted to take his labor philosophies was unbridled. Although he arrived with nothing ("thirteen cents in my pocket and missing a collar"), he was a man with big ideas. When partner Endicott died in 1920 and Johnson became the sole owner of E-J, his long-planned policy of a "square deal" for his workers was fully implemented. As a testament to his success, even today there is a grand archway over the Main Street of Johnson City proclaiming, "Welcome to the Home of the Square Deal."

In Johnson's quest to turn the Southern Tier into a "valley of opportunity," E-J's 24,000-member work force benefited greatly from their

leader's industrial democracy, and they would forever remain loyal to him and to E-J. He built playgrounds for the use of his employees only, constructed E-J homes for those who needed them (provided at well-below market prices), established an E-J health care policy that was the first of its kind in business, and even implemented one of the nation's first revenue-sharing plans. He also began one of the first eight-hour workday, forty-hour workweeks in the country. In return, his workers stayed on their jobs for decades, leading E-J to great success. At one time, his Endicott factory was turning out 175,000 pairs of shoes *a day!*

George F. Johnson died on November 28, 1948.

Grave Location: Johnson is buried in Riverhurst Cemetery, located off East Main Street in Endicott. At your first chance to turn right after entering the cemetery, do so and stop. On your left is a large gravestone with a replica of George F. Johnson's signature scrawled across the front. Numerous family members are also buried in this plot.

Author's Note: There are no shoes made in Endicott anymore. They are mostly made overseas. There are several nice memorials to George F, however, throughout the Southern Tier. These include statues, libraries, highways, and parks. In these parks you will find many hand-carved carousels. Erected under the orders of the company owner himself, these carousels remain in the area and are free to ride. Many signs welcoming you to the region say, "Welcome to the Carousel Capital of the World."

Factoid: When Johnson died, his body lay in state in the parlor of his private residence on Park Street, just across from the main entrance to his factory. More than ten thousand mourners passed through his home to pay their respects, many of them dressed in worker's clothing and many of them weeping in front of the open casket. Later, his funeral was held in En-Joie Park, which he had built. At the park, his body was again made available for viewing, and more than fifty thousand attended. All schools, industries, and retail stores were shuttered at 12:30 p.m. on the day of the funeral as thousands stayed home to listen to the service live on any of the four local stations carrying the event. One national reporter called it "the single largest funeral ceremony for a private citizen ever held in the United States."

For More Information: NPR Radio Diaries, "The Legacy of George F. Johnson and the Square Deal," www.npr.org/2010/12/01/131725100/the-legacy-of-george-f-johnson-and-the-square-deal/.

49

JAMES KONSTANTY

1917–1976

BIG JIM
BURIED IN WORCESTER,
OTSEGO COUNTY

*S*ome baby boomers might remember ballplayer Jim Konstanty from their days of keeping and trading baseball cards. Konstanty was one of the few players depicted wearing eyeglasses on a trading card!

Konstanty came out of rural Central New York to make a name for himself as a professional baseball player. He was a relief pitcher for several teams including the Cincinnati Reds, Boston Braves, New York Yankees, St. Louis Cardinals and, most famously, the Philadelphia Phillies. The highlight of his career came during the glory days of the Phillies' "Whiz Kids" days. This was the sterling Philadelphia team that won the 1950 National League pennant. Among the standouts on that team were Richie Ashburn and Robin Roberts, both of whom were later inducted into the National Baseball Hall of Fame in Cooperstown.

But it was Konstanty who really shined that year. A relief pitcher with a keen eye, a dizzying slider, and a muscular delivery, his wins in relief were enough to put the Phillies into postseason for the first time in thirty-five years. A reliable workhorse of a relief pitcher, he was called into a game seventy-four times that year and amassed a record that included twenty-two saves and sixteen wins. At the end of the season, Big Jim was named the league's Most Valuable Player, beating out Stan Musial, a feat not matched since for a relief pitcher in the National League. He also appeared that year in the All-Star game. In game one of that year's World

Series (against the New York Yankees), he put in a solid performance giving up only four hits in a losing effort (the Phillies lost 1–0).

Leaving baseball at the age of thirty-nine in 1956, he returned to his native Upstate New York and opened a popular sporting goods business in Oneonta. He also served as athletic director at Hartwick College in that city.

Jim Konstanty died on June 11, 1976, at the age of only fifty-nine.

Grave Location: Konstanty is buried in Maple Grove Cemetery in Worcester. Enter the main gate and directly veer to your right. His grave is near the fence facing the road.

Author's Note: Jim Konstanty's grave in Worcester is impressive for the amount of information written on it. The details of his sports career, both as a player and a university athletic director, are listed. A series of illustrations carved on his gravestone include a pair of baseball spikes, a ball and a bat, and a pitcher's glove. Along the bottom is the epitaph: "Teacher. Coach. Referee. Beloved Husband and Father."

National League President Ford Frick (*left*) presents the league's 1950 MVP award to Jim Konstanty as the pitcher's wife, Mary, looks on. Konstanty was the first relief pitcher to ever win the award. Courtesy of the National Baseball Hall of Fame and Museum, Cooperstown, NY.

Factoid: In an era that found only a small percentage of the big name baseball stars armed with a college degree, Konstanty stood out in that respect as well. He earned a bachelor of science degree from Syracuse University before joining the pros.

For More Information: Baseball Reference, "Jim Konstanty," www .baseball-reference.com/players/k/konstji01.shtml.

David Maydole

1807–1882

THE HAMMER KING
BURIED IN NORWICH,
CHENANGO COUNTY

It is hard to wrap your head around the notion that hammer-inflicted wounds were one of the leading causes of injury and even death in the trades industry of the mid-nineteenth century. And I don't mean hitting your finger with a hammer. Hammerheads would often fly off and strike a worker in the head causing severe injuries. Apparently it was very tricky to perfect a hammerhead that would consistently stay on. Several inventors tried, and several failed.

David Maydole of Norwich came up with the idea of improving, lengthening, and securing the hole that attached a steel hammerhead to its handle. One of the most successful and cumbersome methods previously used involved securing the hammerhead to the handle with thin, riveted strips of metal. It was not very efficient, though. Maydole revolutionized the design of the American hammer so that "fly offs" became almost nonexistent.

By the 1850s, Maydole's hammer factory was the leading Norwich industry, and he was turning out his "Maydole" stamped hammers at a rate of hundreds every week. All were made by hand. They were purchased by big companies and small, by individuals and retail stores, and by railroads and the US government. Maydole eventually became one of the richest men in Chenango County.

An early ad in a national magazine described the hammer this way: "A Maydole hammer features a head of press forged polished tool steel and a handle created out of clear, second-growth hickory . . . put on for keeps!" He would end up building one of the largest factories in the county, employing over one hundred men, and giving Norwich the title of Hammer Capital of the United States. After Maydole's death, his hammer company continued on and sold well over a million of his "safety adze head hammers" before it finally closed in the 1960s. During World War II, the US Navy was the largest buyer of Maydole hammers, procuring thousands of them for use in every military naval yard in the country.

David Maydole died October 14, 1882, at the age of seventy-five. His death was met by great sadness in Norwich, and schools and businesses closed in his honor on the day of his funeral.

Grave Location: Maydole is buried in Mount Hope Cemetery in Norwich. Drive through the main cemetery entrance and you will see his monument towering over the others in the first section on the left (across from the flagpole). His grave is the most impressive in the cemetery and features a marble bust of the Hammer King. According to cemetery lore, the bust is turned at an angle so Mr. Maydole could watch over his factory grounds long after he passed away.

Author's Note: Visitors will notice several insignias placed around Maydole's grave by the Norwich Fire Department. The industrialist established the Maydole Hose Company in 1887, making it one of the longest existing fire companies in Upstate New York. He organized the fire company to protect his own factory.

Factoid: The commonly used phrase "to fly off the handle" is purported to stem from the hammer accidents before Maydole's invention.

For More Information: WSKG Public Telecommunications, "David Maydole," wskg.org/history/david-maydole/.

CAPTAIN WILLIAM MCCONKEY

1744–1825

THE MAN WITH THE BOAT
BURIED IN CHARLESTON,
MONTGOMERY COUNTY

$\mathcal{N}$ot a lot is known about William McConkey's life, except what we can glean from old church records. We do know that he came from Scotland as a young boy with his parents and siblings, that he married Hannah Burroughs on January 2, 1769, and that they had two children. Not much else is known. But one other important thing that is known for certain about William McConkey (and earns him a chapter in this book) happened on December 25, 1776.

McConkey was the owner of the ferry that provided the boats for General George Washington's historic Christmas crossing of the Delaware River during the American Revolution.

The general, seeking to strike a much-needed blow to the enemy, chose the early morning hours of the morning after Christmas 1776 to make his move. Knowing the opposing Germanic army would be still groggy after a night of alcohol-primed revelry, Washington struck early and hard. He amassed 2,400 troops at McConkey's ferry crossing. The old river master himself helped to guide boat after boat after boat into the swiftly flowing Delaware River. A lusty winter storm suddenly came blowing down the river flats, bringing with it snow and blinding hail. Large ice chunks bobbed up and down, posing a significant hazard to the troops and ships.

Sixteen Durham boats and flats were also procured to ferry cargo and livestock across the river. It is unknown whether McConkey was actually

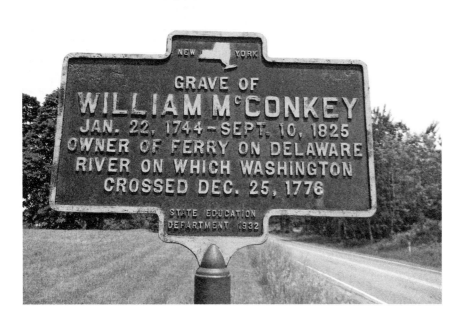

in Washington's boat during the crossing, but historic analysis suggests that he was. If he did accompany the general on the crossing, you can be assured that Emanuel Leutze, the painter who so famously captured the event in his masterpiece "Washington Crossing the Delaware," would have surely put the Scotsman squarely at the rudder!

Grave Location: Captain McConkey is buried in Abram Davis Farm Cemetery in Charleston. This rural cemetery houses just a handful of old, weathered stones. Many of them are hard to read. McConkey and his wife's stones are easy to find because they usually have an American flag posted next to them. A roadside historical marker is the only landmark that would tell a passerby of the cemetery's location. It is exactly one mile south of the Town of Charleston sign on Route 30A. The cemetery is on the western side of the road.

Author's Note: I stumbled upon this grave site while on a "cemetery ride" one day. While traveling north on Route 30A, heading from Cobleskill to Amsterdam in the northern part of the Schoharie Valley,

I caught a glimmer of something shiny in the overgrown brush alongside the road. I stopped to explore. The marker was almost invisible to the unknowing traveler, but it had been freshly painted and the blue and yellow hues of the ubiquitous New York State markers caught my eye. I ventured in and up the bank to the cemetery. This forgotten cemetery holds the remains of about two dozen people, including McConkey, the unsung patriot.

Factoid: McConkey's original ferry and inn are still intact and are now a part of Washington Crossing Historic Park in Pennsylvania. Tours are available, and many visitors come to the park every year. An annual reenactment of the December 25–26 crossing takes place at this site on Christmas Day.

For More Information: Washington Crossing Historic Park, "History," www.washingtoncrossingpark.org/history/.

TIM MURPHY

1751–1818

SAVIOR OF SCHOHARIE
BURIED IN MIDDLEBURGH,
SCHOHARIE COUNTY

*T*im Murphy could neither read nor write. He was a simple man with simple tastes. He was rough-hewn and affable, a man of the soil and a lover of nature. He also had the stealth of a ghost and the eye of an eagle. Some say that "Ol' Tim" Murphy won the Battle of Saratoga for the Americans single-handedly.

Here is his story.

When the British troops were making encroachments against Murphy's home area of Schoharie County in early fall 1777, he went into action. The British, fronted by their Indian allies, had been terrorizing the colonists and spreading fear throughout the valley. Murphy, a natural hunter and a man completely at ease in the bosom of nature, began his own little counterinsurgency. In the thick of an area known as Panther Falls, he engaged in a hit-and-run skirmish with an Indian scouting party over a three-day period. Through lush forests and over cold mountain streams, Murphy navigated the wild terrain as well as they did. At the end, all eleven in the Indian party had been slain by the patient and wily Murphy. Another time, near the same area, he set out to free a white settler, Jennie Swart, who had been kidnapped by four roving Onondaga Indians. Murphy stalked the Indian party for nearly one hundred miles before making his move, killing all four of the captors and freeing the young girl.

Murphy's fame grew far and wide as stories of his escapades were told and retold. One time, on a raiding expedition at Canandaigua Lake (in Central New York), Murphy's group was entirely wiped out, save for himself. With pluck and daring, he evaded capture by a force of fifty Seneca Indians. Murphy, an expert marksman, once fired on a British river barge during a battle near Boston, Massachusetts. Even though the boat was reportedly a half mile away, he was able to pick off ten British soldiers.

Murphy's preferred choice of weapon was an unusual double-barreled Golchar rifle with a hand-rubbed stock. With it, he said, he could "shoot the eye out of a bear at nine hundred feet." So feared was his sharpshooting expertise that British General St. Leger, who normally placed an eight-dollar bounty on a Yankee scalp, doubled it to sixteen for Murphy's.

On Christmas Day, 1776, Murphy accompanied General George Washington across the Delaware River, joined the famous Morgan's Rifle Corps, and soon became its most valuable member. At the Battle of Saratoga (Bemis Heights), Murphy's date with destiny was upon him.

British General Burgoyne attacked American forces with everything he had at Saratoga. The bloodletting was fierce. The British field general, Simon Fraser, pushed his Redcoat army deeper and deeper into American territory. Fraser, sitting high atop a giant white steed, resplendent in his flamboyant battle attire, with feathers and plumes flying, was an intimidating sight. His aide-de-camp, Sir Francis Clark, stayed close to Fraser's side, calculating the enemy losses and planning the army's moves. Dan Morgan, convinced that the American forces were about to meet certain defeat, summoned Tim Murphy to his tent. The task was a simple one, he said. Both British generals must be killed or the battle might be lost.

Murphy, clutching his trusted Golchar, climbed a tall oak tree near the rim of the battlefield and waited. When the British started approaching the area, he patiently waited for the two generals to enter his view. When Clark was three feet away, Murphy let loose with a first volley. Seconds later he fired his last shot at Fraser. Both rounds found their targets. Now, with their commanders dead, the British troops scattered and began an open retreat, and the final victory went to the Americans. British General John Burgoyne said later, "If Dan Morgan's riflemen had marched with me, I'd hold Albany now."

After the war, Murphy moved back to his beloved Schoharie Valley and lived to the age of sixty-seven. Even today, the story of "Ol' Tim" is taught in classrooms up and down the valley. Oh, and his story is also kept alive at the Saratoga battlefield. A marker near the old oak tree where he fired off his fateful shots is highlighted on the battlefield tours.

Grave Location: Murphy is buried in the Middleburgh Cemetery, located off I-88 exit Route 30-Schoharie. Travel south exactly ten miles and you will come to the cemetery off Hunters Land Road on the left. Take the cemetery road all the way to the top to find Murphy's impressive plot (it is across the path from a huge family mausoleum with the name FOSTER across the top). His grave marker reads: "TIM MURPHY. Patriot. Soldier. Scout. Citizen who served distinguishably in Morgan's Rifle Corps. Fought at Saratoga and Monmouth and whose bravery repelled the attack of the British and their Indian allies on Middlefort,

October 17, 1780, and saved the lives of the colonists of his Schoharie Valley. Here too, this warrior sire, with honor rests. Who braved in freedom's cause his valiant breast." A life-sized bronze image of Tim Murphy, dressed in buckskin and holding his Golchar rifle, adorns the front of his grave marker.

Author's Note: Of all of the hundreds of graves I visited in researching this book, none offers a more picturesque view than this one. You can see for ten miles into the distance and you will have an "artist's view" of the famous Vroman's Nose, a most unusual natural phenomenon that is the county's signature landmark.

Factoid: No trip to this historic region would be complete without a visit to the Old Stone Fort just four miles up the road in Schoharie. The fort was built as a High Dutch German Reformed Church in 1772. Inside is a museum with hundreds of artifacts telling the history of this area, which General Washington called the "Breadbasket of the Revolution." There are several remarkable features of this building, including a cannon hole still visible at the roof line dating back to when the church became a fort and was laid siege to by the British in 1780. Also, as was the tradition in that era, early parishioners' names are etched on the exterior walls along the front façade. Patriot David Williams, who captured Benedict Arnold, is buried just steps from the front door.

For More Information: The Old Stone Fort Museum, theoldstone fort.org.

53

HAL ROACH

1892–1992

*FATHER OF OUR GANG
AND THE LITTLE RASCALS
BURIED IN ELMIRA,
CHEMUNG COUNTY*

*H*arold Eugene Roach was one of the most important pioneers in American cinema. He began making movies in Hollywood in 1915 with his friend Harold Lloyd. The two made many successful silent comedies, and Roach went on to expand his early, primitive production studios in Los Angeles into the groundbreaking Hal Roach Studios in the then-quiet California town of Culver City. Roach employed many of the most famous names in movies at the time, including Will Rogers and Laurel and Hardy. In a few short years, Culver City was one of the bustling movie capitals of the West Coast, and Roach was one of the most successful studio heads of his era.

Roach was the man who brought America the *Our Gang* comedies as well as many of the Laurel and Hardy classics. They, and his films with Harold Lloyd, were filmed at his state of the art studios at 882 Washington Boulevard, Culver City, a studio he dubbed "Laugh Factory to the World." It was wildly successful. In total, the Roach studios turned out more than five thousand silent film shorts, westerns, full-length movies, serials, specials, radio serials, and television programs. The movie studio successfully transitioned the rapidly changing film industry, adapting to everything from silent movie potboilers to 1950s sitcoms like *The Gale Storm Show* and *My Little Margie*. Among the famous stars that got their start at Hal Roach Studios were Paulette Goddard, Jean Harlow, Fay Wray, and Boris

HAL E. ROACH
1892 ⟶ 1992

AFTER LEAVING ELMIRA HE FOUND
SUCCESS IN HOLLYWOOD AND
MOTION PICTURES, BUT ALWAYS
LOVED HIS HOMETOWN AND
HAS RETURNED.

Karloff. The studio ceased production in 1959 and was demolished in 1963. If there ever was a birthplace of the American comedy movie, it would be the Hal Roach Studios.

Roach lived a long and fruitful life. In his advanced years he could be found traveling the world accepting honors at film festivals and being interviewed by top entertainment magazines. He appeared on *The Tonight Show with Jay Leno* and even attended the Sixty-Fourth Academy Awards ceremony, both within a few months of his death on November 2, 1992, at the age of one hundred.

Grave Location: Hal Roach was born in Elmira, New York, on January 14, 1892, and left this Southern Tier city at an early age. Although he made his name and fortune in California, he never forgot his roots in Upstate New York and was brought home to be buried at Woodlawn Cemetery a century after his birth. To find his grave, enter the main gate on Walnut Street, and the Roach family plot will be immediately on your right in Section C.

Author's Note: Kudos to the staff and management at Woodlawn Cemetery. There are several famous interments here, and they are all easily found thanks to the concise markers and directional signs leading visitors to the graves.

Factoid: While Roach was attending an Elmira grade school, the humorist Mark Twain visited his school one day to give a presentation. Roach recalled many times that this inspired him as a young boy to explore the world of entertainment. Twain, also a native of Elmira (and the subject of chapter 55), is buried in the same cemetery as Hal Roach. Twain's grave can be found near Roach in Section G.

For More Information: Hollywood Walk of Fame, "Hal Roach," www .walkoffame.com/hal-roach.

54

ALBERT LEO STEVENS

1877–1944

THE HUMAN BOMB
BURIED IN FLY CREEK,
OTSEGO COUNTY

*T*here are a lot of "firsts" in this book. Many of them are innocuous and fairly safe, such as first woman judge or first president to not employ English as his first language or first New York governor. But Leo Stevens took being "first" to a whole new level.

Stevens was a pioneering balloonist. He was among the very first of those daring flying men and women, only in his case he floated rather than flew. His claim to fame was that he might be (records are not clear) the very first person to ever survive a significant jump from a high altitude employing the use of a parachute. It is reported that he conducted this feat in 1895 by leaping off the tall spire of a cathedral in Montreal, Canada.

His fascination with ballooning was really a lifelong passion. He first ascended in a balloon when he was just twelve, began manufacturing them before he was twenty, and is credited with inventing the precursor to the modern day ripcord at the age of thirty-five. In 1909, he opened the first private airfield in America.

Stevens's ballooning feats gave him great fame and fortune, and he attracted huge throngs to gather below and watch his adventures in the sky. Once he lifted his balloon off from the roof of Wanamaker's Department Store in New York City to the cheers of thousands. His greatest feat was an act he called the Human Bomb. As a large crowd watched, a huge hot air balloon would slowly drift across a low sky trailing behind it a long

cord attached to a large ball. Little did the crowd known that Stevens was crouched inside the ball. Suddenly, a small explosion would burst the ball, and aeronaut Stevens would come hurtling out into the sky to the gasps of the crowd. Moments later, a parachute would pop open and the stunt man would float safely to the earth to a chorus of great cheers. He did this to worldwide acclaim at the Pan American Exposition in Buffalo in September 1909.

Stevens was both a true aviation pioneer and a showman who really knew how to draw a crowd. He eventually legally changed his name to Aeronaut Leo Stevens. In 1911, he became the manager of Harriet Quimby, the first licensed female pilot in America. He booked her at air shows throughout the country. On July 1, 1912, Quimby and her partner were performing at an airshow at Squantum, Massachusetts. Unfortunately, as her plane raced across the sky at one thousand feet, it suddenly dipped dramatically and ejected both Quimby and her copilot. Both were killed instantly when they hit the ground.

In retirement, he lived at his farm just west of Cooperstown, New York. The farm was referred to by locals as the Balloon House, as he continued to tinker and make parachutes right up to his death. Stevens died on May 8, 1944 at the age of sixty-seven. Stevens's wife, Laura, had been employed by Ambrose Clark, of Cooperstown's dynastic family, for nearly forty years.

Grave Location: Stevens is buried in tiny Fly Creek, just five miles west of Cooperstown. His grave is near the center of the lower section on the northern side of the Fly Creek Valley Cemetery, located on Cemetery Road just south of Route 80. Do not enter through the main wrought-iron gate, but rather the entrance to the right of it. About twenty rows in, his grave is on the left. If you come to the elaborate stone marked "Clapsaddle," you have gone too far. A bronze medallion on his gravestone depicts a profile of an elderly Stevens looking at a parachute. His grave reflects the change he made to his name: Aeronaut Leo Stevens.

Author's Note: Despite its "rural" name, Fly Creek is a wealthy hamlet with many horse farms, mini-mansions, and historic buildings dotting the rolling landscape. The Fly Creek Cider Mill, a historic 1856 water-powered cider press, mill, gift shop, and retail center, is one of Otsego County's biggest tourist attractions.

For More Information: Hall of Fame of Parachuting, "History of the Leo Stevens Award," www.parafame.org/history_of_leo_stevens_award .htm.

GUSTAV STICKLEY

1858–1942

*FURNITURE MAKER EXTRAORDINAIRE
BURIED IN SYRACUSE,
ONONDAGA COUNTY*

Gustav Stickley's parents came from Germany and settled in Oshkosh, Wisconsin, where he was born on March 9, 1858. By the age of twenty, he was already working in his uncle's furniture manufacturing factory. Eight years later, he and his two brothers formed the Stickley Brothers & Company in Binghamton (eventually five Stickley brothers worked in this enterprise). In the next few years he founded several companies, closed a few others, and actually spent time directing the furniture operations at Auburn State Prison. Between 1892 and 1894 he "employed" more than three hundred prisoners tasked with producing his furniture. It is believed that Stickley designed the first electric chair at the prison—a chair which was first used on August 6, 1890, to execute convicted murderer William Kemmler.

By the turn of the twentieth century, Stickley and his business partners were designing and introducing revolutionary new pieces of furniture to the American scene. His styles were large pieces of furniture with plain, simple lines and a rough-hewn quality that appealed to his middle-class target audience. His pieces, such as chairs, book cases, writing desks, china cabinets, and tables, were soon in high demand. He published a magazine called the *Craftsman*, which carried articles, images of new pieces, prices, and even some current events editorials. Basically a catalog, the magazine was a tremendous success. It cost two dollars for a yearly subscription and

was widely circulated. The motto on the front cover of each magazine read: *"The lyf so short, the craft so long to lerne."* It ran from 1901 to 1960.

As one of the most prominent advocates of the Arts and Crafts style of furniture making, Stickley's name was the most recognizable among a handful of industry leaders. Eventually whole homes—Craftsman Homes—were constructed using the concepts of Stickley's preferred design movement. These homes departed from the accepted norms of house-building and added new features such as lower ceiling heights, large exposed timber beams, smaller bedrooms, and a new invention: the breakfast nook.

To this day, the Stickley imprimatur on a piece of furniture signifies high quality and fine craftsmanship.

Gustav Stickley died in Syracuse on April 11, 1942, at the age of eighty-four.

Grave Location: Stickley is buried in Oakwood Cemetery, located at 904 Comstock Avenue in Syracuse. Enter the cemetery at the gate just south of the main entrance at the office, where you will immediately face Section B. Stickley is buried here with several family members, near the first row, in Plot 233. His gravestone is a marble bench.

Author's Note: There is a Stickley Museum in Fayetteville, New York, which looks at the life and times of the five Stickley brothers and their impact on furniture making and home designs in America. The museum is located on the site of the original Stickley furniture factory. One fun aspect of the museum's website is that it features an "Antique of the Week." Here you can view historic Stickley pieces as they have come up for auction around the country. Some of the final prices are staggering.

Factoid: The Stickley family residence at 438 Columbus Avenue in Syracuse was the first Craftsman Home to be completed. Although quite unremarkable from the outside, the interior is resplendent with all the traditional Stickley touches you would imagine. Wide plank chestnut floors, beveled glass book cases, exposed beam ceilings, doors with many rows of small panes of glass, and slightly lower ceilings heights. The three-story house was built in 1900. Gustav Stickley sold the house to his daughter, Barbara Wiles, and continued to live with her until his death in 1942. Today a nonprofit organization, The Gustav Stickley House Foundation, is overseeing the restoration of the residence. The house was listed on the National Register of Historic Places in 1984.

For More Information: The Stickley Museum, stickleymuseum.com.

THE WARD BOYS

BROTHER'S KEEPER
BURIED IN MUNNSVILLE,
MADISON COUNTY

*B*ill, Delbert, Lyman, and Roscoe Ward were the least likely movie stars you will ever find. They were elderly brothers, illiterate and dirt poor, who shared the same two-room shanty their entire lives. Their shack had no indoor toilet, no running water, and no heat. They slept in pairs. They changed their clothes only a couple of times a year. They tended their small field and had a few chickens, which they kept in an abandoned school bus. They had a small TV and took great pleasure in watching Andy Griffith in *Matlock*.

They were filthy, forgotten, and completely happy. They lived in the threadbare farming community of Munnsville in Madison County. There are approximately five hundred residents in the town. Nobody ever paid much attention to the Ward boys until one of them, Bill, turned up dead in his bed on June 5, 1990.

The death of one of the Ward boys would have slipped by unnoticed if the big city prosecutors hadn't moved in and arrested Bill's brother (and bedmate) Delbert for his murder. Although the death was originally listed as "natural," a case was built against poor Delbert that included everything, it seemed, but the proverbial kitchen sink. Was it a mercy killing? Was it a sex crime? Was it murder? Euthanasia? Revenge? Delbert insisted he did not kill his brother, but after a lengthy interrogation by the New York State Police, he signed a confession saying he had covered his brother's nose and mouth and suffocated him.

Nobody believed him.

Eventually the town, once so distant to the three brothers, roused from its slumber and came roaring to Delbert's defense. Accusing the authorities of everything from political retribution to an unseemly land-grab (the boys' land was small and hardscrabble but in a desirous location), the town rallied to the brothers' cause. The good citizens of Munnsville raised over $10,000 to pay for Delbert's bail and legal defense. The brothers, confused and bewildered by all the fuss, remained isolated on their farm as publicity and national news coverage came calling.

A trial was held.

Grave Location: The Ward brothers are buried in a common grave in the Stockbridge Cemetery in Munnsville. The cemetery is located on Route 46, a mile north of the S-turn in the village off Route 33. Enter the cemetery at the northernmost driveway and proceed to the rear, past the flagpole. In Section K you will find the gravestone marking the final resting place of all the brothers. It identifies them as they were known in life: "The Ward Boys."

Author's Note: I realize that the final line in the main portion of this chapter seems kind of *unfinal.* It is meant to be so.

A movie documentary of the Ward boys' travails was released in 1992 by Joe Berlinger and Bruce Sinofsky and titled *Brother's Keeper.* The film tells of the trial of Delbert Ward and its outcome, and as is the case in any whodunit, I will reveal the ending to you but offer up a spoiler alert here.

The film is gripping and emotional, and it builds to a powerful intensity at the end during the trial. The Wards' confidence in the filmmakers, which allowed them to get close and personal with the brothers over a nine-month filming period, is remarkable. In their childlike naiveté, the elderly brothers emerge as simple, almost reverential figures. The footage of their daily farm routine is quite revealing in its simplicity. From the filming of a pig slaughter to the panoramic vistas of the barren forlorn farmlands in winter, the filmmakers make us part of the story. Once inside, the images of the siblings' living quarters are startling. They live a spare existence in a decrepit garbage-strewn abode that seems barely habitable.

The supporting characters are well defined, especially the rallying townsfolk and the coolly professional prosecuting attorneys. The film is a marvel. The final scene (actual local television news footage of the trial) is unrelenting. Each brother takes the stand to answer questions about what happened on the night of June 5, 1990. No Spielberg production or Tom Hanks performance could be as gripping as the real courtroom drama captured in this documentary. The scene of one of the brothers having a nervous breakdown on the witness stand is about as much as any viewer can take. The film is a masterpiece.

Factoid: The story of the Ward boys is well known in Central New York, but not so much as you leave the environs of the region. The movie, *Brother's Keeper,* spread the story to an international audience. The film won the Sundance Film Festival Audience Award for Best Documentary and the Director's Guild of America Award for Outstanding Directorial Achievement. It was named by *Entertainment Weekly* magazine as one of the "50 Greatest Independent Films of All Time."

(Delbert Ward was acquitted of the murder of his brother.)

For More Information: Internet Movie Database, "Brother's Keeper," www.imdb.com/title/tt0103888/.

Part Five

CATSKILLS

CLAYTON BATES

1907–1998

PEG LEG
BURIED IN PALENTOWN,
ULSTER COUNTY

*C*layton Bates was born on October 11, 1907. His parents were dirt poor sharecroppers from Fountain Inn, South Carolina, and Clayton began working to help support his family at the age of twelve. On only his second day on the job at a local mill, he suffered a terrible accident that would change his life forever . . . for the good!

A sudden power outage plunged the mill into darkness, and young Clayton stumbled into a sugar-grinding conveyer belt, which jolted into action when the power came surging back on. Unable to escape his predicament, his left leg was mangled beyond repair. In those days of the segregated South, with separate whites-only and blacks-only hospitals and no medical insurance for the poor, Clayton's bleeding body was simply carried to his family home, where a neighbor amputated his left leg at the knee. The surgery was performed on his mother's kitchen table.

Before the accident, Clayton had been earning some extra money with a little dance act he did along Main Street. A natural rhythmist, he was an acrobatic tap dancer who made pennies and nickels dancing for the townsfolk of his hometown. He desperately wanted to continue this hobby after the accident and forced himself to recover and rehabilitate with great speed. Within two months of having his leg taken off, he was on his feet and walking with the aid of two crutches made out of broomsticks. Shortly after this, his uncle whittled Clayton a wooden leg and

strapped it onto his left leg stump. Clayton called it his "peg leg," and the name stuck. Within six months, Peg Leg Bates was walking and running on his new leg and began performing his dance routines once more. With one leg.

His unusual dance style (he pounded out the drum cadence of the beat with his wooden leg) drew attention from far and wide. An affable artist with a winning smile and a soaring spirit, Bates devised outlandish feats of tap dancing that drew standing-room-only crowds wherever he went. He became a top draw on the minstrel circuit and eventually caught the eye of a national promoter. He was booked into the famed Cotton Club in Harlem for a three-week appearance in the 1930s, and his fame was secured. His show-stopping final routine was an improvised dance step he called the Imitation American Jet Plane Jump. It called for him to jump his own height straight up, spin crazily in the air and then land on his wooden leg with a tremendous thump, while sticking his good leg out behind him. Crowds leapt to their feet at the exhilaration of this final curtain closer at each of his shows.

Clayton's path to fame and riches took him around the world, and he played in the greatest concert halls to sellout crowds. In the 1950s, he was a headliner with Louis Armstrong's first European tour. In 1936, he was asked to give a command performance in London for the Queen of England. It is reported that at the rousing finale—the Jet Jump—the queen asked from her box for the dancer to "do that one more time, please." Clayton demurred and retreated to his dressing room. The Jet Jump, while being a real show stopper, was also a feat that at times would reduce him to a pain-wracked heap in his dressing room.

Bates made a fortune from dancing and lived a very comfortable life. He and his family lived in beautiful homes and drove fancy cars. He owned thirteen custom-made peg-legs ("one for each color of the suits he owned") and became a supporter of many social causes. He performed more than twenty times on the *Ed Sullivan Show*, more than any other dancer.

Once, while performing at Grossinger's Resort in the Catskill Mountains of Upstate New York, he noticed that his audiences were almost always all-white. This reminded him of the days of his segregated youth, and Bates decided to open up a resort exclusively for African Americans. In 1951, he turned his sixty-acre farm in Kerhonkson, New York, into Peg Leg Bates Country Club and ran it successfully for many years. Here he would greet customers at the front door, sign autographs, and smile for hundreds of pictures. He also danced there regularly. Entertainment legends like Sammy Davis Jr., Ella Fitzgerald, and Nat King Cole all performed there.

Peg Leg Bates officially retired from show-business in 1989, but he never stayed out of the limelight for long. He spoke to countless civic groups about racial harmony, rights for the disabled, and the problems facing disadvantaged youth. He was a motivational speaker of quiet eloquence and sincerity. Many times he accompanied his talks with a video of his life and career.

In his final years, he was honored as a superior talent by many in the entertainment industry. Young dancers found their way to him, and he basked in their admiration. His incredible journey has been told in several television specials and in books. He was awarded the Order of the Palmetto, the highest civilian award given out in South Carolina.

Grave Location: Bates is buried in Palentown, a small crossroads in rural Ulster County near the giant Ashokan Reservoir. To find the cemetery, travel west along County Route 3 (Samsonville-Kerhonkson Road) and veer right on to Palentown Road. The cemetery entrance is on the right. Go into the cemetery at the main entrance and stop at the point where the path bends to the left. Bates's grave is on your left. A large sign is located in the small cemetery signifying many historic graves. Other than Bates, these include several graves of the founding Palen family. Their graves are remarkable in that they are marked with insignias denoting them as veterans of all of America's earliest wars.

Author's Note: The circumstances of Bates's death read like the final chapter of a show-business best seller. At the age of ninety-one, Bates performed to an adoring audience at a benefit at the Fountain Inn High School. The small community was trying to raise funds to build a life-sized statue of their beloved native son, and Bates was the star attraction at the fundraiser. The next day, December 6, 1998, he was walking to church when he dropped dead of a heart attack. The statue has since been erected.

Factoid: Peg Leg Bates's grave marker is one of the most astonishing I have researched. The shiny black granite stone carries an etching on the front that is remarkable for its exactitude. It shows Peg Leg and his wife, Alice, on riding lawn mowers smiling in front of their country club. Dogs frolic in front of them, and Bates is smiling as he waves to all who pass by his final resting place. His peg leg is resting in the front of the mower. The depiction is so precise you can even see the tiny Schaefer Beer neon signs in the club's windows!

For More Information: Knockin' on Wood: Starring Peg Leg Bates, by Lynne Barasch (Lee & Low Books, 2004), is a popular children's book about the dancer's life.

Library of Congress Performing Arts Databases, "Clayton 'Peg Leg' Bates," memory.loc.gov/diglib/ihas/loc.music.tdabio.22/.

GERTRUDE BERG

1899–1966
"YOO HOO, MRS. BLOOM!"
BURIED IN FLEISCHMANNS,
DELAWARE COUNTY

"*Y*oo hoo, Mrs. Bloom!" was the television battle cry signaling an evening of laughter in the 1940s and 1950s. The cry would echo across a small Brooklyn tenement courtyard from the unpainted sill of an open window. The window's only adornment was a flower struggling for life sprouting from an old rusted Sanka coffee can. The large woman leaning far out into the slit of sunlight was the one and only Gertrude Berg, in the persona of one of America's most beloved television characters, Molly Goldberg.

First on radio and then on television (and then movies *and then* Broadway), Molly was the very personification of Jewish motherhood. Sort of an *I Remember Mama*—Yiddish style! Her essayer, Berg, was an enormous talent who was equally blessed as both a writer and an actress. Her forty-year show business career was marked with brilliant creativity and a high degree of professional excellence, both in the spotlight and out.

Berg was born on October 3, 1899, in New York City's Jewish Harlem. Later she moved to the Catskill Mountains to work in her family's summer resort. Inspired by the wisdom and humor of her own immigrant family, she began submitting scripts to radio. After several initial disappointments she hit the big time with her affectionate look at an extended family (much like her own) living in a crowded apartment in New York.

She called the show *The Rise of the Goldbergs*, and it quickly became a national sensation. From the mythical Mrs. Bloom, the unseen object

197

of her opening line bellow, to her husband, Jake, and their two teenage children, Rosalie and Sammy, the entire Goldberg clan and their hilarious Tremont Avenue neighbors became the second most popular comedy show on radio (just behind *Amos and Andy*). In fact, from its opening night show, November 20, 1929, Gertrude Berg would become Molly for several generations of fans. Sure, she tweaked it, refined her character, grew the life story scenario, and expanded the cast (much like Lucille Ball did with her several reincarnations of the Lucy character), but she always kept the core of Molly sacred—wise, funny, inquisitive, loving, and strong.

Later named *The Molly Goldberg Show*, it won every major entertainment award there was, and Berg warmly invited little-known talents to come and hone their craft on her hit show. Anne Bancroft, Van Johnson, John Garfield, and Joseph Cotten were all fairly unknown newcomers who appeared on her show. When she took the Molly franchise to television in 1949, she bagged one of the most lucrative contracts in the business. As the writer, creator, and star of the show, Berg was a power to be reckoned with, again, much like her friendly rival, Lucy. Her steady legion of fifteen million loyal radio fans easily made the transfer to her TV show and she became one of the medium's earliest and biggest successes. Berg won an Emmy Award in 1951 for Best Actress in a television comedy.

While she never completely divorced herself from the Molly character, one could hardly blame her for not trying. She appeared as Molly on radio for nearly two decades, was on television for several years, wrote a bestselling *Molly Goldberg Cookbook*, starred in an autobiographical *Me and Molly* on Broadway for 156 performances in 1948, and got the full-blown Hollywood treatment in the big picture *Molly!* in 1951. America, it seemed, couldn't get enough of "Yoo hoo, Mrs. Bloom!" and Berg laughed with her audience all the way to the bank.

In the late 1950s, she turned her exuberant talents toward Broadway and for the first time away from the beloved Molly. In what she called one of the highlights of her professional life, she starred as Mrs. Jacoby, a widowed Jewish mother, opposite the erudite Sir Cedric Hardwicke's wealthy Japanese widower in the acclaimed *A Majority of One*. The two were friends who had worked together on another Molly-style television show, *Mrs. G Goes to College*. Critics raved at the depth of Berg's Broadway performance and her ability to stay scene for scene with Hardwicke, an honored and respected British thespian, every step of the way. At the age of sixty, she was the hottest ticket on Broadway and walked away with the Tony Award for Best Actress. She would return to Broadway again in 1963, and was cheered for her critically praised performance in *Dear Me, the Sky is Falling*.

In the autumn of 1966, she was rehearsing for yet another play for New York, this one based on her own script, when she fell ill. On September 10, 1966, she went to a doctor's appointment and was admitted into a hospital for routine tests. She died four days later of a massive heart attack. She was sixty-six years old.

Grave Location: Gertrude Berg is buried in the Catskill Mountain community of Fleischmanns. Clovesville Cemetery is one of the smallest cemeteries discussed in this book. Coming north into town on Route 28 (in Delaware County), take the second exit into the village and cross the bridge on Depot Street. Make a left on what is known as "old" Route 28, and the cemetery is on the right about a half mile down the road at the intersection of Grochall Road. Enter the cemetery and proceed to the gated Jewish section in the rear on the right (Congregation B'nai Israel). On the highest knoll in this section is the Berg family plot.

Author's Note: Fleischmanns Museum of Memories is located at 1017 Main Street in the village, behind the historic Skene Library. The museum houses a collection of Gertrude Berg memorabilia.

Factoid: Fleischmanns was once one of the Catskill Mountain region's great playgrounds for the rich and famous. One of the wealthiest early families here was the Fleischmann family, which created the first commercially produced yeast in the United States. Their sprawling compound was one of the region's grandest, containing five large mansions.

For More Information: Fleischmanns Museum of Memories, www.skenelib.org/dpq/memorabilia.php.

59

JOHN BURROUGHS

1837–1921

THE SAGE OF SLABSIDES
BURIED IN ROXBURY,
DELAWARE COUNTY

John Burroughs was a simple man with simple tastes. He dressed casually (some would say raggedly) and sported a chin full of flowing white whiskers. He trudged lonely forgotten country roads as if a man on a mission. For seventy-five years he was a familiar, solitary figure along the dusty back roads of the northern Catskill Mountains of Upstate New York. A study in contradictions, Burroughs's rough-hewn demeanor masked a timid soul, a keen mind, and a deft sense of purpose. Having been brought up in an area he compared to "paradise," he was determined to become one with nature and to preserve for the future the beauty of the land he so loved.

Born in rural Roxbury, New York, the young Burroughs would climb the hilltop behind his home and gaze out across the pristine valleys from his favorite vantage point, a place he called Boyhood Rock. It was from this viewpoint that one of America's greatest naturalists first came under the spell of Mother Nature. His first essays, written when he was still only in his twenties, captured the imagination of his reading audience immediately, and he soon focused on becoming a writer.

Burroughs found that being a writer meant infrequent paydays and empty cupboards, so in 1869, to support his young family, he made a fateful move from the wilderness of Upstate to the hustle and bustle of our nation's capital, Washington, DC. Although the job he landed was

mundane (a clerk at the US Currency Bureau), a chance meeting with his idol, Walt Whitman, changed the course of Burroughs's life forever. The two men became close friends, and a tutorial relationship grew out of their mutual respect and admiration. Burroughs would later reflect that he owed much of his career to the teachings of "Master Whitman." In tribute, Burroughs published *Notes on Walt Whitman as Poet and Person* in 1867. In 1871, his first great nature study, *Wake Robin*, was published (the title was suggested by friend Whitman). The book was favorably reviewed, and his future works were eagerly anticipated.

Burroughs's prose and poetry were provocative, passionate and pro-lific. His writing output was astonishing—*Locusts and Wild Honey* (1879), *Signs and Seasons* (1886), *Leaf and Tendril* (1908), *The Summit of the Years* (1913), *Under the Apple Trees* (1916), and *Field and Study* (1919) were all major Burroughs works. For the last forty years of his life, he averaged one book every two years. In all, he sold over a million copies of his twenty-three books.

Although he disdained the outward trappings of fame, many of the great personages of his era sought audience with him for both advice and friendship. He even camped with President Theodore Roosevelt at Yosemite. He was heralded as one of the fathers of the American conservation movement, and even in his final years his speaking schedule was enough to tire a much younger man.

Having traveled to California in the spring of 1921 to fulfill a speaking commitment, Burroughs suddenly fell ill and, perhaps sensing that his time had come, directed that he be transported back to his Catskill Mountain aerie at once. He never made it. On March 29, 1921, he died on the train heading east. He was just shy of his eighty-fourth birthday.

Grave Location: John Burroughs is buried directly in front of Boyhood Rock behind his home in Roxbury. Travel into the village on Route 30 and veer off at Hardscrabble Road. Take that road to the top, and on your right you will find his home, Woodchuck Lodge, and grave site. As rural as all of this sounds, New York State has wisely marked the area with signs, exhibits, and photographic panels illustrating Burroughs's life, both here on the mountain and abroad. A picnic area has been set up in the woods for those who wish to stay and enjoy the surroundings so admired by Burroughs as a young man. A path leads you to his grave, where you will find one of the most unusual things I have ever found at a grave site. A metal box is situated on a small podium. Inside the box are pencils and a journal. Visitors are encouraged to leave notes, poems, thoughts, dedications, and messages.

Author's Note: Burroughs's official home is in West Park, New York. Named Slabsides, and open all year, it usually hosts several open houses annually with speakers, presentations, and discussions. Inside Slabsides you will find photographs of the famous visitors who came to reflect and collaborate with the writer, including Walt Whitman, Thomas Edison, John Muir, and Henry Ford. His old straw hat still hangs on a peg by the front door.

Factoid: Jay Gould, one of the most ruthless robber barons of the late 1800s, was also born near Burroughs's home. He was a famous financier and at one time one of the richest (and most reviled) men in America. Gould was born in 1836, one year earlier than Burroughs. His children honored their late father by building one of the Catskill's most beautiful churches in Roxbury in his memory, the Jay Gould Memorial Reformed Church. It contains original Louis Comfort Tiffany stained glass windows.

For More Information: Woodchuck Lodge, The Catskills Home of John Burroughs, jbwoodchucklodge.org.

60

GOVERNOR GEORGE CLINTON

1739–1812

FATHER OF NEW YORK
BURIED IN KINGSTON,
ULSTER COUNTY

*I*n the pantheon of legendary New Yorkers, surely no name would shine brighter than that of its first governor, George Clinton. An astute politician of untiring ambition, he was one of the most popular leaders of his or any other era. From his early political beginnings in his home area, Ulster County, George Clinton would rise to lead the state for an unprecedented *seven terms* as governor and then go on to become vice president under both Jefferson and Madison.

A lifelong resident of New York's Catskill region, he was on call to lead the defenses of the Hudson River Valley during the hostilities of 1775. Clinton never pretended to possess great military skills and was eager to transition into his more natural arena of politics. A regrettable footnote to his rather undistinguished military career is the fact that his soldierly duties prevented him from attending the signing of the Declaration of Independence, so he missed the glorious opportunity of affixing his signature to the most famous document in American history.

Once well-pointed along his political journey, George Clinton proved unstoppable. In June 1777, he defeated the well-known Philip Schuyler in the gubernatorial race by such a lopsided margin that he was elected to both the governorship and the lieutenant-governorship at the same time (he resigned from the latter post). He earned a sterling reputation as a tightfisted financial manager and as an adroit negotiator.

An iron horse in New York politics, Clinton served as governor for an astounding twenty-one years. As a fighter for New York's future, he supported greater manufacturing growth, better schools and roads, and greater power for the states in the realm of internal affairs (he was a vocal antifederalist). His interest in establishing a sophisticated interconnecting series of waterways and canals to join the Hudson River with the Great Lakes was championed later by his famous nephew, DeWitt Clinton, who also became a governor of New York.

George Clinton was born on July 26, 1739, and died on April 20, 1812. He never retired from public life and was the sitting vice president of the United States at the time of his death.

Grave Location: Clinton was first buried with full honors at the Congressional Cemetery in Washington, DC. In 1908, his body was moved and reinterred with pomp and ceremony in the historic cemetery at the Old Dutch Church in Kingston. His tall monument can be viewed from the sidewalk, although the cemetery is open and makes for an interesting stroll through early New York history. In 1989, his imposing monument, complete with a marble profile of Clinton on the front, underwent a total refurbishing to commemorate the 250th anniversary of his birth. The church and cemetery are located in the heart of downtown Kingston at 272 Wall Street.

Author's Note: During a visit to George Clinton's final resting place, take a few moments to go inside the historic Old Dutch Church. It carries significant history within, having established its first congregation in 1659. This makes it one of the oldest continuously operating religious communities in the nation. In retaliation for the church's passionate support of the Americans in the Revolutionary War, the British burned it to the ground when they sacked the city of Kingston in 1777. After the church was rebuilt following the British defeat, General Washington came to present the congregation with a letter of gratitude for their support of the cause of liberty. The church still exhibits the letter.

Factoid: The church's steeple rises to 225 feet. The city of Kingston enacted a law in 1984 stating that no other structure in the historic Stockade section of the city could exceed that height.

For More Information: Old Dutch Church and Graveyard, "Our Story," www.olddutchchurch.org/history.php.

61

THOMAS COLE

1801–1848

MUSE OF THE MOUNTAINS
BURIED IN CATSKILL,
GREENE COUNTY

*A*rtist Thomas Cole painted, among other things, his surroundings. And today, stepping into those surroundings feels like walking into one of his lush, evocative works of art.

Cole was born in 1801 in England and came to America as a teenager. He was a self-taught artist who honed his craft at studios in Ohio and Pennsylvania before "discovering" the Catskill Mountains in 1825. Cole would paint dozens of landscapes over his life, but it is his hauntingly beautiful paintings of his beloved Catskills that would be his lasting legacy. He is considered to be a founder of the Hudson River school, which was America's first formal art movement. A stint in Europe allowed him to paint the images of that continent's sweeping mountains and verdant river valleys, and upon his return in 1832 he exhibited those European landscapes to great acclaim in New York City. For the most part, Cole's paintings all began in his small, rural studio in the aptly named village of Catskill.

Cole's studio and home, named Cedar Grove, are today a wonderful museum to his life and works. From the front porch of his residence a visitor can easily see the far-off Catskill Mountains looming over the horizon, virtually unchanged from the time he first picked up a brush in his studio here. Cole and his wife, Maria, were married in the parlor of this modest mansion on November 22, 1836.

Thomas Cole did not live to see his fame spread down through newer generations of wilderness landscape painters. He died of pleurisy on February 11, 1848, in his bed at Cedar Grove. He was just forty-seven years old.

Grave Location: Thomas Cole is buried less than a mile from Cedar Grove. He was originally buried near his home, but his remains were reinterred in the Thompson Street Cemetery in 1858. Travel south on Spring Street from his home and veer right on Thompson Street. Enter the northern gate of the cemetery, and you will find the Cole family plot on the right approximately thirty rows in, near where the cemetery ends and the nearby residences begin. He is buried with his wife, Maria, and three children.

Author's Note: Cole's son Thomas is buried near a large Celtic cross near the family plot. His stone reads: "Thomas Cole. Catskill 1848—Saugerties 1919. Rector of Trinity Church Saugerties for Forty Years."

Factoid: This area is an art lover's heaven. Both Thomas Cole and Frederic Church, two of America's most famous landscape artists, had homes within a few miles of each other. Church's mansion, Olana, is located in nearby Hudson, New York, on the other side of the Hudson River. At one time Church was a pupil of Thomas Cole. Guided hikes up and into the mountains offer guests a unique opportunity to literally step into the landscapes of Thomas Cole, Frederic Church, Jasper Cropsey, and other Hudson River School painters (arrangements can be made at Cedar Grove).

For More Information: Thomas Cole National Historic Site, thomas cole.org.

62

JENNIE GROSSINGER

1892–1945

THE CATSKILLS' INNKEEPER
BURIED IN LIBERTY,
SULLIVAN COUNTY

*W*hen I first met Frank Kubiak, his face was a road map of wrinkles and his hands showed the roughness of a person who has never shied away from hard work. He was retired then, well into his seventies, and living with his longtime wife in a cottage in the hills overlooking Worcester, New York. He had worked for many years at Grossinger's Resort in the Catskills, "back in the good old days" as he called them.

His time served at the famed resort was in the kitchen. During the 1930s he was part of a kitchen crew that helped grow this resort into the most famous one of them all. He closed his eyes and shared his memories of that time. "It was a big family place. Lots of families came to stay there, and Jennie's family all worked there together taking care of them," he started in his thick Eastern European accent.

"Harry, Jennie's husband, was the real brains of the outfit. They were third cousins and both had the last name of Grossinger. He was the money man, the bookkeeper. He did all the buying for the place himself. The mother, Malke, was tough as nails. I remember one time when she came into the kitchen while I was working. She discovered a milk pot being used for a meat dish. Since Grossinger's adhered strictly to all kosher dining rules, she had a fit. Actually it was a rage. She grabbed the milk pot out of my hands and dumped the contents on the floor. She then lugged that big old pot into the cellar where she took an axe and smashed it to

bits. But Jennie," Kubiak whispered with a twinkle in his eye, "she was a sweetheart. She was the real charmer of the bunch. She knew all of us workers by name and treated us with fairness and kindness. She showed real affection for her employees. I will never forget her."

Such were the feelings many people harbored for famed Catskill hotel owner Jennie Grossinger. In 1914, she and her husband moved into a dilapidated seven-room country house near Liberty, New York. Strapped for money, she rented out several rooms during their first summer there and netted a grand total of eighty-one dollars for her efforts. Later, she would add on, buy up the surrounding farms and homes, and eventually build her rooming business into a large hotel. Tourists fled the steamy summer confines of metropolitan New York for the cool mountain setting of her country resort. Her hotel eventually grew to accommodate more than five hundred guests at a time.

Jennie Grossinger's secret weapon was her genuine friendliness. An attractive, elegant hostess, she remembered all of her guests' first names and treated each visitor as if he or she were a celebrity. And many were!

During the hotel's heyday, one would not be surprised to scan the cavernous dining room and see the likes of Eleanor Roosevelt, Jonas Salk, Bobby Kennedy, Frank Sinatra, and her two favorite Rockies—boxing champion Rocky Marciano and New York Governor Nelson Rockefeller. In fact, the boxer even wore a white satin robe into the ring for his fights with the hotel's name emblazoned across the back. Singer Eddie Fisher sang there as a struggling, unknown singer and then came back many years later and married actress Debbie Reynolds on the grounds of the resort.

The memories of Grossinger's are of a time of laughter and fun in the historic Borscht Belt of the Catskills. By 1972, the 1,200-acre resort was taking in over $7 million a year and boasted its own ski lodge, lake, airport, and post office. The resort also had its own ski slope, and in 1952 they were the first ski slope in America to use artificial snow.

A few years in the early 1950s, however, were difficult ones for the famed hotel when two devastating fires tore through the structures and brought death and destruction to its idyllic grounds. The most serious fire, on March 1, 1954, killed eight employees and injured another thirty. Still, the glamour and the reputation of this Catskill Mountains icon would not die, and the landmark resort was fully restored through commitment and hard work. It remained one of the great success stories for several more decades.

Jennie Grossinger lived a happy and full life surrounded by family and friends at her hotel. When she died of a stroke on November 20, 1972, at the age of eighty, she could truly have claimed to have been loved by all who had met her. She remained loyal to her hotel even after her daily responsibilities were diminished by her age. She died at Jay Cottage, a small home that was built for her directly on the hotel grounds so she could be near "her place."

Grave Location: Jennie Grossinger is buried in Ahavath Israel Cemetery in Liberty. Follow Route 52 to the intersection of Hysana Road and continue for a half mile, past a pond, where you will enter the cemetery on your right. From this first unmarked entrance you can see the Grossinger family plot immediately on your left near a slight knoll. Jennie is buried here with many family members. Paul Grossinger, Jennie's son and co-owner of the resort, is remembered on his gravestone as "a true big leaguer."

Author's Note: The decades of the 1980s and 1990s saw the ultimate demise and slow death of the Borscht Belt, as this resort area had been known for many years. Grossinger's went broke and closed. Cheap airfares, second vacation homes, other nearby entertainment meccas (like Atlantic City), and air conditioning in the city all but made the need for summer escape to the aging Catskill resorts a thing of the past. Huge, lumbering hotels, once filled with the smells of Jewish cooking and the sounds of "dirty dancing," are mere ghosts of an era long gone.

Businesses are more for sale here than not. The Liberty area still struggles economically. But, like the basket in which all of the proverbial eggs are placed, legalized gambling in the form of a large casino is beginning to look like a potential savior for this phoenix waiting to rise. Years after its final closing, Grossinger's was sold to a consortium promising a new "all improved" resort in the future. It never happened. In fact, the present day Grossinger Golf Course on the property is still thriving, but their publicity advises visitors to "not let the passing of the abandoned hotel on your way to the golf course dull your senses or enthusiasm."

Factoid: Jennie Grossinger was a tireless supporter of causes for the State of Israel. There is a convalescent home named after her in Safed, Israel, as well as a medical center in Tel Aviv.

For More Information: *Growing Up at Grossinger's,* by Tania Grossinger (Skyhorse Publishing, 2008).

Out of Babylon: Ghosts of Grossinger's, by Richard Grossinger (Frog Books, 1997).

Grossingers Country Club (golf), www.grossingergolf.net.

63

LEVON HELM

1940–2012

MIDNIGHT RAMBLER
BURIED IN WOODSTOCK,
ULSTER COUNTY

Levon Helm was the famed drummer and vocalist for the legendary rock group The Band. For many years, Helm, who lived in the Woodstock area, would hold late night (and often all night) music parties at his home studio dubbed "the barn." These joyous congregations would include many of the greatest names in music all attending an off-the-cuff, free-for-all jam session that would usually begin with a potluck supper and end with the passing of a hat to help Helm pay various debts that were closing in on him, from mortgage to medical expenses. Ticket prices were around a hundred bucks, and the barn only sat about two hundred people. There was never an empty seat.

Among the many performers who participated in these house parties, from the stage or in the audience, were Elvis Costello, Norah Jones, Emmylou Harris, Dr. John, Allen Toussaint, and others. The studio was a rustic, acoustically superior recording complex that Helm built to rehearse and record. The setting for the rambles was informal, as in kick-your-shoes-off-and-pull-up-a-pillow informal. In the 1990s, Helm was diagnosed with throat cancer, and these rambles helped to pay his skyrocketing medical bills. His voice was a mere shadow of its former self due to the chemotherapy sessions he underwent, but Helm was always behind a set of drums cranking along with a mile-wide grin on his face. Many of these "mini-Woodstocks" were recorded for posterity's sake.

Helm was born in rural Arkansas and fell in love with early country music he heard on his radio. Many of the great founding figures of
the nascent rock and roll era travelled through his rural mountain home
region, and he saw them all perform, from Elvis Presley to Chuck Berry
to Little Richard. He later worked with a variety of rock bands through
the 1950s and 1960s and had a musical relationship with Bob Dylan. His
work with The Band is legendary, and the group—with original members Helm, Rick Danko, Robbie Robertson, Richard Manuel, and Garth
Hudson—played on the final day of the famed 1969 Woodstock Music
Festival in Bethel, New York. They performed a dozen songs in a set that
included their signature song, "The Weight." Among the group's other
best-selling songs were "The Night They Drove Old Dixie Down" and
"Up on Cripple Creek."

Levon Helm was a sometimes-actor who appeared in *The Right Stuff*
(1983) and *End of the Line* (1987). He appeared as himself in *The Last
Waltz*, an acclaimed 1978 Martin Scorsese documentary about The
Band's final concert, and he acted with Jane Fonda in *The Dollmaker*

(1985). Perhaps his most famous role was that of Ted Webb, Loretta Lynn's father, in the Academy Award–winning *Coal Miner's Daughter* (1980). It was his debut movie.

Helm died on April 19, 2012, at the age of seventy-one.

Grave Location: Levon Helm is buried in Woodstock Cemetery, located on Rock City Road just two blocks from the main downtown business district. Enter the main gate of the cemetery and stay to the right as you continue on. Levon Helm's grave will be on the right in front of a large section of stockade fence wall that bears music notes.

Author's Note: Four of the original five members of The Band were Canadians, with Helm the lone American. This explains a number of Canadian flags that can usually be found left in tribute to his musical legacy. Rick Danko, one of The Band's founding members, died on December 10, 1999, at his home in nearby Marbletown, New York. He is also buried in this cemetery.

Factoid: Levon Helm's funeral was a celebration of the beloved local figure in Woodstock. More than a thousand people lined the streets of the tiny business district to witness a funeral procession of one hundred cars carrying the musician to his final resting place. His body was escorted into the cemetery by a rousing New Orleans–style Dixieland band.

For More Information: Rock and Roll Hall of Fame, "The Band," www.rockhall.com/inductees/band.

64

LEWIS W. HINE

1874–1940

EYE ON AMERICA
BURIED IN FRANKLIN,
DELAWARE COUNTY

$\mathcal{L}$ewis Hine saw more, revealed more, and interpreted more through the lens of his camera than most Americans see in real life. Although he was an educator by training, his keen view of the working poor (mostly children) and Depression-era happenings made him one of the most famous photographers in the country.

While a teacher, Hine and his students endeavored to document immigrant children coming through Ellis Island in the early 1900s. With his students, he produced what many have called the first photo documentary to ever gain wide respect. Hine had worked in menial, difficult jobs as a child, and his heart and his camera became the tools of his trade in uncovering the disgrace that was child labor in America at the turn of the twentieth century. He took more than five thousand photographs of poor children working in mills, factories, farm fields, and coal mines. His scathing photographic commentary led to many important social changes in this area, and in 1908 Hine joined the National Child Labor Committee, which was tasked with solving draconian child labor issues in America. His photographic portraits of these waifs toiling in filthy, unsafe, and backbreaking adult jobs remain stunning in their simplicity. They continue to haunt the viewer over a century later.

In 1930, Hine famously photographed, in stages, the construction of the Empire State Building in Manhattan. Even though he was fifty-six

years old, the wiry cameraman lugged his equipment up hundreds of feet in the air, where he dangled out of windows and balanced on steel beams to capture the progress in the building of America's greatest skyscraper. His images of sweaty construction workers, complicated construction processes, and the hurly-burly of the city streets below remain iconic. A book of these photographs, *Men at Work*, was a publishing success in 1932.

As work dropped off in the late 1930s, Hine struggled to find employment as a photographer. He was broke when he died on November 3, 1940, in New York City at the age of sixty-six.

Grave Location: Hine was a frequent visitor to the small hamlet of Franklin, in rural Delaware County, where he had family through marriage. He is buried in Ouleout Valley Cemetery on Route 357 just outside the community. To reach his grave, enter the ornate iron gates of the cemetery and drive to the highest point, marked by an American Flag and a Civil War monument. About twenty rows behind that, toward the trees, Hine's grave can be found just where the lawn begins to slope downhill. Look for the tall nearby monument for the Noble family as your marker.

Author's Note: Ouleout Valley Cemetery is one of Upstate's loveliest. The imposing Victorian-era iron-gated entrance welcomes you to a sprawling, beautifully landscaped series of rises, which surround ponds, a historic iron fountain, and many historic graves, including several from all of America's wars dating back to the Revolutionary War. Also buried here is publisher James McCall, the founder of *McCall's* magazine.

Factoid: For many years Lewis Hine was given credit for snapping one of the most popular and recognizable photographs ever taken by an American cameraman. "Lunch Atop a Skyscraper" shows eleven men, some with hats on, some shirtless, taking a lunch break 850 feet above the streets of Manhattan. They are sitting on an I-beam jutting out over the New York skyline. No safety harnesses support them. Some are lighting cigarettes, some are eating, some are conversing, and a few are just staring blankly forward with the backdrop of New York City rolling out in the distance behind them. The year is 1932. They were part of the construction crew building Rockefeller Center. It wasn't until a few years ago that a documentary on the photo, titled *Men at Lunch,* tried to find the real photographer of the iconic image. Most experts now believe that the famous picture was taken by Charles C. Ebbets and not Lewis Hine.

For More Information: Mornings on Maple Street, "Lewis Hine Project," morningsonmaplestreet.com/lewis-hine-project-index-of-stories/lewis-hine-project/.

E. Z. C. JUDSON

1821–1886

NED BUNTLINE:
KING OF THE DIME NOVEL
BURIED IN STAMFORD,
DELAWARE COUNTY

*N*ed Buntline was a bit of a fraud.

Born Edward Zane Carroll Judson in rural Stamford, New York, his life was filled with unverifiable tales of daring, his military career was undistinguished (yet he called himself Colonel), and his success as a writer hinged on the embroidered tales of a glorified buffalo hunter. Despite all of this (or perhaps because of it), E. Z. C. Judson, known as Ned Buntline, was one of the most famous and colorful figures of the literary Old West.

One remarkable event in his life, and a verified one at that, certainly must place his name in the forefront of frontier legends. In March 1848, Judson killed a man named Robert Porterfield, with whose wife Judson was having an affair in Tennessee. At Judson's murder trial, the late Porterfield's brother opened fire on him, and Judson flung himself out an open window and escaped. Soon he was recaptured, jailed, convicted, and sentenced to death. Unbelievably, at the time of his hanging, the hangman's noose broke when the trap door swung open, and Judson, his neck still intact, was freed as the law dictated.

Later, in New York City, he founded a popular scandal sheet, *Ned Buntline's Own*, which was the most successful of its kind anywhere. He was convicted of starting a riot in the city, the famous Astor Place Riot on

May 10, 1849, and this time actually served a year in prison. In 1852, he was indicted on charges of inciting yet another riot, this one on Election Day in St. Louis, but escaped prosecution by skipping bail. Eventually he relieved himself of all his many legal entanglements and concentrated on his writing career. Through skillfully placed news reports of his antics and through the power of his own prose (in which he usually was the prototype of his fictional heroes), Judson became a cause célèbre and a tremendously popular personality on the national stage.

Using the pseudonym of Ned Buntline, he wrote more than four hundred inexpensive adventure books, none of which ever cost more than a dime. Each was more eagerly anticipated than the previous. These dime novels made him a wealthy man. It was reported that at his peak he was making more money annually than established writers like Mark Twain and Walt Whitman. In 1869, he met a twenty-three-year-old buffalo hunter named William F. Cody. Christening him Buffalo Bill, Judson brought the man's daring tales of life on the frontier to the public through several books and articles featuring the intriguing plainsman. By the time he wrote the stage play, *Scouts of the Prairie*, starring Cody, each man's public stature was at its zenith.

Judson was married four times and was chased by ex-wives most of the last decades of his life. In 1871, at last a wealthy, aging man, he retired to his comfortable mansion in Stamford, Eagle's Nest. There he continued to write until his death on July 16, 1886, at the age of sixty-four. In these twilight years, Colonel Judson was a familiar sight in the upper circles of Catskill society. With his drooping white walrus moustache and his bemedaled vest, he was always a welcome and sought-after dinner guest. Eagle's Nest was the scene of many sparkling galas attended by the literati of the region, all eager to hear once more the tales of Ned Buntline, Buffalo Bill, and the stories of the Wild West.

Grave Location: Judson is buried in Stamford Rural Cemetery, located off Route 23 near the southern entrance to the village. A five-hundred-foot drive up Cemetery Road will bring you to the first entrance to the cemetery. Continue in all the way until the path starts to bend to the left. His grave, on your right and marked by a tall, polished red-brown obelisk, reads "E.Z.C. Judson."

Author's Note: The Stamford Village Library at 117 Main Street has a collection of information about Stamford's most famous resident. In fact, Judson was one of the committee to raise funds to found a library in Stamford in 1872.

Factoid: Judson's moniker, Ned Buntline, was appropriated by the makers of the Colt .45. It is said that Judson commissioned the long-barreled pistol as a payment for a large delivery of his books for which he was not paid. It is believed that one of the first recipients of the new Buntline Special was the legendary marshal Wyatt Earp.

For More Information: Stamford Village Library, www.svlny.org.

66

ZADOCK PRATT

1790–1871

AMERICA'S FIRST MOUNT RUSHMORE
BURIED IN PRATTSVILLE,
GREENE COUNTY

Zadock Pratt was one of the most important men in the Catskills during the early part of the nineteenth century. He was a businessman, a tanner, a politician and banker. His home base was near the Northern Catskills village of Windham. Eventually, when he entered the tannery business, he located his company along the Schoharie Creek on the western side of Windham, an area that eventually was named after him.

When it was founded, Prattsville was a small, poor farming community. But it was rich in natural assets. Pratt built an enormous leather tannery here, the largest in the world. He hired hundreds of workers, and the population of little Prattsville more than doubled as the business grew. The surrounding hills were thick with hemlock trees, which he used in the tanning process. Over time, more than 1.5 million hemlocks were felled for the tanning business.

Some regard Prattsville as one of America's first planned communities. To attract workers from a long distance, Pratt built more than one hundred homes, which he sold at a generous price to those who worked the tannery. He made Prattsville a lovely community in which to work and live, and he spent a great deal of time mapping out the streets, planting trees, and beautifying the community. In a short time, Prattsville boasted two thousand residents and had several mills and machine shops and a handful of retail businesses. Pratt financed the building of all of the

village's churches. The success of the tannery and his namesake community made Pratt the wealthiest man in town. In 1829, he built a home for his family on Main Street. Today it houses the Zadock Pratt Museum.

Zadock Pratt served in the War of 1812 and later pursued a career in politics. He was elected to two terms in the US Congress. His passion was the lowering of postal rates, which he succeeded in doing several times. Pratt was married five times, including to two pairs of sisters. He died following a fall on April 5, 1871, at the age of eighty.

Grave Location: Pratt is buried in a small cemetery near the north end of town known as the Lower Cemetery. Upon entering Prattsville from the north on Route 23, make a sharp left-hand turn just after crossing the bridge that goes over the Schoharie Creek. The cemetery is just a few hundred yards up the road on the right. Numerous family members are buried here also, and a historical marker along the roadside notes Pratt's final resting place. The cemetery has very few plots in it, and Pratt's is unmistakable in the center. It is the tallest grave marker in the cemetery,

The amazing carvings found at Pratt Rock have caused it to be known as America's First Mount Rushmore.

and the face of his tombstone recites some of his accomplishments, including the fact that "while a member of Congress he moved for the reduction of postage."

Author's Note: While the Schoharie Creek was vital to the early success of Pratt's mills and Prattsville itself, the creek is famous for being one of the most cantankerous water passages in Upstate. Prone to flooding, the village of Prattsville suffered greatly during Hurricane Irene in 2011. Virtually no building in the village was left untouched, and almost all of the 650 residents were left with no place to return to after the mandatory evacuation. Governor Andrew Cuomo called Prattsville the hardest hit community in the state. Over time, the village has rebounded in an inspiring way. Although several empty, off-kilter homes remind passersby of the storm's terrible destruction, Prattsville is now up, back, and open for business. The Zadock Pratt Museum, in Pratt's former home, was also heavily damaged in the flood but has reopened and hosts many interesting events.

Factoid: No visit to Prattsville is complete without hiking up Pratt Rock. You will find this curious roadside oddity at the southern entrance to the village on Route 23. A small park with picnic tables is located at the base of a trail. After a short hike up the mountain, you will emerge into a rock canyon with the most amazing carvings on its stone walls. They depict an odd mix of local history, plus personal touches referring to Pratt's own businesses and his family. Pratt carved a large hemlock tree into to the cave wall, signifying the importance of the tree to his business. He wrote family names and dates and carved a large horse and an arm wielding a hammer. One carving pays tribute to his son, George, who was killed during the Civil War. Some historians have referred to Pratt Rock as "America's first Mount Rushmore." It should be noted that other historians have more accurately called it "America's first Civil War monument."

Zadock Pratt had hoped to be buried in the stone canyon, but local lore said that he could not find a place that didn't leak so he settled for the cemetery in town. Six of his favorite animals, including horses, are buried in a common grave at Pratt Rock.

For More Information: Zadock Pratt Museum, zadockprattmuseum .com.

67

CATHERINE VAN DEBOGART

1803–1821

DOOMED BRIDE OF WOODSTOCK
BURIED IN WOODSTOCK,
ULSTER COUNTY

*O*ver the many years of my travels throughout New York State, I have come face to face with many great folktales, legends, and homespun campfire stories. One of the most bizarre and memorable of these concerns the grave of a girl named Catherine Van Debogart, in Woodstock, New York.

Catherine was a beautiful eighteen-year-old girl in 1820 when she married a much older John Van Debogart in Woodstock. Soon after they were married, their marriage turned into a troublesome affair. John was a drunkard who would often become violent after too many tankards of ale, and usually it was poor Catherine who was the object of his inebriated fury.

One night in August 1821, Catherine chanced to visit a nearby neighbor who needed some medical ministering. Catherine was eight months pregnant at the time. John had been on a binge for days and was home only infrequently. The rule laid down by the man of the house was that when he was not at home Catherine must not leave their dwelling. And that when he did come home, a hearty supper was to be prepared and ready to be served. This night, John came home and his wife was nowhere to be found. He immediately conjured up drunken imaginations of her out and about perhaps cavorting with a younger man. His jealous rage was not to be contained. He stole out into the backyard of their home and tore off a large branch from a towering elm tree. He then waited behind the front door for his young wife to come home.

Within an hour, Catherine entered the front door and John exploded at her. He threw her to the ground and beat her so badly that a doctor had to be called. When the physician arrived, he and John carried the young woman to her bed. The unborn baby had already died from the mother's injuries, and Catherine would not live to see the morning. John professed his innocence and said that she was injured when he came home and no assailant was found. In her final breath, she called her husband to her side and whispered to him that she knew it was he who had beaten her and that she forgave him for what he did. But she had one request. "I want you to bury the elm tree branch with me so that you will always remember the terrible thing you did to me and our baby." He agreed, and she died an hour later.

John buried his wife and unborn infant in the same coffin, along with the elm tree branch. Seized with remorse, he would visit his wife's grave every week for the rest of his own life. He became a pathetic and lonely sight along the streets of Woodstock, trudging out to the cemetery regularly. One day, about a year after his wife's death, John was visiting her grave when he noticed an elm branch growing out of Catherine's grave.

He pulled the small but growing bush out of the ground but it sprouted anew within days. In frenzy he did everything within his power to keep this demonic reminder of his terrible deed from reappearing. It was to no avail.

John went half mad trying to kill this living reminder of what he had done to his wife and infant. He eventually decided that he could no longer visit her grave, but after a month or so he returned for a visit. He was horrified to see that the elm branch, rooted in Catherine's coffin, had grown out of the ground and had risen up to and gone through her stone marker. *It had actually split the stone into two pieces.* The bottom half of the gravestone was now in front, and the top half bearing Catherine's name and birthdate jutted out from the ground behind it. Sensing this was a message of revenge from beyond, John began drinking heavily again and slowly dissolved into an inebriated oblivion.

"The Split-Elm Grave of Catherine Van Debogart" is one of the truly great legends of the Catskill Mountains. Whether the story is true or just an interesting yet apocryphal tale (told perhaps too many times) is for you to decide. But one thing is certain. If you visit Catherine Van Debogart's grave today, there is most assuredly an elm tree rising up and splitting her aged stone in half!

Grave Location: Catherine Van Debogart's grave is in the center of Woodstock Cemetery, located on Rock City Road. Her gravestone reads: "In Memory of Catherine Van Debogart, wife of John Van Debogart and also her Infant. Who died on August 2, 1821, Aged 18 Years, 2 Months and 13 Days."

Author's Note: From Catherine's grave you can see the final resting place of Levon Helm, member of the legendary rock group The Band. They are buried about one hundred yards apart. He is featured in chapter 63.

Factoid: Van Debogart is a well-known name in Woodstock today. There is even a Van Debogart Road. I know of no connection between today's Van Debogarts and the subject of this chapter.

For More Information: Legendary Locals of Woodstock, by Richard Heppner and Janine Fallon-Mower (Arcadia Publishing, 2013), www .arcadiapublishing.com/Products/9781467100670.

Part Six

HUDSON VALLEY/WESTCHESTER

68

ANDREW CARNEGIE

1835–1919

RICHEST MAN IN THE WORLD
BURIED IN SLEEPY HOLLOW,
WESTCHESTER COUNTY

*A*ndrew Carnegie was a man who had everything. Once the richest man in the world, he displayed one of the most storied runs of consistent financial luck in the annals of American business history. He was a super-millionaire by the time he was thirty and would come as close to becoming America's first billionaire as anyone of his era could. And yet he was a restive man, a man unsatisfied with the game of wealth-building that was played so ruthlessly by his nineteenth-century contemporaries. At the age of sixty-five he made a decision to give his vast fortune away, piece by piece. *All of it* . . . and he almost did.

The biographical backstory to the life of this famous man has been told many times over the years. We know that he was born in Scotland and came to this country at the age of twelve. Raised in stark poverty, the young Carnegie was a quick student who possessed an ambitious nature. He started work as a five-dollar-a-month bobbin boy in a Pittsburgh cotton factory. In quick succession he rose to office manager, then telegraph operator, and finally assistant to the president of the Pennsylvania Railroad. He lived a Spartan life and invested his growing salary wisely. One of his earliest investments was in the fledgling American steel industry. As the American Industrial Revolution roared along, his investment grew wildly, and eventually he was able to claim ownership of a large steel company. He was a tightfisted and shrewd financier who soon found himself to

be the top producer of steel in America. And even as this country grew up and out, Carnegie's own fortunes grew to an astronomical amount.

Carnegie had a Midas touch, and his ensuing investments amassed him hundreds of millions of dollars. In one uncharacteristic setback, he mishandled a labor strike at a company mill, and the ensuing troubles, known as the Homestead Steel Riot of 1892, would haunt him for the rest of his life. Finally, in January of 1901, he sold his empire to J. P. Morgan for a half billion dollars. The story goes that at the closing of this titanic deal, Mr. Morgan, who was dressed in satin tails and a tall silk top hat and standing imperiously above the diminutive Scotsman, stuck out his hand to Carnegie and said quietly, "Congratulations, Mr. Carnegie, you are now the richest man in the world."

It was at this point in his life that Carnegie turned reflective about his unheard-of-sized fortune. He adopted the credo that "to die wealthy is to die disgraced" and set his life course on the task of giving away his millions for the betterment of society. His beneficiaries were innumerable to say the least.

He established the Carnegie Corporation of New York with an endowment of $125 million. The purpose of this fund was to award educational grants for research, and since its formation in 1911 the fund has awarded over a half billion dollars in awards. Carnegie was a lover of books, and he oversaw the construction of 2,500 public libraries across the globe. He built Carnegie Hall in New York City, perhaps the most prestigious concert venue in the world. He supplied eight thousand organs for churches nationwide, at no cost to them. He gave $10 million to establish a Scottish University trust in honor of his homeland, where he also built his second home, Skibo Castle. He founded Carnegie Mellon University in Pittsburgh in 1900 (as The Carnegie Technical Schools). One of his most recognizable legacies, the Carnegie Hero Fund, has awarded millions of dollars to ordinary citizens who have performed extraordinary acts of bravery.

Dedicating oneself to the dispersal of a fortune amounting into the hundreds of millions of dollars was a daunting task. But Carnegie acted with an inspired urgency. By the time he died, on August 11, 1919, his will revealed that, save for personal bequests and family obligations, Andrew Carnegie had given away almost all of his money. A sum totaling more than $350 million (nearly $80 *billion* in today's money).

Grave Location: Andrew Carnegie is buried in Sleepy Hollow Cemetery, located on Route 9 just north of the Old Dutch Church. Upon entering the cemetery's main gates, you will find that Carnegie's grave is the first of many final resting places of the rich and famous (a kiosk at the front gate is stocked with maps to the graves of the many famous and infamous buried here). Located just a few yards away from the main office, Carnegie is buried beneath a simple, Celtic cross made out of stones taken from his home in Scotland. In this cemetery of millionaires (Rockefellers, Chryslers, Astors, Helmsleys, etc.) the onetime "richest man in the world" rests eternally in a plot marked only by a stone cross.

Author's Note: Carnegie libraries still stand throughout the land. Many of them are denoted as Carnegie gifts and highlighted as local historic landmarks. Carnegie was called the Patron Saint of Libraries, and his largess was not exclusive to the United States. He built 1,681 libraries in

America, 660 in the United Kingdom, 125 in Canada, and dozens more around the world. He even built one in Fiji.

Factoid: You could take Andrew Carnegie's word straight to the bank. As a young man he vowed to his mother that he would never marry while she was alive. She finally died when he was fifty-one years old. Carnegie married Louise Whitfield one year later.

For More Information: Carnegie Corporation of New York, "Andrew Carnegie," www.carnegie.org/interactives/foundersstory/#!/.

69

LIEUTENANT COLONEL GEORGE ARMSTRONG CUSTER

1839–1876

LITTLE BIGHORN
BURIED AT WEST POINT
MILITARY ACADEMY,
ORANGE COUNTY

George A. Custer was a soldier's soldier. Not comfortable staying in the rear, he was often seen cutting a dashing figure at the very front of a company charge during the Civil War. He fought for the Union cause and was an unforgettable presence on and off the battlefield. He was unmistakable among the long, anonymous lines of blue uniforms advancing across a wheat field or charging on horseback down a forested hillside. He had a dramatic handlebar mustache, flowing hair that covered his uniform collar, and a floppy hat that fastened under his chin. His uniform glistened with medals, ribbons, and brass buttons, and he often wore heavy, cavalry officer's leather gloves that reached halfway up his arm. He was fearless, a motivator of men, and an important player in many of the war's most important battles.

He also graduated dead last in his West Point class of 1861.

Custer was a cavalry officer who saw duty from the beginning of the war to its completion. He was in its first engagement, the First Battle of Bull Run on July 21, 1861, and was present for the signing of the surrender of Lee's Confederate army at Appomattox, Virginia, on April 9, 1865.

Custer stayed in the army after the Civil War, where his services were employed to fight against the Indians in the American West. He led his

men, the Seventh Cavalry Regiment, into the Montana Territory in 1876 with orders to secure the territory from the Indians who were frequently breaking treaties and causing unrest. On June 25, 1876, Custer and his men were attacked by a large group of enemy Indians at a place known as Little Bighorn, the center of the Crow Indian Nation.

The Battle of Little Bighorn is one of those great, towering tales of the American military that has been told in various forms for over a century and a half. Known now as Custer's Last Stand, the battle pitted the US Cavalry against an overwhelming force of American Indians made up of warriors of several tribes. Although not certain, some historians placed the strength of the two warring factions at about 650 for the US Army against approximately 2,000 to 2,500 Indians. The battle by all reports was a savage bloodletting.

The fatality count on the army side was total, with many of the soldiers being scalped and mutilated. In a desperate attempt to provide cover for themselves near the end of the battle, the cavalrymen shot their own horses and piled them up to use their bodies as protective berms from which to fire. It was to no avail.

When reinforcements arrived, they found all of Custer's men dead on the battlefield. Custer himself had been shot twice, once in the chest and once in the head. The final casualty account listed about 268 US dead and less than forty Indian dead. The soldiers were buried on the battlefield where they "died with their boots on."

Lt. Col. George Armstrong Custer was thirty-six when he died.

Grave Location: Custer is buried at West Point Post Cemetery at the United States Military Academy. His impressive monument is in Section 27, Row A, Grave 1. Around the base of his tall memorial obelisk are several bronze plaques that describe his military career, including all of the battles he fought in. Most remarkable are the three-dimensional buffalo heads that protrude from the base of the grave monument. Custer's grave is the most visited final resting place in this hallowed cemetery of American military heroes. Visitors can conduct their own walking tour of the cemetery, as maps to the numerous notable graves are available in a kiosk behind the main office.

Author's Note: This cemetery and Sleepy Hollow Cemetery are perhaps two of the most famous cemeteries in Upstate New York. Other military heroes buried at West Point Post Cemetery include Gen. George Washington Goethals, chief engineer of the construction of the Panama Canal; Gen. Frank Merrill, whose "Merrill's Marauders" gained fame for their hindrance of the Japanese advancement in the Pacific during World War II; Gen. William Westmoreland, commander of US forces during the Vietnam War; and Gen. Norman Schwarzkopf, who led US troops during Operation Desert Storm. Also buried here are Air Force Lt. Col.

Edward White, an astronaut who died in a training exercise in 1967; Maggie Dixon, a basketball coach and an Army veteran who led the Black Knights to their first NCAA berth; and movie star Glenda Farrell, whose husband, a US Army veteran, served on Gen. Dwight Eisenhower's staff.

Factoid: Custer has been the focus of dozens of magazine articles, books, television shows, and full length feature films. He was portrayed by actors in more than two dozen Hollywood films. Ronald Reagan portrayed him in *Santa Fe Trail* (1940), and Errol Flynn played him in *They Died with Their Boots On* in 1941.

For More Information: National Park Service, Little Bighorn Battlefield, "Lt. Col. George Armstrong Custer," www.nps.gov/libi/learn/history culture/lt-col-george-armstrong-custer.htm.

70

ENOCH CROSBY

1750–1835

REVOLUTIONARY WAR SPY
BURIED IN CARMEL,
PUTNAM COUNTY

Although Enoch Crosby was born in Massachusetts in 1750, his family moved to Putnam County when he was just an infant. He learned the trade of shoemaker in his teens. At the outbreak of the Revolutionary War, he enlisted to fight for the American forces and was stationed in Danbury, Connecticut. A series of unusual happenings found Crosby inadvertently invited to a meeting where Loyalists were discussing plans to back the British and organize a militia. Crosby was able to leave this meeting and take the information he had overheard to the American side, where he personally gave it to John Jay, a leader of Patriot soldiers, organizer of counterintelligence operations, and member of a quasi-shadow government called the Committee of Safety. Upon hearing this information, Jay ordered the arrest and detainment of those plotting against the patriot forces.

Recognizing his talents, Jay made Crosby an important spy for the American army, and Crosby shrouded his identity by identifying himself as a British spy with British General Howe. This gained him entrance into many strategic meetings with enemy officers, where he was privy to (and delivered back to the Americans) much important information. Once, the American's staged a mock trial after which Crosby was "allowed" to escape, further enhancing his reputation as a wily spy. Because of his creative subterfuge, Crosby was arrested many times, even by American

forces who would later learn of his double life. He was considered to be a favorite spy of General George Washington.

The danger involved in his military life of deceit caused Crosby great worry that if he was caught or killed his family might be the subject of scorn by compatriots who did not realize he was actually an American spy and not a British one. John Jay assured him that, if this happened, he and the full Committee of Safety would step forward and reveal Crosby's patriotic contributions on his behalf.

It is believed that the writer James Fenimore Cooper heard stories of Crosby's derring-do (perhaps from his friend John Jay) and fashioned a lead fictional character, Harvey Birch, after him when he wrote his classic *The Spy: A Tale of the Neutral Ground* (1821). Crosby is considered by many to be the first federal agent intelligence officer.

After the war, Crosby returned to his home state of Connecticut and became a farmer. He died on June 26, 1835.

Grave Location: This famous spy is buried in the small Revolutionary War–era Old Gilead Cemetery in Carmel. The cemetery can be found at the intersection of Mechanic Street and Northgate Road. It is a lovely burial ground filled with old stones and monuments and surrounded by a four-foot fieldstone wall. Crosby's grave is prominently located in the back, and his monument is the largest in the cemetery. For many years the connection between Cooper's novel and Crosby was speculation, but the epitaph on his stone seems to dispel any questions about it. It reads: "In memory of Enoch Crosby ('Harvey Birch'). Patriot spy of the Revolutionary War. June 5, 1750 to June 26, 1935. He braved danger and death that this land might be free to the cause of liberty. He offered his all, without hope of reward, honored by Washington, revered by his countrymen. We who inherit the freedom for which he toiled raise this monument to his glorious memory."

Author's Note: The stone wall around this quiet cemetery is beautiful, and the entrance is guarded by two towering black wrought-iron gates (which are easy to open). Because the cemetery is so small, it is pleasant to wander the rows of gravestones and read the names, dates, and epitaphs of so many who were around during the American Revolution. Crosby's grave is tended by the Enoch Crosby chapter of the National Society Daughters of the American Revolution, formed in Carmel and named in Crosby's honor in 1926.

Factoid: Sybil Ludington, the Female Paul Revere, is buried in Patterson, New York, just seven miles north of Carmel (she is the subject of chapter 73). Ludington's father, Colonel Henry Ludington, and Enoch Crosby were close friends. A famous life-sized statue depicting young Sybil on her own famous "midnight ride" is located in Carmel's lakefront area, where visitors would begin their drive up Mechanic Street to the Old Gilead Cemetery.

For More Information: Daughters of the American Revolution, "Enoch Crosby, American Patriot and Spy," www.rootsweb.ancestry.com /~nyeccdar/enoch_crosby_american_patriot.htm.

71

GOVERNOR THOMAS E. DEWEY

1902–1971

RACKET BUSTER
BURIED IN PAWLING,
DUTCHESS COUNTY

*T*homas E. Dewey first came to national prominence as an indefatigable, relentless crime buster. From his perch as a New York City prosecutor in what many called the "lawless 1930s," Dewey strong-armed many of the most illustrious, headline-grabbing crime figures right into prison cells where they were sentenced to long terms behind bars. One account said Dewey engineered the capture and conviction of more than seventy well-known New York City crime figures in less than two years. His dogged pursuit of criminals, Mafia members, bootleggers, and street gangsters earned the stern, controlled district attorney headlines of his own. Praised by the press and public alike, Dewey found himself thrust into the limelight of state and national politics.

Hailed as "Public Hero #1" by the media, Dewey was handpicked by the New York State Republican Party to run against incumbent governor Herbert Lehman in 1838. Dewey lost. Dewey ran again in 1942 and won. He was reelected in 1946 and 1950 by some of the widest margins ever registered in a New York gubernatorial race.

Dewey had his eye on the presidency for several years, but national and international events—as well as the entry into the races by more well-known politicians—prevented him from securing the nomination until 1948. With incumbent President Harry Truman in the White House, Dewey ran a lackluster campaign and was accused by many political

experts of treating his party's nomination as a coronation of sorts that virtually assured him the White House. Truman conducted an aggressive,
bulldog campaign right up until the night before the election. With most
polls and pundits predicting a Dewey win, Truman pulled off a political
miracle by beating the popular New Yorker. As a sidebar to the exciting
campaign finish, the election also gave us one of the most famous newspaper errors ever printed when the *Chicago Daily Tribune* prematurely
published the blaring headline "Dewey Defeats Truman." The 150,000
copies with the embarrassing headline became instant collectors' items.

After his defeat by Truman, Dewey retired from elected political life
but became one of the great lions of the Republican Party. His advice
was sage and sought after by Presidents Eisenhower and Nixon, as well as
New York Governor Nelson Rockefeller. He also made a sizable amount
of money from his well-heeled New York City law firm Dewey, Ballantine,
Bushby, Palmer & Wood, located at 140 Broadway in Manhattan.

On March 16, 1971, after playing a round of golf in Florida, Dewey
returned to his hotel room to dress and pack for a flight to Washington,

where he had been invited by President Nixon to attend a celebration of Mrs. Nixon's fifty-ninth birthday. Dewey's golf partner, baseball player Carl Yastrzemski, was alarmed when the governor didn't respond to phone calls. He and hotel management went to the suite and found that Dewey had died of a massive heart attack.

Grave Location: Governor Thomas E. Dewey is buried in Pawling Cemetery, located on the west side of Route 22. From the main entrance, proceed through the first section and over a small bridge. A series of mausoleums will be on a rise to your left. Dewey's is the first one.

Author's Note: Admiral John L. Worden, Civil War hero of the "Battle of the Ironclads," is also buried in this cemetery (see chapter 83).

Factoid: A quick search of completed auctions on eBay shows that an original "Dewey Defeats Truman" *Chicago Daily Tribune* newspaper can bring anywhere between $500 and $2,000, depending on its condition.

For More Information: New York State Hall of Governors, "Thomas E. Dewey," hallofgovernors.ny.gov/ThomasDewey/.

72

ANN TROW LOHMAN

1812–1878

WICKEDEST WOMAN IN NEW YORK
BURIED IN SLEEPY HOLLOW,
WESTCHESTER COUNTY

*A*nn Trow Lohman was hated by almost everyone. Hers is a remarkable story.

Time has been just a little bit kinder to the reputation of Ann Trow Lohman than real life actually was. In the mid-1840s all of New York was abuzz with the news, stories, and backyard gossip of this despised woman, called the Wickedest Woman in New York by the tabloids of the time.

As a young woman, Lohman married a quack doctor and changed her own persona to that of a mysterious creature called Madame Restell (an invented name). She was an abortionist by trade. Her clientele included many of New York's high-society women, and she gained fame and influence over the course of a few short years. Madame Restell had many friends in high places and was said to have carried everyone from politicians to police chiefs on her payroll.

Restell's fame grew even wider following several widely publicized skirmishes with women's groups and law enforcement agencies. Although she was arrested many times, her political clout allowed her to escape harsh treatment. In March 1846, however, following the enactment of stringent new laws that made abortion the equivalent of murder, she was arrested, charged, and convicted. She was sentenced to serve time in the infamous Blackwell's Island Prison. A newspaper uncovered the fact that Restell was spending her confinement in comfort and luxury in private

quarters at the jail, and a scandal erupted. At the height of the controversy, the warden of the prison was fired and Restell found herself again front-page news.

Although she grew quite wealthy through her abortion practice, she ultimately became a pariah to all. She was so despised and hated by her neighbors that the building adjoining her mansion stood vacant for years for want of a tenant. Ostracized by society, she took considerable delight in riding her fancy carriage up and down ritzy Fifth Avenue in full view of her shocked detractors.

Her husband died in 1876, and she retired and vowed to walk the straight and narrow. This was not to be the case. With her influence vastly diminished, she was arrested again in 1878 on what many considered to be trumped up charges of "possession of immoral articles." Everyone sensed this was payback time for Madame Restell, and it became obvious that she was the victim of a vendetta by the New York Society for the Suppression of Vice.

Perhaps too tired to once again face the harsh, scornful eye of the public and the press (or perhaps just to get the last word in), Ann Trow Lohman, the infamous and made up Madame Restell, slit her own throat with a large carving knife while taking a bath in her mansion on April Fool's Day 1878.

Through suicide, she would finally be left alone. She left an estate valued at close to $1 million.

Grave Location: Ann Lohman is buried in Sleepy Hollow Cemetery, one of the most famous in the state. Many notables are buried here, and a cemetery kiosk provides maps guiding visitors to the graves of well-known personalities. Lohman's grave is in the middle of the Hudson Hill section. Upon entering the cemetery, veer right onto Camp Grove Avenue, which becomes Ivy and then Lawrence. Here, on the left, is a section of very old graves, and Lohman's is near the center.

Author's Note: The road in front of this cemetery is Route 9 (called Broadway). Traffic barrels along, and the entrance to Sleepy Hollow Cemetery is easy to miss on your first pass.

Factoid: Eerily, Lohman's grave, which is a tall Victorian obelisk, is topped with the marble image of a sleeping child!

For More Information: Smithsonian, "Madame Restell: The Abortionist of Fifth Avenue," www.smithsonianmag.com/history/madame -restell-the-abortionist-of-fifth-avenue-145109198/.

73

SYBIL LUDINGTON

1761–1839

THE FEMALE PAUL REVERE
BURIED IN PATTERSON,
PUTNAM COUNTY

*S*ybil Ludington was just sixteen years old when she rode out into the darkness on April 26, 1777, to warn her neighbors, "The redcoats are coming!" Her father, Colonel Henry Ludington, had heard that the British were quickly advancing on nearby Danbury, Connecticut. As the head of the local militia, he knew time was short so he sent his young daughter out, riding her beloved horse Star, to warn others of the oncoming enemy and to rally an opposing force.

The young woman's journey that night covered more than forty miles. She rode through thick forests to evade capture and oftentimes walked her horse through near total darkness so as not to attract attention. When she saw some British soldiers approaching, she pulled Star even deeper into the woods and quieted him with some carrots she brought in her coat pocket. Afterward, she jumped back on the horse and rode at breakneck speed through the small villages of rural Putnam County. She was so small that her feet didn't reach the stirrups, so she rode the distance side saddle, prodding her steed on with a tree branch. At first she stopped at houses and farms and knocked on each door to arouse the sleeping towns- folk. Realizing that this was too time consuming, she resorted to riding into the center of a small town and rearing her horse back on its hind feet and then screaming out the warning to any and all who could hear. Then, in an instant she was gone, leaving an ever increasing number of flickering

candles in her wake. Her ride was actually farther than the more famous midnight ride of Paul Revere, as Ludington was gone from about 9:00 am until dawn the next day.

By the time she had finished her route and returned home, more than four hundred locals had gathered at her father's house to march on the British. Although too late to save Danbury from the enemy torch, Colonel Ludington's troops forced the British to retreat to their ships in Long Island Sound.

Young Sybil was declared a heroine of the Revolutionary War and was even visited by George Washington, who came to thank her and "pat her on the head."

Ludington married Edmond Ogden in 1784, and they later moved to Unadilla (Otsego County). She died there on February 26, 1839, at the age of seventy-seven.

Grave Location: Sybil Ludington is buried near her father in Maple Avenue Cemetery in Patterson. To find her simple grave, walk between the two small churches in front of the cemetery (Christ Church Episcopal and Patterson Community Church). The Ludingtons are buried approximately twenty cemetery plots from the road in Section A. Sybil's grave is in the third row from the south side of the Patterson Community Church. Her grave is marked with an American flag. Curiously, the name on her gravestone is spelled Sibbell.

Author's Note: The two churches come up quickly as you travel Route 311. It is a very busy intersection, and you probably will miss it your first time through. There is a historical marker near the road telling you of the Ludingtons buried in the cemetery.

Factoid: An amazing statue of Sybil Ludington, astride Star and in full flight, stands near Lake Gleneida in nearby Carmel, New York. The sculptor was Anna Hyatt Huntington, and it is one of the most exciting statuary tributes I have seen in my travels. In 1976, Sybil was honored with her own postage stamp depicting her during her famous ride.

For More Information: National Women's History Museum, "Sybil Ludington," www.nwhm.org/education-resources/biographies/sybil-ludington.

74

EDNA ST. VINCENT MILLAY

1892–1950

PULITZER PRIZE
BURIED IN AUSTERLITZ,
COLUMBIA COUNTY

$\mathcal{D}$uring the 1930s, Edna St. Vincent Millay was the foremost woman poet in America.

In 1917, she published her first volume of poetry, *Renascence and Other Poems*, to great critical acclaim. In fact, "Renascence," a beautiful depiction of nature's poetic glory, would remain one of her most famous works. That same year, she moved from her home in Rockland, Maine, to Greenwich Village, where she commiserated with the other "free spirits" of the burgeoning American poetry culture and immersed herself in the wild living offered in New York's Little Bohemia. Her poems began to reflect her newfound freedom. She wrote famously of "burning the candle at both ends" and of having no regrets at having done so.

Her 1923 release, *The Harp Weaver and Other Poems*, was hailed as a masterpiece by literary critics and earned her the Pulitzer Prize for Poetry. Millay was the first American woman to win this award.

She spent the last thirty years of her life in the quiet, rural setting of her 650-acre country home, Steepletop, in the tiny mountain community of Austerlitz. She died of a heart attack there on October 19, 1950. She was fifty-eight years old.

Grave Location: Although visiting Millay's remote grave site can be a daunting task, it is well worth the effort. No other grave in this book more

fully reflects the persona and spirit of the subject. Steepletop is located at 436 East Hill Road just outside of Austerlitz. Millay's home atop this mountain road is now a museum, and tours are given. Just a few hundred yards north of her home, you will see a well cleared path on the left that goes into the woods. A sign greets you at the entrance: "Millay loved this trail so much that she chose it for her final resting place." Her grave is a half-mile trek into the woods down this path.

The walk is easy and fairly level. Visitors will pass through thick forests and thinned-out clearings before reaching her grave. Along the way signs are posted with snippets of some of the poet's most famous works. Among them are passages from "Renascence" (1912), "The Little Ghost" (1917), "Afternoon on a Hill" (1917), "Elegy Before Death" (1918), "Portrait by a Neighbor" (1922), "The Goose-Girl" (1923), "Counting-Out Rhyme" (1928), "From a Very Little Sphinx" (1929), and "Through the Green Forest" (1940).

The first grave along the path is that of Cora Buzzell Millay (1864–1931), Edna's mother. Another grave marks the final resting place of Norma

Millay (d. 1986), Edna's sister. At the end of the trail is a large boulder with a bronze plaque affixed to it. This is the grave of Edna and her husband, Eugen Jan Boissevain. A small wrought-iron chain fence surrounds the grave, and there is a stone bench nearby where visitors can sit and reflect. The surroundings here, deep in the forest, are stunning, peaceful, and a fitting location for the poet's final resting place.

Author's Note: No visit to this remote grave location would be complete without taking a tour of Millay's hilltop home and museum in her honor. At the museum you can see an interesting exhibit from Millay's 1924 around-the-world honeymoon journey with her husband, Eugen. She was a tireless collector of bric-a-brac and souvenirs, and the museum displays many of them. There are Japanese paper fans, a lacquered money case from Burma, several gorgeous Chinese silk kimonos, brass swords from Java, a porcelain pitcher from India, and other artifacts from her travels. Also on display are copious handwritten notes from her personal journal of the trip.

Factoid: Steepletop is owned by the Millay Society, which acts as the "keeper of the flame" regarding the poet's legacy. Also onsite is the Millay Colony for the Arts, founded in 1973, which is a writer's residence, retreat, and workshop center.

For More Information: Edna St. Vincent Millay Society, "Visit Steepletop," millay.org/visitsteepletop.php.

VICE PRESIDENT
LEVI PARSONS MORTON

1824–1920

SERVANT OF A NATION
BURIED IN RHINEBECK,
DUTCHESS COUNTY

*F*ew official positions in the US government are subject to such scorn and ridicule as that of vice president. Being largely a ceremonial role, the vice presidency has swallowed up more dedicated public servants than almost any other position. A sage political observer, John Nance Garner (once a vice president), called the job "akin to a bucket of warm spit." The roll call of number-two men in the White House is a litany of forgotten names obscured by time and the job itself. The names of Schuyler Colfax, George Mifflin Dallas, Charles Fairbanks, and Thomas Hendricks scarcely evoke a glimmer of recognition when spoken of today. The name of Levi Parsons Morton probably is equally unknown. But most of these men, in their pre-veep days, were men of great political stature who had carved out respectable, if limited, public service careers. None, however, could match the impressive resume of Morton.

Born in Vermont in 1824, he early on established a personal and public life in neighboring New York State. Working in the wholesale goods business, he built up and headed Morton and Grinnell Company, one of the largest firms of its kind in the East. He rode through the mid-1800s on a wave of prosperity and good fortune until he suffered a near fatal business setback in 1861. His business went broke because of forfeiture of Southern debts owed to his company before the Civil War. He reorganized the firm

256

and eventually gained back his reputation, stature, and fortune. He was a wise and flinty financier who became a leader in the American banking business. Due to his vast expertise in both national and international business, it wasn't long before the major political parties came calling looking for a candidate.

Morton's first foray into politics ended in defeat when, as a Republican nominee for the Forty-Fifth Congress in 1876, he was soundly beaten. He reestablished his political base and won two years later, then won again in 1880. President James A. Garfield then named Morton to be his minister to France, where he served for five years.

In 1889, Morton went to Washington, DC, as Benjamin Harrison's vice president.

A strict rule enforcer, Morton adhered to the tightest dictates of Senate procedures when called upon to officiate over that body. One story tells of Morton forgoing lunch breaks so as to prevent the Senate from "acting out of sorts" in his absence.

After leaving Washington, Morton returned to his Hudson Valley and ran for governor. He won and spearheaded civil-service reform as the major goal of his administration. He retired from public life in 1897 at the age of seventy-three but would enjoy a fruitful life for many years to come. He reorganized his substantial financial holdings, created the Morton Trust Company, traveled extensively, and enjoyed the lively companionship of his many friends. He entertained lavishly at his Rhinebeck estate, Ellerslie, and it was at this home that he died peacefully on May 16, 1920, his ninety-sixth birthday.

Grave Location: Morton is buried in Rhinebeck Cemetery, located on the left as you enter town from the south on Route 9. His family plot is located in the back of the cemetery near the western edge tree line. A black railing surrounds the plot, which holds the remains of more than a dozen family members. The cemetery intersection is Park and Grasmere. His large tombstone reads: "A Servant of the Nation. Member of Congress. Minister to France. Governor of New York. Vice-President of the United States."

Author's Note: Morton had five daughters and held many festive parties for them at Ellerslie over the years. Little is left of the original mansion, and it is privately owned. Its grounds, which were once tended by fourteen gardeners, are still intact. Morton was the wealthiest and most famous resident of Rhinebeck, a quaint village on the east side of the Hudson River, two hours north of New York City. He employed many of the residents of Rhinebeck in his businesses and at his many interests, homes, and farms. At the age of eighty-five he sold his Morton Company to J. P. Morgan, who then changed its name to the now familiar Morgan Guaranty Trust Company.

Factoid: As minister to France, Morton actually personally accompanied the Statue of Liberty to New York City where it was erected!

For More Information: Morton Memorial Library and Community House (constructed by Morton and his wife and donated to the village of Rhinecliff in memory of their daughter, Lena), morton.rhinecliff.lib.ny.us.

76

FLOYD PATTERSON

1935–2006

*THE GENTLEMAN OF BOXING
BURIED IN NEW PALTZ,
ULSTER COUNTY*

*F*loyd Patterson's beginnings were inauspicious. Born in a dirt-floor cabin to a poor family in Waco, North Carolina, he was known as a troublemaker, rarely attended school, and by age eleven was still unable to read or write. His frustrated parents sent him to a reform school for African American youngsters, the Wiltwyck School for Boys, in Esopus, New York. The school was located across the Hudson River from Franklin D. Roosevelt's mansion in Hyde Park, and in fact, Eleanor Roosevelt was one of its great benefactors.

Patterson's life took a dramatic turn for the better after his enrollment at Wiltwyck. Although socially reserved, he learned to read and write, and he was taught the art of boxing. He left Wiltwyck and returned home, where he was enrolled in a school for troubled youth, and then later joined a vocational school to learn a trade to help support his family. He was painfully shy and almost never spoke unless spoken to, but early boxing mentors saw a champion in the sweet-faced, gentle man who could unleash a flurry of powerful punches in the ring. Good fortune shined on Patterson when he was fourteen and joined the famous Gramercy Gym in New York City, where he came into the sphere of boxing legend Cus D'Amato, the owner of the club.

Under D'Amato's tutelage, Patterson became a championship contender at a very young age. At age sixteen, he won the New York State

Golden Gloves middleweight title, and the following year he won the gold in the middleweight category at the 1952 Helsinki Olympics. By the mid-1950s he had turned pro and was earning up to five hundred dollars a fight. Headlines called him a star on the boxing horizon. His boxing career would last two decades and amass him a fortune of $8 million, a record at that time.

Patterson had many memorable moments in the ring, including defeating two heavyweights, Archie Moore and Ingemar Johansson, for the title in that weight category. He holds several boxing records, including being the youngest boxer to win the heavyweight title (age twenty-one) and the first heavyweight champion to regain his title after losing it. He had lost his title to Johansson on June 20, 1959, after being knocked down seven times by the Swedish boxer. He stole the crown back exactly a year later, June 20, 1960, when Patterson knocked Johansson out in the fifth round.

Patterson fought all the great boxing legends of his time with varying degrees of success. He lost twice to both Sonny Liston and Muhammad Ali, but was victorious over Archie Moore, Canadian boxer George

Chuvalo, Henry Cooper from Great Britain, and Oscar Bonavena from Argentina. His last fight was a loss against Ali on September 20, 1972. He was thirty-six years old at the time.

In retirement, Patterson became chairman of the New York State Athletic Commission. A growing forgetfulness caused Patterson to retire from this commission. He was later diagnosed with Alzheimer's disease, which he would endure for eight years until his death on May 11, 2006, at his home in New Paltz. The champ was seventy-one.

Grave Location: Boxer Floyd Patterson is buried in New Paltz Rural Cemetery. His gravestone, which reads "A Champ Forever," is located in Section Q-6 Center West. When you enter the cemetery, go in about one hundred yards and Patterson's grave will be on your right, alone in a large section near the road.

Author's Note: Celebrity hotelier Oscar Tschirky, known as Oscar of the Waldorf, is also buried in this cemetery. He was the maître d' of the famed Waldorf Astoria Hotel in New York City and is credited with inventing the Waldorf salad and eggs Benedict. He is buried in Section E-1.

Factoid: During the 1960s, Floyd Patterson appeared on several popular television series, including roles on *The Wild, Wild West* (1968) and *Daniel Boone* (1969).

For More Information: International Boxing Hall of Fame, "Floyd Patterson," www.ibhof.com/pages/about/inductees/modern/patterson.html.

77

LYNN REDGRAVE

1943–2010

GEORGY GIRL
BURIED IN LITHGOW,
DUTCHESS COUNTY

Like so many of her other family members, Lynn Redgrave was a star with many facets. She was a major force on the New York boards, on television, and in motion pictures. She made her Broadway debut in 1967 opposite Geraldine Page in *Black Comedy*. Over her thirty-year stage career, she would return often to New York, scoring Tony nominations for George Bernard Shaw's *Mrs. Warren's Profession* (1976), her one-woman show *Shakespeare for My Father* (1993), and *The Constant Wife* (2005). Her father was the patriarch of a long family line of award-winning performers, Sir Michael Redgrave.

In film, Redgrave starred in several productions from the 1960s to the 1980s. Perhaps her most famous role was that of the loveable, frumpy, overweight and naïve twenty-two-year-old London woman named Georgy Parkin in the 1966 box-office hit *Georgy Girl*. Lynn Redgrave's mother, Rachel Kempson, costarred in this movie, along with such British heavyweights as James Mason and Alan Bates. Critics loved this endearing film, and Lynn Redgrave was nominated for a Best Actress Academy Award. More than three decades after *Georgy Girl*, she was nominated for another Academy Award, this time as Best Supporting Actress for her role in *Gods and Monsters* (1998).

In her later career, Redgrave became a familiar and popular figure with the American public through her roles in television movies, as a

spokesperson for a well-known series of commercials for Weight Watchers, and for her books about dieting and health. She costarred with Wayne Rogers for three seasons in the sitcom *House Calls* and received an Emmy nomination for her work in this series.

Lynn Redgrave's life and career were not without controversy. She was married to actor John Clark, whom she divorced after he revealed he was the father of a love child. The tabloids made much out of this nasty court proceeding. The actress also was relieved of her role in *House Calls* when she refused to follow the studio's instructions not to bring her newborn baby to work on the set, where the actress routinely breastfed her child. After much public fanfare, she was let go and replaced midseries by actress Sharon Gless.

The actress was much-honored over the course of her career, and despite being nominated for a Grammy, Emmy, Tony, and Oscar, she never won any of them. Redgrave died of breast cancer on May 2, 2010. She was sixty-seven.

Grave Location: Lynn Redgrave is buried in St. Peter's Episcopal Church Cemetery, located at the corner of Route 44 and Shunpike Road in Lithgow, about four miles from Amenia, New York. It is a very small, rural cemetery surrounded by an old stone wall. Although there are few grave sites in this cemetery, the Redgrave family plot in the rear makes this place definitely worth a visit. Lynn Redgrave; her niece, the actress Natasha Richardson (chapter 78); and her mother, Lady Rachel Kempson, are all buried here. Each grave is marked with a poignant, beautiful statue. Lynn Redgrave's stone reads: "No one dies who is remembered. Mother. Actor. Playwright. Friend."

Author's Note: The small cemetery is near the border of the property making up the eight-hundred-acre campus of the exclusive Millbrook School. This preparatory school, founded in 1931, lists among its alumni Robert F. Kennedy Jr. and New York Senator James L. Buckley.

Factoid: Lynn Redgrave was the first of many celebrity spokespersons for Weight Watchers food. She signed on with the company in 1984 and made its advertising catchphrase—"This is living!"—part of the pop landscape. Following Redgrave came Sarah Ferguson, Jenny McCarthy, and others, but the company acknowledges that Redgrave's personable appeal to American women was a key component of the advertising campaign's success.

For More Information: Internet Movie Database, "Lynn Redgrave," www.imdb.com/name/nm0001655/.

78

NATASHA RICHARDSON

1963–2009

SALLY BOWLES
BURIED IN LITHGOW,
DUTCHESS COUNTY

*N*atasha Richardson was trained as a classical British actress but eventually evolved into a dynamic entertainment triple threat. Early in her career she could be found starring in Anton Chekov's *The Seagull* in London's West End. Shortly after that, in 1993, she came to the United States, where she appeared on Broadway in *Anna Christie*. Critics praised her work in this classic, and she became a steady presence on the Great White Way for several years after. Her big breakthrough stage performance came as the high-spirited Sally Bowles in the acclaimed 1998 revival of *Cabaret*, for which she won the Tony Award for Best Actress in a Musical. She later starred in perennial Broadway favorites *A Streetcar Named Desire* (2005) and Stephen Sondheim's *A Little Night Music* (2009).

The actress appeared in a number of Hollywood films including *Nell* (1994), *The Parent Trap* (1998), and *Waking Up in Reno* (2002). She also appeared in *The Handmaid's Tale* (1990) opposite Robert Duvall and Faye Dunaway, and portrayed the famous fugitive heiress in the Paul Schrader film *Patty Hearst* (1988).

Richardson was a member of the legendary Redgrave acting family, and in 1994 she married the actor Liam Neeson. That same year, the couple spent nearly $4 million on a secluded thirty-seven-acre estate in the rolling hillsides of rural Dutchess County. The home, which included a swimming pool, tennis court, horse barn, and paved courtyard, became

the center for the Neeson, Richardson, and Redgrave clans to gather for family events.

While taking skiing lessons at Quebec's Mont-Tremblant, the actress had an accident on the beginner's trail and suffered a head wound. Although she appeared to be fine and insisted on staying in her lodge and not going to the hospital, her conditioned worsened. Her husband was in Toronto, Canada, filming *Chloe* at the time. He rushed to her side and was with her when she was transferred to New York City's Lenox Hill Hospital. She died on March 19, 2009, with her mother, the actress Vanessa Redgrave, and her husband at her side. She was forty-five.

Grave Location: Natasha Richardson is buried in the Redgrave family plot in the rear section of St. Peter's Episcopal Church Cemetery at the corner of Route 44 and Shunpike Road in rural Lithgow, New York. The cemetery is near the home she and her husband shared. Her grave is located near that of her aunt, actress Lynn Redgrave, and her grandmother, Rachel Kempton. Richardson's final resting place is marked by a graceful statue of a young girl kneeling and holding a bowl of water. The inscription reads: "Though your days were brief, your spirit was alive, awake and complete. Beloved daughter, sister, aunt, and true friend. Cast your bread upon the waters."

Author's Note: This quiet corner of a small, country graveyard holds the remains of several members of one of the most honored families in show business. The Redgrave family plot is in the rear of the cemetery, near a stone wall. It is in a shaded, peaceful section, and the family graves are marked by beautiful sculptures.

Factoid: Natasha Richardson belonged to an acting dynasty that included her grandmother Rachel Kempton (who appeared in five films with her daughters), aunt Lynn Redgrave (whose achievements are discussed in chapter 77), mother Vanessa Redgrave (an Oscar winner and six-time nominee), grandfather Sir Michael Redgrave (esteemed English stage and film actor), father Tony Richardson (a director, and Oscar winner for *Tom Jones*), sister Joely Richardson (who appeared in more than forty films and television shows), and half-brother Carlo Nero (a director, and the son of Vanessa Redgrave and pianist Peter Nero).

For More Information: Internet Movie Database, "Natasha Richardson," www.imdb.com/name/nm0001670/.

79

WILLIAM ROCKEFELLER

1841–1922

*MILLIONAIRE SALESMAN OF STANDARD OIL
BURIED IN SLEEPY HOLLOW,
WESTCHESTER COUNTY*

*I*n a state so indelibly imprinted with the name Rockefeller, it is interesting that the little-known William Rockefeller is the only member of this famous family whose grave site is accessible to the public. Although it was his lot to stand in the shadow of his legendary brother, John D., William was able to carve out a profitable piece of the Rockefeller pie that eventually became known as Standard Oil.

While the brothers shared many attributes, it was William's success as a salesman that gained brother John his own fortune. John and William started Standard Oil from scratch and shepherded it to its position as the country's leading source of oil products. William was extremely successful in introducing oil to the far-flung, growing markets around the world. He invested in copper, railroads, mines, and banks.

It was his participation in a copper company in the late 1890s that nearly was his undoing, however. With the government investigating reports that he had rigged the market and caused the failure of a major bank, William Rockefeller came under an excruciating public spotlight that tarnished the family name. He was spared the agony and humiliation of an official public inquiry only because his health turned conveniently bad. A judge mercifully ruled him unfit to stand trial, and the charges were ultimately dismissed. Shortly after the case receded from the headlines,

it was discovered that William was suffering from throat cancer and truly was in failing health during the time of the scandal.

A second scar on the Rockefeller image was the infamous 1914 Ludlow Massacre at a family-owned mine in Colorado, in which guards killed about two dozen striking miners and their family members. It took millions of dollars and many years for the Rockefellers to clean up what many considered to be a major public relations disaster.

Reflecting the sentiments of his more famous brother, William Rockefeller was a magnanimous philanthropist. While he always preferred to remain anonymous, many of his huge contributions were well noted in the press. For one cause alone—the United States War Relief Fund of World War I—he wrote a personal check for $1 million.

He worked steadily into his eighties and in fact was walking to work in the rain, on a Saturday no less, when he developed a severe cold. He died a week later on June 24, 1922, at the age of eighty-one. His estimated fortune was put at well over $100 million.

Grave Location: William Rockefeller's tomb in the historic Sleepy Hollow Cemetery is one of the largest, most expensive personal tombs in America. He is the only major Rockefeller family member not to be buried in the private family cemetery at their estate, Pocantico Hills, which adjoins the Sleepy Hollow Cemetery. Maps are available at the front office that will guide you to the many grave sites in this cemetery. William Rockefeller's mammoth tomb occupies its own section of the cemetery.

Author's Note: For history lovers, a day wandering the paths and roads of Sleepy Hollow Cemetery is well spent. Although William Rockefeller's tomb is the largest in the cemetery, there are many other final resting places here that are jaw-droppers, including those of millionaires Walter Chrysler and Leona Helmsley. Each of these, and many others, cost huge sums to erect. On the other end of the spectrum, Washington Irving, one of America's most famous writers, is also buried in Sleepy Hollow Cemetery. His simple grave marker cost about one hundred dollars.

Factoid: William Rockefeller oversaw the construction of his own mausoleum. It was created using the talents of several of the nation's most respected sculptors and artists. Welles Bosworth was the main architect, and French sculptor Gaston Lachaise did the bas-relief artwork over the entranceway. The structure is enormous—thirty-five feet wide, forty-four feet deep, and thirty-eight feet high. The mausoleum, made out of Vermont granite, weighs in at thirty-two tons. Inside are twenty wall crypts reserved for Rockefeller family members. In the center are two marble sarcophagi holding the remains of William and his wife of fifty-six years, Almira. The total cost was over $250,000. Although there is no mistaking this grave when you come to it, you will have to search for a moment to find his name on it. Rather than inscribe it across the top of this majestic tomb, the name ROCKEFELLER can be seen etched on the front of the bottom step leading up to the door of the mausoleum.

For More Information: Sleepy Hollow Cemetery, sleepyhollow cemetery.org.

PRESIDENT FRANKLIN DELANO ROOSEVELT

1882–1945

*THIRTY-SECOND PRESIDENT
OF THE UNITED STATES
BURIED IN HYDE PARK,
DUTCHESS COUNTY*

*F*ranklin Roosevelt is almost always judged by historians to be among the top three or four most respected US presidents. He guided our country through the Great Depression and was commander in chief of our military during World War II. More words have been written about FDR than perhaps any other US president.

There is little left to be said about his historic tenure as president or his everlasting legacy to our nation, so I will instead share some observations about his Upstate New York final resting place. Roosevelt is buried at Springbrook, the estate where he was born and which he called home all of his sixty-three years. This historic estate in Hyde Park, New York, is also the site of the FDR Presidential Library, for many years the most visited presidential library in the country (now surpassed by the Ronald Reagan Presidential Library).

The home and library exhibit vast displays of FDR memorabilia and offer guided tours, prize-winning rose gardens, miles of footpaths, inspiring peeks at the Hudson River out back, and much more. Roosevelt personally oversaw the planting of 400,000 trees on the eight-hundred-acre estate and, despite his extended term in the White House, was a frequent and welcome visitor to the tiny village of Hyde Park over his presidential

years. In fact, from 1933 to his death in 1945, the president made more than two hundred visits to his ancestral home.

From his infant crib, which is still on display here, to his grave site in the front garden, this place bears the remarkable footprint of a true son of the Hudson Valley. In his waning days and in perilous health, Roosevelt was said to have remarked, "All that is within me cries out to go back to my Hudson River home."

Grave Location: President Roosevelt had said many times that he wanted to be buried near his mother's sundial in the rose garden next to the mansion. And so it was to be. When Roosevelt's body arrived here for burial it was said that "every man, woman and child in Hyde Park came out to say thank you and goodbye to their famous neighbor." Eleanor Roosevelt was buried next to her husband beneath the majestic white marble tomb when she passed away in 1962.

Author's Note: Franklin Roosevelt's home and his presidential library are a major visitor attraction in the Hudson Valley. Thousands come here every year to take tours, enjoy a lively calendar of public events, and visit the Henry A. Wallace Visitors and Education Center for its remarkable library and gift shop. The FDR Presidential Library was the first of all presidential libraries and was also the first one designed by *and used* by a sitting president.

Factoid: Roosevelt's little dog Fala remains the most famous of all presidential pets. At the Franklin D. Roosevelt Memorial in Washington, DC, Fala is prominently represented in bronze (the only presidential pet so honored). The Scottish terrier died on April 5, 1952, and is buried near the sundial behind his master's grave. The president's less famous dog, a German shepherd named Chief, is also buried in the Rose Garden.

For More Information: National Park Service, "Home of Franklin D. Roosevelt," www.nps.gov/hofr/index.htm.

81

LOWELL THOMAS

1892–1981

"SO LONG, UNTIL TOMORROW"
BURIED IN QUAKER HILL,
DUTCHESS COUNTY

*F*rom an early age, Lowell Thomas began to carve out a remarkable public life in journalism, both in print and on the screen. He pioneered the travelogue genre, presenting moving and still images with his own narration while traveling through exotic and faraway places. The first of these trips was to remote Alaska, which would lead to travels around the world over the next seven decades. In the beginning, he presented these travel shows in live performances at large theaters and concert halls. Later, he tailored them for radio and television, where he was a constant and popular presence for over thirty years.

Lowell Thomas is the man credited with finding and promoting Lawrence of Arabia, helping to turn this historical figure into a legend. He discovered the dashing Englishman while covering the British campaign in the Empire in Palestine around 1915. He followed the enigmatic and brazen British swashbuckler as he successfully led a ragtag army of Bedouins to victory against the powerful Turks. He became friends with Lawrence and interviewed and photographed him extensively. When he returned to the United States, Thomas mounted a full-scale cinematic production based on the life of this modern day swashbuckler. Called "The Last Crusade," it was set in the then-strange and distant lands of Egypt and other Near East countries. The stage production had a large dash of Hollywood

glitz and glamour to it, including special effects, pyrotechnics, and dancing harem girls. The shows were wildly successful, playing hundreds of
performances around the world. They made Lawrence a household name
and Thomas a millionaire.

Thomas was one of America's legendary radio broadcasters, with a
career that spanned more than four decades and included many historic
firsts. In 1940, he was the first to cover a national political convention, the
Republican Convention in Philadelphia. Looking back over his career he
could count hundreds of famous sports stars, movie celebrities, and for-
eign leaders as interview subjects as well as personal friends.

Long a resident and benefactor of tiny Quaker Hill, a tight-knit mountain community outside of Pawling, New York, Thomas died at his home
there on August 29, 1981. He was eighty-nine. At the time of his death, the
New York Times reported that his broadcasting career was the longest ever
(since surpassed by Paul Harvey), and that his audience had been in the
billions of listeners.

Grave Location: The famed newsman is buried under a giant boulder in the side yard of Christ Church, located at 17 Church Street in Pawling (Quaker Hill is in the Town of Pawling). There are no other graves near his, and the stone is adorned with only a simple bronze plaque bearing his name.

Author's Note: Next to Thomas's grave you will find remembrances of other recognizable residents of Quaker Hill who were Thomas's neighbors and friends. Dr. and Mrs. Norman Vincent Peale lived across the street from the church and are memorialized at the church with a peaceful garden and reflection area near Thomas's grave. Also, a small stand of trees here is identified as "being planted in memory of New York Governor Thomas E. Dewey and his wife," friends of Thomas. Edward R. Murrow, the famed CBS newsman and contemporary of Thomas, had a horse farm here, and after his death his ashes were scattered over his pastures.

Factoid: Thomas ruled Quaker Hill with a determined focus. His horse farm was the largest in the hamlet, eventually encompassing nearly three thousand acres, and he became the star resident when he began recording his radio programs from his residence. Upon his direction, no commercial development was allowed "on the hill" so as to keep it in its simple, pristine condition. The only exception was his encouragement of the Quaker Hill Country Club, designed by Robert Trent Jones. Across from Thomas's grave site sits the magnificent Akin Free Library (known as Akin Hall), built in 1908. Thomas took a great interest in the renovation and securing of this copper-topped Victorian showplace for future residents of the hamlet. It is open to the public.

For More Information: Historical Society of Quaker Hill and Pawling, www.pawling-history.org.

82

MATTHEW VASSAR

1792–1868

BREWER PHILANTHROPIST
BURIED IN POUGHKEEPSIE,
DUTCHESS COUNTY

*M*atthew Vassar started out in life to be a beer maker. His father ran a successful brewery in Poughkeepsie, and when it burned down in 1822, young Matthew built a new one. It became a highly profitable endeavor for him and quickly made him a very rich young man. Although he would remain involved in the brewery business for nearly a half century, the source of his everlasting fame would come from a much different source (albeit one that was funded by his "beer money"), the field of women's education.

Vassar enjoyed spreading his wealth. A curious investor, he provided the seed money for his nephew's efforts to settle and develop a new territory that we now know as the state of Michigan. Even today, the town of Vassar, Michigan, stands as a proud tribute to the fruits of his investment.

He also invested heavily in the whaling industry and eventually built one of the largest whaling docks of the time. It was during this income-amassing period of his life that Vassar chose to turn his financial energies to more socially relevant issues. His young niece, Lydia Booth, had been the headmistress at an all-girls' school in Poughkeepsie, and it was through his association with her that Vassar charted the establishment of a school for the higher education of women.

In 1861, he donated the land and nearly a half million dollars toward the building of Vassar Female College. With an illustrious board of

trustees that included Samuel F. B. Morse and Henry Ward Beecher, Vassar College quickly grew into the model of its kind in the nation. Faced with strong competition from older, more entrenched female schools, Vassar College soon found itself fighting for each and every student and eventually had to turn to its founder for help.

In what became an innovative new tactic, Vassar began advertising his college in hopes of attracting new students from near and far, and was the first such institution to do so. The marketing ploy worked, and soon his sparkling new campus in the Hudson Valley was on sound footing and attracting a student body from around the world. As Vassar College became one of the premier women's colleges in the United States, Vassar's niece, Lydia, commented to the press that, "Vassar College stands proudly as a monument more lasting than the Great Pyramids of Egypt."

The oft-told campus legend recalls that on the morning of June 23, 1868, Matthew Vassar uncharacteristically went out and splurged on buying a shiny, new three-piece suit for himself. He was attending an important board of trustees meeting at the college and, despite being more than seventy-five years old, wanted to make an impression with his colleagues. As the meeting ended, Vassar reached into his vest pocket and pulled out a slip of paper from which he began to read. It was an announcement of his final retirement from the college board after decades of tireless service. When he finished his speech, he silently sat back down in his chair, put his head down on the conference table, and died of a massive heart attack. He was buried three days later in his shiny new three-piece suit.

After a large funeral service at the First Baptist Church of Poughkeepsie (a church also financed by his "beer money"), Matthew Vassar was laid to rest next to his wife, Catherine, in the family plot.

Grave Location: Vassar is buried in Poughkeepsie Rural Cemetery at 342 South Avenue. It is a sprawling place with thousands of graves, miles of walking paths, and many glens, hills, and ponds to enjoy. Vassar is buried in Lot 17, Section L. From this section you can view the Hudson River. His grave is unmistakable—a towering acorn, the ancient symbol of education!

Author's Note: Vassar College still stands today as one of the great learning centers of the country. Located seventy-five miles north of New York City, it has an enrollment of 2,600 students at its beautiful campus on Raymond Avenue in Poughkeepsie. With more than two hundred varieties of trees, shrubs, and flowering bushes beautifying its more than one thousand acres, the *entire campus* is treated as an arboretum. Vassar was the first all-women's college to go co-ed in 1969, and today men count for nearly 50 percent of its enrollment.

Factoid: Poughkeepsie Rural Cemetery is one of the great Upstate cemeteries to explore. There are dozens of famous people buried here, and the different styles of astonishing funereal architecture are fascinating (Vassar's acorn, for example). Two famous names buried here are Andrew and William Smith, the bearded brothers whose faces grace a billion boxes of their famous cough drops. Yes, Andrew and William, not "Trade" and "Mark."

For More Information: A History of Vassar College, info.vassar.edu /about/vassar/history.html.

83

ADMIRAL JOHN L. WORDEN

1818–1897

THE MONITOR AND THE MERRIMACK
BURIED IN PAWLING,
DUTCHESS COUNTY

*A*dmiral John Worden was one of the greatest of all the legendary US Navy heroes.

Born in in Ossining, New York (a historical plaque marks his place of birth on Route 9), he went on to become one of the most storied military leaders of the Civil War. After being captured and held by the South for nearly seven months during the war, Worden was rewarded by President Lincoln with the prestigious assignment of helming the experimental metal-clad ship *Monitor*.

Fitted with impenetrable steel sheathing, the ship was the technological marvel of her day. Not to be outdone, the Confederates scuttled a 4,600-ton frigate named *Merrimack* and transformed it into the CSS *Virginia*. On March 9, 1862, all eyes were on Hampton Roads, Virginia, where the two seagoing iron giants met in mortal combat for the first time. Admiral Worden was severely wounded during the ferocious engagement when a shell exploded near him, blinding him temporarily. He was evacuated from his *Monitor*. The two ships fought to a stalemate, and both survived, albeit dented and misshapen from the volleys of cannon shot. It was the first battle of ironclad ships in history and was the single major naval engagement of the Civil War. The battle ushered in a new phase of naval warfare.

Admiral Worden was a close friend of President Lincoln, and his patron gladly repaid the naval officer's heroism by naming him in 1868

to the rank of commodore. In this role, Worden would continue to help design and construct ironclad ships. One year later, he was named superintendent of the United States Naval Academy. During his four-year term at the academy, his rank was raised again, to rear admiral. In 1886, he was retired and awarded a full pay pension for life from Congress.

He died in 1897 at the age of eighty-nine.

Grave Location: John Worden is buried in the small and quite beautiful Pawling Cemetery, located on Route 22. Enter the main gate and proceed to the second section in the back. Here, near the end of this section on the left, is Worden's unmistakable gravestone. It is a five-foot-tall anchor with his last name in large letters along the bottom. He is buried here with his wife, Olivia. New York State Governor Thomas E. Dewey is buried in a large tomb nearby.

Author's Note: What became of the original ironclads? Worden's *Monitor* sank in a hurricane off Cape Hatteras, North Carolina, on New Year's Eve 1862. Four of its officers and twelve crewmen died. On August

5, 2002, the *Monitor*'s large intact gun turret was found on the Atlantic Ocean floor and raised. The nine-foot-tall, 160-ton turret is now on display at the Mariners' Museum in Newport News, Virginia. The *Merrimack* (CSS *Virginia*) was sunk by the Confederates shortly after the Battle of Hampton Roads so as not to be captured by the North.

Factoid: Just inside the main gate of Pawling Cemetery is a large stone with a brass plaque affixed to it. This plaque tells the story in detail of Admiral Worden's heroics. Just behind the boulder, in the same section, is the grave of Italian actress Silvana Mangano. She was a beauty pageant winner, "Miss Rome," at sixteen and came to America three years later. Her first film was *Bitter Rice* (1949). She made many movies from the 1950s to the 1970s. In 1949, she married famed movie producer Dino de Laurentis. Her granddaughter is Giada de Laurentis, a major star on the *Food Network* and famed cookbook author.

For More Information: The USS *Monitor* Center at the Mariners' Museum and Park, "Biography of John Lorimer Worden," www.monitorcenter .org/donate-now/captain-worden-challenge/biography-of-john-lorimer -worden/.

Part Seven

CAPITAL DISTRICT
AND SARATOGA REGION

84

PRESIDENT CHESTER A. ARTHUR

1829–1886

TWENTY-FIRST PRESIDENT
OF THE UNITED STATES
BURIED IN ALBANY,
ALBANY COUNTY

Chester Arthur the *man* was much more inspiring than Chester Arthur the *president*. In fact *Time* magazine once rated President Arthur as one of America's biggest presidential failures.

He was the second US vice president to become chief executive upon the assassination of his predecessor (Andrew Johnson followed Lincoln). When President James A. Garfield was shot in the back while waiting for a train in Washington, DC, Arthur was immediately whisked away to the capital. Garfield hovered between life and death for more than ten weeks while Arthur slowly insinuated himself into the Oval Office. When the president finally succumbed to his wounds, Arthur became the first president to assume office without ever having been elected to anything before (except the vice presidency, of course).

Arthur was a steady, if uninspiring, steward, and what his administration lacked in innovation it made up for in integrity and moral leadership. Arthur was not renominated for a second term in his own right, and he retired from public office and returned to a practice in a private law firm.

Chester Arthur's public and private personas were as different as night and day. Although perhaps a bit haughty or regal in his public stature, in private he was an engaging, gregarious, and charming socialite who enjoyed ballroom dancing, female companionship, and natty attire. He

owned more than eighty suits. He was an avid outdoorsman and passionate fisherman. Arthur would have preferred to have had a much longer
retirement than he did. He died on November 18, 1896, just eighteen
months after leaving the White House. He was fifty-seven years old.

Grave Location: President Arthur's grave in Albany Rural Cemetery
is marked by one of the most dramatic funereal sculptures I have ever
seen. His enormous black marble sarcophagus is lorded over by a towering bronze guardian angel. It is one of the most striking grave sites in a
cemetery filled with historic graves. The president's wife and other family
members are also buried in the plot. A Seal of the President of the United
States is embedded under the tomb. President Arthur's final resting place
is in Section 24, Lot 8.

Author's Note: Albany Rural Cemetery is considered to be one of
America's greatest because of its natural beauty, its thoughtful four-hun-
dred-acre layout, and all of the many historical figures who are buried
here. Unfortunately, the signage is a bit woeful. Visitors would be advised

to look for one of the only flagpoles flying the American flag in the cemetery as the directional marker to Arthur's grave. Also, as is the case in many of the cemeteries mentioned in this book, the front office personnel are always eager to help with directions if the office is open.

Factoid: The Division of Military and naval Affairs always conducts a memorial wreath-laying ceremony at President Arthur's grave on his birthday, October 5.

For More Information: University of Virginia Miller Center, "Chester A. Arthur," millercenter.org/president/arthur.

These Exalted Acres: Unlocking the Secrets of Albany Rural Cemetery, by Paul Grondahl (Albany Times Union, 2013).

SERGEANT THOMAS A. BAKER

1916–1944

MEDAL OF HONOR
BURIED IN SCHUYLERVILLE,
SARATOGA COUNTY

*T*here are so many heroes who have fought for our country's freedom over the many years that I wanted to find a way to honor them all. Clearly, that would be impossible in a book as limited as this one. So how to do it? I finally came up with the idea of choosing just a single serviceman or woman to represent all of those who have served from New York and who have paid the ultimate sacrifice. There was no method for coming up with my choice for this chapter. In fact, I picked the person almost totally at random. All who served are heroes to me, and so I will tell the story of Tom Baker of Troy, New York, and let him stand as a representative of all of his brothers and sisters who have worn our nation's uniform.

There are more than fourteen thousand military graves at the Gerald B. H. Solomon Saratoga National Cemetery in Schuylerville, representing those who fell in every US military engagement since World War I. The cemetery's name honors an area congressman who worked for many years in Washington on military issues, and it is the final resting place of military personnel of all ranks and from all services. Scattered among the undulating rows of identical white tombstones are markers that tell some unusual stories, such as the grave of John Quinlan, who was the tail gunner on the famous bomber the *Memphis Belle*, or Almon Wilson, a legendary rear admiral who championed the Navy's modern mobile hospital

system. At this printing, only three graves are marked with the insignia of the Medal of Honor, our nation's highest military award.

Sgt. Thomas A. Baker is one of them.

Each and every story of those who have received the Medal of Honor is thrilling, inspiring, and almost beyond comprehension to the average person. Their achievements and sacrifice were above and beyond the call of duty. One must pass a high bar, almost impossibly high, in order to become a recipient of the medal.

There is no way I could ever translate the incredible act of courage that Tom Baker, of Troy, New York, performed on the afternoon of July 7, 1944. I will let his Medal of Honor citation speak for itself:

For conspicuous gallantry and intrepidity at the risk of his life above and beyond the call of duty at Saipan, Mariana Islands, 19 June to 7 July 1944. When his entire company was held up by fire from automatic weapons and small-arms fire from strongly fortified enemy positions that commanded the view of the company, Sgt. (then Pvt.) Baker voluntarily took a bazooka and dashed alone to within 100 yards of the enemy. Through heavy rifle and machine gun fire that was directed at him by the enemy, he knocked out the strong point, enabling his company to assault the ridge. Some days later while his company advanced across the open field flanked with obstructions and places of concealment for the enemy, Sgt. Baker again voluntarily took up a position in the rear to protect the company against surprise attack and came upon 2 heavily fortified enemy pockets manned by 2 officers and 10 enlisted men which had been bypassed. Without regard for such superior numbers, he unhesitatingly attacked and killed all of them. Five hundred yards farther, he discovered 6 men of the enemy who had concealed themselves behind our lines and destroyed all of them. On 7 July 1944, the perimeter of which Sgt. Baker was a part was attacked from 3 sides by from 3,000 to 5,000 Japanese. During the early stages of this attack, Sgt. Baker was seriously wounded but he insisted on remaining in the line and fired at the enemy at ranges sometimes as close as 5 yards until his ammunition ran out. Without ammunition and with his own weapon battered to uselessness from hand-to-hand combat, he was carried about 50 yards to the rear by a comrade, who was then himself wounded. At this point Sgt. Baker refused to be moved any farther stating that he preferred to be left to die rather than risk the lives of any more of his friends. A short time later, at his request, he was placed in a sitting position against a small tree. Another comrade, withdrawing, offered assistance. Sgt. Baker refused, insisting that he be left alone and be given a soldier's pistol with its remaining 8 rounds of ammunition. When last seen alive, Sgt. Baker was propped against a tree, pistol in hand, calmly facing the foe. Later Sgt. Baker's body was found in the same position, gun empty, with 8 Japanese lying dead before him. His deeds were in keeping with the highest traditions of the U.S. Army. (Courtesy of the Congressional Medal of Honor Society)

This chapter honors the memory and service of Sgt. Thomas Baker, as well as the memories of all US servicemen and women who have fallen in the line of duty.

Grave Location: Sergeant Baker is buried in Section 8, Plot 530 in Gerald B. H. Solomon Saratoga National Cemetery, located at 200 Duell

Road in Schuylerville. As with all military cemeteries, the gravestones are marked for easy locating. Each has the section number on the back, and then they are all numbered in sequence. Baker's stone is marked 8-530 on the back, and the front carries the insignia of the Congressional Medal of Honor.

Author's Note: There are seven national military cemeteries in New York State. Two of them are full and closed (Cypress Hills Cemetery in Brooklyn, and the Soldier's Plot at Albany Rural Cemetery), two are utilized for cremation only (Woodlawn in Elmira, and Long Island Cemetery in Farmingdale), and three are open and accepting burials (Bath National Cemetery in Bath, Gerald B. H. Solomon Saratoga National Cemetery in Schuylerville, and Calverton National Cemetery in Calverton).

Factoid: The Battle of Butterfly Ridge, on the island of Saipan, was a bloody encounter between the US Army and a much larger Japanese force. It is also one of just a handful of World War II battles in which two Medals of Honor were given. One of them went to Sgt. Thomas Baker and the other went to Lt. Col. William J. O'Brien. Amazingly, both Baker and O'Brien were from the same Upstate city—Troy.

Lieutenant Colonel O'Brien is buried in the cemetery at Troy's Saint Peter's Church.

For More Information: Congressional Medal of Honor Society, "Baker, Thomas A.," www.cmohs.org/recipient-detail/2623/baker-thomas -a.php.

86

GEORGE CRUM

1824–1914

INVENTOR OF THE POTATO CHIP
BURIED IN MALTA RIDGE,
SARATOGA COUNTY

As Ripley would say, "believe it or not," George Crum, an Upstate New Yorker whose father was African American and whose mother was Native American, was the inventor of the potato chip!

Crum, a chef at Cary Moon's Lake Lodge, a classy Adirondack Mountain inn in Saratoga Springs, New York, was a crusty, curmudgeonly character known far and wide for his talents in the kitchen. This lodge on the shores of beautiful Saratoga Lake was a popular spot with the well-heeled of the mid-1800s who would flee the stuffy confines of summer in New York City to hobnob with the millionaires and celebrities in the cooler Adirondacks. One of those bluebloods was none other than Commodore Cornelius Vanderbilt, then one of the richest men in America.

As the story is told, on August 24, 1853, the commodore was dining at the swanky hotel when he voiced his displeasure at the thickness of the potato wedges he and his companions were served. He told the waiter to tell the chef to cut the potatoes thinner. This went back and forth for several minutes between the millionaire and the chef until finally Crum decided to give Vanderbilt his comeuppance.

Crum sliced half a dozen potatoes so thin you could almost see through them. He then deep fried them and sprinkled them with salt and sent them out with the waiter to the commodore's table. To the surprise of almost everyone, Vanderbilt loved the "new" taste sensations. Other diners

also asked for them. Crum named them Saratoga chips, and a legend was born. Soon the rich and famous began bringing the chips back to New York City in their fancy railroad parlor cars. One struggles to imagine the conversation among the Astors and the Vanderbilts and the Goulds as they excitedly chatted about "Indian George's chips."

On the heels of his new fame and notoriety, Crum, a descendant of Huron warriors, a fur trapper, and an Adirondack guide, opened up his own lakeside hotel, Crum's House, in Saratoga. The restaurant featured complimentary baskets of Saratoga chips on each table. Over his life, Crum had five wives who, along with much of his extended family, made up the core of his employees at this popular restaurant. The fame of Saratoga chips spread nationally when they were included in one of the best-selling cookbooks of the day, *Buckeye Cookery and Practical House-keeping,* by Estelle Woods Wilcox.

Crum died on July 22, 1914, at the age of eighty-six.

Grave Location: Crum is buried in Malta Ridge Cemetery on Route 9 about ten miles from Saratoga Springs. The cemetery is on the west side of the highway and is located just yards from Exit 13 of the Adirondack Northway (I-87). His grave can be seen in the center of the cemetery from the road. The name on the gravestone is "Speck."

Author's Note: Finding the grave of the inventor of the potato chip was one of my great challenges in writing this book. I found it years ago, before GPS had even been thought of, and at the time there was little information on his burial location. It took me several walks through a few Saratoga cemeteries (St. Peters, Greenridge, etc.) to realize I was coming up empty-handed.

The key to finding his grave was in a long lost story regarding his name. Some had told me that George Crum hated the comic overtones of his last name and had it changed for legal reasons to George Speck when he was a young man. He continued to use Crum professionally. In fact, however, it is known that his name at birth was Speck and he adopted the name Crum at his customer's suggestion. Now, looking for a Speck instead of a Crum, my task became easier. I found that a George Speck had been born in Malta in 1828. Another little piece of the puzzle.

In my search of the Malta area, one man came to my rescue. Mike Peters was the Malta cemetery historian, and it was a lucky day when I found him. He took me to his home, where he dug out the old cemetery record logs and started to flip through them. But then even he became stumped. He found an entry that was illegible and thought that might be it. A quick call to a friend confirmed that Speck (Crum) was in fact buried just up the road from Peters's house in the old Malta Ridge Cemetery on Route 9. He dug out the grave charts, pored over them with a strong magnifying glass, and then exclaimed, "There! There he is." I said good-bye to this kindly gent and his wife and traveled up to the cemetery.

And there it was, just as Mike Peters had written down for me on the back of an old envelope. "Malta Ridge Cemetery, Lot #79, seven burial plots north of the driveway."

Factoid: To add to all of the confusion about where Speck/Crum was buried was the confusion about his age. His gravestone reads, "George Speck. Born Malta, 1828. Died July 22, 1914. 86 years old." Mike Peters's handwritten cemetery records showed Crum age at death to be ninety-six. And, any biographical references to the inventor of the potato chip shows him dying at the age of ninety or ninety-two.

Confusing? Yes.

For More Information: The Original Saratoga Chips, "The Story of George Crum and America's First Kettle Chip," originalsaratogachips.com/our-story/. The company still makes these chips in Saratoga; note that the website lists George's birth date as 1822, while his actual grave marker lists it as 1828.

VIRGINIA O'HANLON DOUGLAS

1889–1971

"YES, VIRGINIA, THERE IS A SANTA CLAUS!"
BURIED IN NORTH CHATHAM,
COLUMBIA COUNTY

$\mathcal{E}$ight-year-old Virginia O'Hanlon was disturbed when some of the poor children in her neighborhood blamed their bleak Christmas on Santa Claus. They told her that if Santa was real they would have received more presents than they actually did. Later, at home, she asked her father if there really was a Santa Claus. Dr. Philip O'Hanlon, a respected surgeon with the New York City Police Department, advised his young child that while he believed there really was a Santa Claus, she should write to the *New York Sun* newspaper and ask them. "If you see it printed in the *Sun*, then it is so," he told her. From that innocent father-daughter chat emerged one of the most inspiring, enduring, and charming pieces of Christmas folk history.

Virginia took pen in hand and poured out her confusing situation in what would become one of the most famous letters to the editor ever written.

> Dear Editor: I am 8 years old. Some of my little friends say there is no Santa Claus. Papa says, "If you see it in *The Sun*, it is so!" Please tell me the truth. Is there a Santa Claus?

She signed it "Virginia O'Hanlon, 8 years old, 115 W. 95th Street, New York City, New York."

Virginia's letter landed on the desk of Francis Pharcellus Church. He was one of the many editorial writers at the paper, and it was prophetic that the little girl's letter was given to him to answer. A crusty, twenty-year veteran of journalistic battles (and real ones, for he was a former war correspondent), Church seized this opportunity to reveal a softer, more sentimental side to his readers. In a direct and gentle manner belying his dour demeanor, Church recognized the child's heartfelt sincerity and answered in kind.

> Yes, Virginia, there is a Santa Claus! He exists as certainly as love and generosity and devotion exist, and you know that they abound and give to your life its highest beauty and joy. Alas! How dreary would be the world if there was no Santa Claus. It would be as dreary as if there were no Virginias! There would be no childlike faith then, no poetry, and no romance to make tolerable this existence. We should have no enjoyment except in sense and sight. The eternal light with which childhood fills the world would be extinguished.

He signed the letter anonymously as the *New York Sun*.

The response to this exchange of letters was overwhelming. The *Sun* was deluged with requests for the editorial, and media outlets all over the country wanted to know more about the little girl who started the whole thing. While the commotion over the "Yes, Virginia" letter soon died down, it has remained a holiday fixture ever since. Both the child's letter and the editor's response have been printed and reprinted thousands of times during holiday seasons over the years. Since it first appeared on September 21, 1897, it has been reprinted around the world in more than twenty-five languages.

What became of little Virginia? Well, she grew up to pursue a career in education and attempted to remain far from the limelight for the rest of her life. Still, on Christmas Day, it was not unusual for some intrepid news reporter to try to track her down for a retelling of her Santa story and to see what she was doing. Her career was a stellar one: she received a bachelor's degree from Hunter College in 1910, a master's degree from Columbia University in 1911, and a doctorate in education from Fordham University in 1935, then went on to become a highly respected educator. She spent nearly a half century teaching in New York City public schools before retiring. Her last position was as principal of PS 401 in Brooklyn, New York, a school for chronically ill children.

Francis Church died on April 11, 1906. Because of the *Sun's* policy of having their editorials printed unsigned, no one knew that it was he who was responsible for the paper's now-immortal reply. Even his own obituary in the *Sun* omitted his contribution to Christmas lore.

Virginia O'Hanlon (Douglas) spent her final years Upstate living with her daughter, Mrs. Robert Temple. Even in her autumnal years, people would refer to her as the "Yes, Virginia" lady. She died in a Valatie, New York, nursing home on May 13, 1971, at the age of eighty-one.

Grave Location: Virginia O'Hanlon Douglas's grave is in the North Chatham Cemetery, located just north of the village near the intersection of Route 203 and Route 32. Virginia's grave is easy to find in this small, rural cemetery. Enter at the first set of stone pillars, and one hundred feet in one of the first graves on your right is hers.

Author's Note: This cemetery can be a little tricky to find if you are using a GPS. There is a North Chatham, a Chatham, an Old Chatham, and a Chatham Center all near each other. While in the area, consider a visit to the world-famous Shaker Museum and Library in Old Chatham. Thousands of people visit each year to enjoy the "premier center for the interpretation and exhibition of Shaker life and culture in America." If you ever wanted to know how the Shakers made those round wooden boxes or why they hung their chairs on wall pegs, well, this is the place to get your answers. It should be noted that Mother Ann Lee, the founder of the Shakers in America, is also buried in Upstate New York (Albany) and is featured chapter 91.

Factoid: In 1969, while recovering from a serious illness, Virginia was forced to spend Christmas at Columbia Memorial Hospital in Hudson, New York. On Christmas Eve, a jolly old man in a red suit with a white beard came in to give her a Christmas kiss. The newspapers recorded the event with the headline, "Virginia Finally Meets Santa!" She died two years later.

At the entrance to the Barnwell Nursing Home, where she lived until her death, is a small plaque that reads: "Virginia O'Hanlon Douglas. 1890–1971. Shortly before her death Virginia expressed 'Remember the children at Christmas!' The little girl of 'Yes, Virginia, there is a Santa Claus!' spent her final years in Valatie, NY, at this nursing facility."

For More Information: Newseum, "Yes, Virginia, There Is a Santa Claus," www.newseum.org/exhibits/online/yes-virginia/. This collection includes photos of Douglas and Church, and both the little girl's letter and the printed *Sun* editorial.

Barnwell Nursing Home, Valatie (which houses the plaque), barnwell nrc.com.

88

COLONEL ELMER E. ELLSWORTH

1837–1861

FIRST UNION OFFICER TO DIE IN THE CIVIL WAR
BURIED IN MECHANICVILLE,
SARATOGA COUNTY

*H*ow many of us can actually say that we ended up doing exactly what we originally wanted to do as a child? How many librarians out there really wanted to be an astronaut? How many accountants wanted to be a dancer? Well, Elmer Ephraim Ellsworth *always* wanted to be only one thing—a soldier!

He dreamed of being a soldier as a young child, and he was determined never to waver from that path. Upon his high school graduation, he applied to the military academy at West Point. He was rejected. His family could not afford to send their young son to a private military academy, so he drifted off to Chicago where he began to study law. His fascination with all things military continued unabated during this time, and he was especially fascinated with a French military organization called the Zouaves. He studied their unique and intricate training methods and even learned the French language so he could better translate French Zouave manuals. He eventually attached himself to a group of "weekend soldiers" that was on the verge of disbanding. At last able to put his extensive military expertise to work, Ellsworth organized the disheveled group into a tight, precision brigade that became highly respected for their discipline and professional abilities.

He named his new group the U.S. Zouave Cadets and exhibited their skills at public shows. Thousands would turn out to see the spectacle of

colorfully uniformed soldiers performing their precision formations and intricate drills. The unit became a major attraction in the Chicago area, and Ellsworth was persuaded to take his soldiers on a nationwide tour. The popularity of the group grew so widespread that he was named assistant general of the Illinois National Guard, and his Zouaves were named to the prestigious position of Governor's Guards.

In 1860, Ellsworth joined the law office of Abraham Lincoln and worked tirelessly for his election to the presidency. He personally accompanied Lincoln to his inauguration in Washington. He urged his friend, now president, to oversee a complete restructuring of the US military in preparation for the anticipated hostilities ahead. Lincoln, completely charmed by this young New Yorker, agreed to all of his recommendations. So close were the president and the young soldier at this point that Ellsworth had rare access to all sections of the White House, would dine with the president frequently, and became a favorite playmate to Lincoln's young son. Mary Todd Lincoln considered him family.

At the very dawning of the Civil War, Ellsworth was sent over the Potomac River at Washington to evict Confederate supporters in nearby Alexandria, Virginia. Not a shot was fired as the Union soldiers entered town. Colonel Ellsworth spied a large Confederate flag flying from the top of the city's largest hotel and personally went to the roof to take it down. While coming back down the stairs, he was confronted by the upset hotel manager, who shot and killed Ellsworth in the stairwell. The Confederate flag was still tucked into Ellsworth's jacket. Doctors could not save the young soldier, and he died on the spot. An onlooker noticed the large medallion around the dead soldier's neck. It read: "*Non Sul Nobis Sed Pre Patriae*" (not for ourselves, but for our country).

Colonel Elmer E. Ellsworth became the first noteworthy Union death of the Civil War.

Upon hearing of Ellsworth's death, Lincoln collapsed at his desk and sobbed uncontrollably. "I cannot talk. Ellsworth is dead, and it has unnerved me greatly." The president ordered a state funeral of unprecedented grandeur for the soldier. His funeral was held in the White House, where hundreds passed his casket to grieve. His body was then moved to New York City, where it lay in state for three days. Five thousand mourners passed his casket here. Ellsworth's body was then placed on a funeral boat which traveled up the Hudson to Troy, New York. From there a special "mourning train" was commissioned to take him to his hometown of Mechanicville. There, he was buried with full military honors in Hudson View Cemetery.

Because of the extensive mourning period, some believe that Ellsworth was one of the first famous person in the United States to have been successfully embalmed (a new technique at the time).

A direct reaction to Ellsworth's death was a surge of recruits joining the Union cause. The popular phrase of the day was "Remember Ellsworth!" One large unit from New York was named Ellsworth's Avengers.

At the time of his death, Elmer Ellsworth had just turned twenty-four years old.

Grave Location: Hudson View Cemetery is located off South Street on a hill in the southern area of Mechanicville, which is eighteen miles north of Albany. At the cemetery, markers guide visitors to his grave site. His grave monument is magnificent—a towering obelisk topped by an eagle with wings spread makes for a dramatic setting for his final resting place. An inscription on the monument reads: "I am confident that he who knoweth even the fall of the sparrow will have purpose even in the fate of one like me."

Author's Note: Ellsworth's grave is tended by the local historical organizations in Mechanicville and is usually resplendent with flowers and patriotic adornments.

Factoid: The New York State Military Museum in Saratoga Springs has an exhibit on Col. Ellsworth. The most arresting artifact is the actual uniform he was wearing at the time of his death. A blood-stained hole in his uniform over his heart shows where the fatal bullet hit him.

For More Information: New York State Military Museum and Veterans Research Center, dmna.ny.gov/historic/mil-hist.htm.

89

JOHNNY EVERS

1881–1947
"TINKER TO EVERS TO CHANCE"
BURIED IN TROY,
RENSSELAER COUNTY

*I*mmortalized in the now famous Franklin Adams 1910 poem "Baseball's Sad Lexicon," the tongue-friendly phrase "Tinker to Evers to Chance" was chanted by sandlot ballplayers for decades. But who was Tinker? Evers? And who, by chance, was Chance?

All three were Chicago Cubs baseball stars shortly after the turn of the twentieth century. The three were famed (and feared) for their ease in turning a simple ground ball into a double play. In fact they were the best trio in baseball history at carrying out this feat. Johnny Evers was from Upstate New York, so let's start with him.

Evers (rhymes with beavers) was the important center cog at second base in this historic trio. He joined the Cubs full time in 1903 and helped lead them to three straight National League pennants. A powerful hitter as well as one of the league's most dominant infielders, Evers batted .350 in both the 1907 and 1908 World Series. Nicknamed the Trojan for his roots in Troy, New York, and also called the Crab for his low-crouching fielding style, he was one of the two or three key players for the Cubs during those years. He also had a part in what has been called one of the most controversial baseball games ever played.

On September, 23, 1908, with the National League pennant at stake, the Chicago Cubs and the New York Giants were locked in a 1–1 tie, men on first and third, bottom of the ninth with the Giants at bat. The

hitter drove a hard single to the outfield, easily scoring the man on third to end the game. Except that in order for the play to be ruled completed, nineteen-year-old Fred Merkle, making his first start of the year as a pinch runner on first, had to actually touch second base. When the Giants runner at third crossed home plate, swarms of fans streamed onto the field in jubilation and chaos. In this scrum, Merkle simply turned and walked toward the outfield clubhouse, considering the game finished and won by the Giants. At this point, Johnny Evers, seeing that Merkle had failed to touch second base, started screaming for the ball, got it, and ran and tagged second base, essentially putting Merkle out. A riotous confrontation between the teams ensued, and finally the exasperated umpires could not make a ruling one way or the other. Considering the strangeness of the play, they ruled that it was a tie game and that it must be replayed. It was, and the Cubs won the game and took the pennant away from the New York Giants. Poor Fred Merkle was never spoken of again in New York except when fans recalled the Merkle Boner, as it became known. Evers's knowledge of the game and its rules gave the team the win.

Tinker, Evers, and Chance all ended up managing the Cubs. In fact, Johnny Evers managed both Chicago teams, the White Sox and Cubs, and is the only player to ever do so. While they were forever linked by the singsong sound of their famous double play sequence, the three players were hardly close friends off the field. One time a feud erupted in the clubhouse between Chance and Tinker, and it quickly escalated into fisticuffs. They would not speak to each other for more than thirty years after the altercation.

Johnny Evers, always a fan favorite, was honored with his own day, a rare tribute, on May 10, 1913. Johnny Evers Day took place at the Polo Grounds in New York City, and a large contingent of his friends, family, and fans made the trip down from his hometown of Troy, New York. He performed well that day, slamming a single and a double, and he even scored the winning run in the Cubs' victory over the Giants.

Johnny Evers spent his retirement years mixing business and baseball in Albany. His health declined in retirement, but he still could be found in a wheelchair behind the counter of his sporting goods store regaling customers with stories of his playing years. He suffered a stroke in 1942 and died five years later on March 28, 1947, of a cerebral hemorrhage in St. Peter's Hospital in Albany. He was sixty-five.

Evers was the second in the famed trio to pass away. Frank Chance, the first baseman, was the first to go. Known as the Peerless Leader, he had a knack for attracting the beanball and eventually was forced to retire from baseball with head injuries. He suffered brain disease and died at the age of forty-eight on September 24, 1924. He is buried in Los Angeles. Shortstop Joe Tinker, who once stole home twice in a single game, suffered from diabetes most of his life and, after a double leg amputation, died on his sixty-eighth birthday, July 27, 1948. He is buried in Florida.

All three players were inducted into the National Baseball Hall of Fame in Cooperstown in 1946. Evers and Tinker, who hadn't spoken to each other in decades, were moved to tears at the emotion of the moment.

Grave Location: Johnny Evers is buried in St. Mary's Cemetery, located at 79 Brunswick Road in Troy. Follow the main road into the cemetery to Section B. Evers is buried in Lot 237, Grave 3, next to his wife,

Helen, who died in 1974. A five-foot-tall statue of Christ atop the nearby Hannum family tomb will guide you to Evers's grave site.

Author's Note: Actress Maureen Stapleton (chapter 95) is also buried in this cemetery.

Factoid: Evers's plaque at the National Baseball Hall of Fame refers to him as "the middleman of the famous double play combination of Tinker to Evers to Chance," and it also notes that he shares the record for hitting the most singles in a four-game World Series.

For More Information: Baseball Reference, "Johnny Evers," www .baseball-reference.com/players/e/eversjo01.shtml.

BEGORDIUS HATCH

1761–1836

*STRONGEST MAN IN WASHINGTON'S ARMY
BURIED IN NEW LEBANON,
COLUMBIA COUNTY*

*T*he history of the Upstate New York is filled with tales of strange happenings and colorful people. Some are true and some are fable. Generations have been dazzled by tales of everything from a headless horseman to a monster-sized man of stone called the Cardiff Giant to a sixteen-year-old girl who rode through the hills warning "The Redcoats are coming! The Redcoats are coming!" Like I said, some are true and some not. The man who lost his head and the stone giant are fun and interesting but obviously fictitious tales. The sixteen-year-old rider story is true.

Here is another one that is true.

Begordius Hatch was born in Ticonderoga, New York, and survived an Indian massacre at the age of four. His parents were killed. He was raised by relatives on a farm near New Lebanon, about twenty-five miles southeast of Albany. He fathered thirteen children and was a popular and beloved figure in his native area. He rests eternally there today, in a small family cemetery surrounded by numerous family members.

When Hatch was sixteen, he ran away from his New Lebanon home to join General Washington's army at the Battle of Boston Heights. Washington was intrigued by this towering yet gentle fellow, and he signed the new recruit on as his personal bodyguard. Hatch pledged his total allegiance to the general and accompanied Washington everywhere. In fact, Hatch was one of only a handful of men to serve in all of Washington's battle campaigns.

During the years that Hatch was in the army, there were long periods of inactivity between hostilities. During this peaceful time, the soldiers would keep fit by boxing, wrestling, and holding weight-lifting contests. No one dared challenge Hatch, though. Washington would prod the gentle giant into putting on amazing shows of strength for the troops. Often, Hatch would hoist a cast-iron cannon onto his massive shoulders and parade around in front of his astonished fellow soldiers. Washington took great pleasure in showing Hatch off, but he was also sincerely grateful to his bodyguard for getting him through the war without a scratch.

At the close of the war, General Washington expressed his great thanks to Hatch and dismissed him. Hatch shyly smiled and simply turned away and walked home. All the way home. Some 160 miles!

At home in New Lebanon, the man who was known as one of the strongest men in the country took up farming and began to raise a large family. The Indians in the nearby wilderness respected his great strength and calm demeanor and left him and his farm in peace. A man of deep compassion, Hatch was a personable man with a cheery disposition. He was always the first one to help with a neighbor's harvest or barn raising (and because of his might, he was asked to do both often).

The stories of Hatch's great power are legendary. Locals say that at the site of the Hatch farmstead one can still see an eighty-foot-deep cobblestone-lined well. Hatch is said to have dug it by hand.

Another story that still makes the rounds around New Lebanon happened in 1836, the last year of Hatch's life. Although he was then seventy-five years old, some of his neighbors invited him to a barn raising, and he accepted. The neighbors schemed a trick on the aging strongman. They positioned him in the middle of a large beam and put six farmhands on each side of him. At a signal, the farmhands would feign lifting the heavy wooden beam and leave all the work to Hatch. At the command of "heave" they stood limply to the side as Hatch hoisted the beam onto his back, climbed a ladder, and placed it where it belonged. He then descended the ladder, looked at the wide-eyed farmhands, gave them a sly wink of the eye, and strode off to his home. The crowd broke into applause.

Hatch died on May 24, 1836.

Grave Location: Hatch is buried in a family cemetery, and his grave is difficult to find. Once you are in New Lebanon, turn off Route 20 on to West Street at the firehouse. Travel up this road approximately four miles (it will turn into Presbyterian Hill Road). Keep an eye out for a small, overgrown cemetery on your right. The Hatch Family Cemetery is located about one hundred yards from the road. Although it was once a beautiful family plot surrounded by an elegant stone wall, today it is unkempt and difficult to walk through. Hatch's grave is usually the only one marked with a US flag.

Author's Note: There is no sign or historical marker along this road. It is much easier to spot the cemetery coming down Presbyterian Hill Road from the north than going up the hill from the south.

Factoid: Hatch's thirteen children didn't move far from home, and there are still sixth- and seventh-generation Hatch family members living near New Lebanon today.

For More Information: Hometown Tales, "Begordius Hatch," stephen towngenealogy.com/hometowntales.html.

91

ANN LEE

1736–1784

THE WORD
BURIED IN COLONIE,
ALBANY COUNTY

*A*nn Lee dropped out of school in her native England at a very young age and went to work. She toiled as a house cleaner or some other domestic servant for several years. She was a hard worker who had few social interests. In 1762, she married a local blacksmith named Abraham Standerin and bore him four children in quick succession. Each birth was a painful and difficult ordeal for Ann, and sadly each of her four children died in infancy. This unhappy occurrence led Ann to become reluctant to enter into any other sexual relationship whatsoever. She became a member of a sect that preached disdain for sexual activity. The sect, operated by preacher James Wardley and his wife, Jane, was a precursor to the Shaker religion.

The Shakers—so named because of their wildly shaking gyrations performed during dances attempting to exorcise sin from the worshipper—had a small yet loyal following in England. Ann was an enthusiastic convert and quickly became one of their leaders. In 1770, she was imprisoned for "acts against the Sabbath" and became a martyr to her followers. When she emerged from jail, she announced that she had had a vision in her cell and that vision had convinced her that all of mankind's ills were brought on by the sex act. She began referring to herself as Mother Ann or "The Word." Following several more years of persecution and jailings, Ann led her group to America.

Things did not go much better for Mother Ann in her new country. Her followers considered her to be the "second coming of Christ," and this led to some angry and even violent reactions from those she tried to enlist in her sect. She travelled New England preaching the ways of the Shakers, and while some listened and even joined her, others called her a charlatan and physically attacked her. At one New England appearance she was even stoned by her audience.

She continued to be harassed and imprisoned, and in 1780 she was jailed for high treason for preaching nonviolence and pacifism during the Revolutionary War.

Exhausted, frail, and in ill health, The Word passed away in Watervliet, New York, on September 8, 1784, at the age of only forty-eight.

Grave Location: Ann Lee is buried near the site of the first Shaker community in America. The Shaker Cemetery, located on Watervliet Shaker Road, is adjacent to Albany International Airport. A tall black wrought-iron fence surrounds the cemetery, which contains the identical stones of 144 of Ann's followers and disciples. Her grave marker is in the center and is about four inches taller than all of the others.

Author's Note: This cemetery is small and surrounded by tall trees, but the graves of Ann Lee and her followers can easily be seen from the road. A New York State roadside historical marker tells of the history of the cemetery and of its most famous burial.

Factoid: Nestled up to the hustle and bustle of Albany's busy airport is the 770-acre Shaker Heritage Society and Historic District, with several interesting, original Shaker buildings. This small and relatively unknown museum hosts an active schedule of public events, and it is an important historical site for those wishing to learn about the Shakers. The Shakers were known for their creative, simple innovations, and it was here at this site that the flat broom, vacuum-sealed tin cans, and individually packeted garden seeds were first invented and sold. The site was also a refuge for runaway slaves.

For More Information: Shaker Heritage Society of Albany, shaker heritage.org.

92

JANE MCCREA

1752–1777

TRAGIC BRIDE OF FORT EDWARD
BURIED IN FORT EDWARD,
WASHINGTON COUNTY

$\mathcal{J}$ane McCrea was a beautiful, well-liked, twenty-four-year-old woman living in a quiet region north of New York State's Capital District when the battles of the Revolutionary War darkened her idyllic life. She was engaged to Lieutenant David Jones, a senior officer with the British troops under the command of General Burgoyne. Because of her close relationship with a British officer, Jane was afforded a somewhat "protected status" by the British. On July 27, her intended wedding day, she and a friend, Sarah McNeil, were riding in the forest when they were kidnapped by Indians loyal to Burgoyne. One of them took McCrea, and the other took McNeil prisoner. By the time they got to base camp at a nearby fort, McNeil noticed that McCrea was not there. Thinking that their safe status would prevent them from being harmed, McNeil was shocked when two Indian scouts arrived bearing a white woman's scalp. She knew in an instant that her friend had been murdered by her captors.

Lieutenant Jones was heartbroken and demanded severe action against the Indians. Burgoyne, in the unenviable positions of having to arrest and alienate his Indian allies, chose to do nothing. Various reports declared that McCrea had been shot in error by the British, murdered and scalped by the Indians, or even shot by the Americans who were pursuing them.

News of Jane McCrea's murder swept the region, portrayed as an act of betrayal by the British and an act of savagery by the Indians. The story

of the doomed "Bride of Fort Edward" was told and retold all along the northern battlefront of New York State. Long lines of volunteers answered the call to march with their neighbors to avenge her death. Troops from as far away as the Green Mountains of Vermont came to stand with the patriots. This great surge in troop strength proved to be the ultimate downfall of the indecisive Burgoyne when he was soundly defeated by these same troops several months later at the Battle of Saratoga, the defining turning point of the war.

Jane McCrea was buried in her wedding dress just two miles from her home in Fort Edward, New York.

Grave Location: Jane McCrea is buried in Union Cemetery on Route 4 between Hudson Falls and Fort Edward. Her original gravestone, more than two centuries old, was plainly visible from the highway for years and was encased in glass. The epitaph read: "Here rests the remains of Jane McCrea age unknown and murdered by a band of Indians while on a visit to a relative (around AD 1777). Commemoration one of the most thrilling incidents in the annals of the American Revolution." Today, new grave-stones for McCrea and McNeil are located just inside the gates of Union Cemetery. A historical marker identifies their final resting places.

Author's Note: Despite the fact that she was buried and reburied at least three different times, no proof remained of McCrea's cause of death or even if she was buried here. In 2004, the History Channel aired a full-length television documentary on her death entitled "Buried Secrets of the Revolutionary War." DNA experts were interviewed, distant family members of McCrea and McNeil were located, and science was loosed upon this age-old mystery. To make matters more complicated, it was discovered that some of McCrea's bones were missing, including her skull, perhaps stolen by souvenir hunters during one of her many interments. Also, her family line had completely died off or was not found, so no certain identification of her bones was possible. The results were murky, but one thing was clear: More than one body had been buried in Jane's grave. And that other person was . . . Sarah McNeil, who died twenty-two years after Jane!

Factoid: The Fort Edward train station is of historical significance. It was built as a Delaware & Hudson railroad depot in 1900 and now serves as an Amtrak station. It is an elegant station, designed in the Victorian style of the era. In 1991, locals rallied to save this landmark when the railroad's new owner, Canadian Pacific, decided to demolish it. Today it serves passengers and has a gift shop and a small restaurant.

For More Information: Old Fort House Museum (houses books and prints about Jane McCrea), www.oldforthousemuseum.com.

93

ANNA MARY ROBERTSON MOSES

1860–1961

GRANDMA MOSES
BURIED IN HOOSICK FALLS,
RENSSELAER COUNTY

*W*hat a life she had!

Born before the Civil War and living through both world wars, Anna Robertson preferred to look at life on the brighter side. Born in poverty, she had only a few short months of schooling before her father pulled her out of school and instructed her on the "womanly arts" of cooking, sewing, keeping house, candle making, gardening, and canning. She was raised in a family of ten, and at age twenty-seven she married Thomas Salmon Moses, with whom she would then have her own ten children (only five survived infancy). She first took up painting at the age of seventy after arthritis prevented her from creating and selling needlework. By this age she was known to all as Grandma Moses.

She lived most of her life in the area around Eagle's Bridge and Hoosick Falls. The legend of her fame began in 1939, when she placed several of her paintings in a drugstore window on Main Street of Hoosick Falls. She had given many of her pieces to friends before this. One day, Louis Caldor, an art collector from New York City, happened by the window and saw her paintings. Caldor asked the druggist how much the paintings cost and if there were more of them. He was told that Moses had ten more paintings out at her farm near the edge of the village. Caldor headed out to see her. One amusing story is that the druggist called Grandma in advance to let her know there was an art collector on his way to see her to

buy all of her ten paintings. Realizing that she only really had nine, she cleverly cut the largest one in two to make ten!

Caldor took all of Moses's artwork to New York and exhibited three pieces at the famed Museum of Modern Art in a show called "Contemporary, Unknown Painters." The show was a success, and within one year Moses was mounting a one-woman show at Galerie St. Etienne in Manhattan. Art fans from around the city were clamoring for her work. She was seventy-nine years old when fame found Grandma Moses.

She produced more than two thousand paintings during her career, most of them on crude masonite board, using her typical primitive style of starting the painting at the top with the sky, then the trees and the mountains next, and then the buildings, people, and the animals. She only painted what she called "old timey things" from her rural past—holiday meals, Christmas in New England, barn raisings, pumpkin patches, apple pickers, and similar subjects. In 1945, Hallmark Cards purchased the rights to reproduce her paintings on greeting cards and sold six million of them *the first year!*

Grandma Moses defined the word prolific. Incredibly, of the two thousand paintings she produced in her lifetime, more than 250 were done after she reached her one hundredth birthday!

Near the end of her life, in 1955 at the age of ninety-six, she was the guest on the Edward R. Murrow interview show *See It Now.* She charmed the nation. When Murrow asked her what uniquely qualified her to be an artist, she gave him a crinkly smile, shoved a piece of paper on front of him and said, "Here. Now draw a tree. Anybody can paint!"

She died on September 13, 1961. President John F. Kennedy, in a tribute, called her "our national treasure."

Grave Location: Grandma Moses's grave is in Maple Grove New Cemetery, just south of the village of Hoosick Falls. Enter the main gate and signs will direct you to the final resting place of the village's most famous native daughter.

Author's Note: The Bennington (Vermont) Museum just ten miles east of Hoosick Falls hosts the world's largest collection of original Grandma Moses paintings. The museum is also the home of the Grandma Moses Schoolhouse, the fully renovated actual schoolhouse that Grandma Moses attended in Eagle Bridge. The building was moved to Bennington in 1972.

Factoid: The original drug store building where Grandma Moses first displayed the paintings that caught Louis Caldor's eye still stands on Main Street in Hoosick Falls. It is currently a bagel shop and a florist.

For More Information: Bennington Museum, "Grandma Moses," benningtonmuseum.org/portfolio-items/grandma-moses/.

94

RUSSELL SAGE

1816–1906

MONEY KING
BURIED IN TROY,
RENSSELAER COUNTY

"*A*ny man can earn a dollar, but it takes a *wise* man to save it."

Russell Sage once boasted that he still possessed "the first dollar he ever earned," and he lived by his own personal "Saving Golden Rule" his entire life. When he died in 1906, he almost *could* claim that he did have every dollar he ever earned. One of the richest men in America, Sage left a fortune of over $90 million.

A true Wall Street titan, Sage dealt with all the great moneymen and financiers of his era, including his good friend (and fellow Upstater) Jay Gould. He amassed a huge fortune, first as a successful merchant and then as a money manager on Wall Street. Later, as a railroad tycoon, he is said to have bragged that he was the president of twenty different railroads *simultaneously!*

Sage was a teetotaler of simple habits who married the love of his life in 1840, eighteen-year-old Marie-Henri Winne. Sage adored his beautiful wife unabashedly. When she died unexpectedly at the age of forty-five, he grieved deeply. He would mourn his sweet Marie-Henri for the rest of his own very long life.

Although he spent time as a US congressman, he was reclusive by nature. His devotion to his businesses kept him behind closed doors and insulated him from the outside world through most of his Wall Street

career. One startling episode, however, thrust Sage uncomfortably onto the front pages of every newspaper in America and changed his life forever.

On December 4, 1891, a disgruntled investor, Henry Norcross, came to Sage's private Wall Street office in an attempt to extort money from the millionaire. The man was carrying a bomb, which he accidentally detonated so that it blew up right in front of Sage before the extortion deal could be consummated. The intruder was blown out the window to his death on the street below. Sage's longtime clerk was also killed, and eight others were seriously injured. Sage himself walked out of his destroyed office unscathed.

One of those injured, William Laidlaw, asked Sage to cover the cost of his long hospitalization. The tightfisted financier refused to make any payments, and Laidlaw took his employer to court. At the proceedings, the clerk testified that at the exact moment of the bomb blast Sage had thrown Laidlaw in front of him to shield himself from harm. This public accusation of cowardice enraged Sage, and he vowed that his clerk "would never receive a cent." Although Laidlaw only sued for a modest sum to cover his hospital bills ($25,000), Sage mounted a major legal offensive. The trial lasted seven years and cost Sage more than $100,000. Needless to say, he was victorious. Shortly after the trial, Laidlaw died penniless.

In 1869, aware that it was a social necessity for a man of his stature to have a wife, Sage made a marriage of convenience to one Margaret Olivia Slocum. She was an austere woman whose regal bearing would hide a soon-to-be-revealed heart of gold.

On July 22, 1906, Russell Sage died at the age of ninety years old. Few mourned the passing of the once-powerful Money King.

Now one of the richest women in America, Sage's widow immediately began distributing the tycoon's wealth. To her eternal credit, she was benevolent on an unprecedented scale. In total, she donated almost *all* of her late husband's fortune in just over ten years. Perhaps no woman before or after has so generously dispersed so much of her husband's fortune than did Margaret Olivia Slocum Sage. Of the nearly $50 million dispensed, a significant sum went to the founding of a college in Troy, New York. Fittingly, it is called Russell Sage College.

Grave Location: Sage's massive Parthenon-inspired tomb is located in Oakwood Cemetery in Troy, New York. Enter the cemetery off Oakwood Avenue through the main gate. Make your first major right turn, and you will see his grave site on a small hill to your right between Sections I-1 and K-1. It is one of the largest mausoleums in the cemetery. Several other famous people are buried in Oakwood Cemetery, and the main office can provide visitors with a map to their graves.

Author's Note: It is reported that Sage's widow, fearing that her husband's body would be dug up and held for ransom, ordered bizarre measures to keep grave robbers at bay. The diminutive millionaire was buried in a huge *six-ton* coffin that cost $22,000 and took twenty-five men to lift. A burglar alarm was installed to prevent thieves from entering his tomb.

Factoid: For all its size and grandeur, Sage's tomb is unmarked. It sits anonymously in all its gloomy glory bereft of the Sage family name.

Marie-Henri Winne, the only person perhaps to ever reach the crusty old miser's heart, is buried in a separate grave just a few feet from his tomb.

For More Information: Oakwood Cemetery, www.oakwoodcemetery .org.

Russell Sage College, www.sage.edu/about/mission-history/.

95

MAUREEN STAPLETON

1925–2006

ACTRESS EXTRAORDINAIRE
BURIED IN TROY,
RENSSELAER COUNTY

*A*ctress Maureen Stapleton had a tense, fidgety, kinetic on-screen persona that made her unforgettable. A hit with audiences from a very young age, she was already being featured on Broadway at age twenty-one. Her debut, *The Playboy of the Western World* (1946), was met with glowing critical reviews, and she performed in several other Broadway shows in the ensuing years. In 1951, she received her first Tony Award for Best Actress for her role in the Tennessee Williams classic *The Rose Tattoo*. She would eventually become a six-time Tony nominee.

She made her screen debut in 1958 in *Lonelyhearts*. Even though the drama was top-heavy with well-known actors, including Montgomery Clift, Robert Ryan, and Myrna Loy, it was newcomer Stapleton who garnered a Best Supporting Actress Academy Award nomination. She was later nominated for Oscars for *Airport* (1970) and for her role in Woody Allen's *Interiors* (1978). Although she didn't win the Oscar for any of these performances, she was nominated again in 1981 for her portrayal of anarchist Emma Goldman in Warren Beatty's *Reds*. She won the coveted Best Supporting Actress award for this movie. As her hometown friends and family watched the Oscar telecast that night, one could hear a collective cheer go up throughout the city as the actress announced, "I want to thank Troy, New York, and all my family and friends" to a viewing audience of millions.

Stapleton was a show business legend. In addition to winning Oscar and Tony awards, she was also nominated several times for her work on television. She won the Emmy Award for Best Actress in 1968 for her role in the ABC television movie *Among the Paths to Eden*. Her performances in other nonnominated movies and television performances remain familiar, popular, and sometimes immortal. She was memorable as Mae Peterson in the 1963 film *Bye Bye Birdie* and is remembered fondly her role in the heartwarming 1985 film *Cocoon* (as well as its sequel).

As if to add a cherry to the top of her show business career, she also received a Grammy nomination for her 1975 spoken word recording of the novel *To Kill a Mockingbird*.

The actress's last years were spent in semiretirement in the Berkshires of western Massachusets, where she appeared in a few movies and local productions to raise money for cultural venues in Lenox. She battled alcoholism most of her adult life and was a longtime cigarette smoker. She was eighty when she died on March 13, 2006.

Grave Location: Maureen Stapleton is buried in Saint Mary's Cemetery, 79 Brunswick Road, in her native Troy. Her gravestone can be found in Section R. Curiously, the face of her stone identifies her only as "Mrs. Stapleton."

Author's Note: On December 15, 1981, Hudson Valley Community College in Troy dedicated a theater in Stapleton's honor. The 350-seat Maureen Stapleton Theater is located at the north end of the Siek Campus Center.

Factoid: Maureen Stapleton is one of the most awarded actresses of our time for her work in film, television, and on stage. She was nominated an astounding sixteen times and had eight wins. In 1981, she became the tenth actor to win the Triple Crown of Acting (Oscar, Tony, and Emmy awards). An amazing footnote to this achievement is that in 1959 she had been nominated for all three of these honors in a single year—*The Cold Wind and the Warm* (Tony), *All the King's Men* (Emmy), and *Lonelyhearts* (Oscar). The actress was also famous for her deathly fear of flying. She reportedly turned down several major film roles because they required her to fly to distant locations. She traveled by boat to England to film her Oscar-winning role in *Reds*.

For More Information: Playbill, "Maureen Stapleton," www.playbill .com/person/maureen-stapleton-vault-0000067064.

96

KATE STONEMAN

1841–1925

FIRST FEMALE LAWYER
IN NEW YORK STATE
BURIED IN ALBANY,
ALBANY COUNTY

Kate Stoneman was born in far western New York to a father who was a justice of the peace. She was the seventh of eight children. The family was destined to leave its mark on the United States in several ways. One brother, Major General George Stoneman, was a West Point roommate of General Stonewall Jackson who, unlike Jackson, led troops for the North. As the Civil War was ending, he and General William T. Sherman led successful raids throughout North Carolina and Virginia. These raids were the inspiration for the folk and pop song "The Night They Drove Old Dixie Down." He later served as governor of California. Another brother, Edward, served for many years on the Illinois Supreme Court. Still another brother, John, was a judge and popular politician in Iowa.

Kate Stoneman's path to fame was much more difficult than that of her brothers. She wanted to be a lawyer at a time when there was not a single female lawyer in New York State, nor were there any female students attending law school. She attended college in Albany and clerked for the New York Court of Appeals. She took up many of the women's rights movements of the day and became a celebrated activist. She trained for a legal profession but was repeatedly turned down because of her gender. She agitated for a change in the law that would open the doors to law

school for females, and she prevailed. In 1886, she was admitted to the New York State Bar.

Although Stoneman's formal experience in the field of law was limited to a stint of clerking in a court, she gained fame as an outspoken voice for revisions to the rules that prevented women from entering legal and educational professions. She was fifty-seven years old when she became the first woman to graduate from Albany Law School in 1898. She toured the nation speaking out on issues ranging from international peace to women's suffrage. In 1918, she was able to witness women voting for the very first time in the United States.

She continued to practice law in the Albany area until age finally slowed her down. She died on May 19, 1925, at the age of eighty-five.

Grave Location: Kate Stoneman is buried in Albany Rural Cemetery. You can find her final resting place in Lot 28, on the south side of Section 56. Her marker is near the edge of a large, deep creek bank. It is a simple white stone with her name on the front. There is a special commemorative bronze plaque in front of her grave celebrating her historic achievements. It reads:

> Kate Stoneman was the first woman admitted to practice law in New York State. After training in a private firm, her application to join the bar was rejected because of her gender. She then successfully campaigned to amend the Code of Civil Procedure to permit the admission of qualified applicants without regard to gender or race. Her admission to the New York State Bar in 1886 paved the way for thousands of women and minorities who followed. Ms. Stoneman continued her legal education by attending Albany Law School and in 1898, became the first woman to graduate.

Author's Note: There are many famous people buried in Albany Rural Cemetery, a beautiful, 460-acre site with many hills, winding paths, ponds, and wooded areas. Revolutionary War hero Brig. Gen. Peter Gansevoort is buried in the area next to Stoneman (Lot 1, Section 55).

Factoid: Albany Law School has never forgotten one of its most famous graduates. In 1994, the institution began an annual Kate Stoneman Day celebration in her honor, and in 2000 a visiting professorship was established in her name. In 2009, Stoneman was inducted into the National Women's Hall of Fame in Seneca Falls. Her fellow inductee that year was author Emma Lazarus.

For More Information: Albany Law School, "Kate Stoneman," www.albanylaw.edu/katestoneman/.

97

SAMUEL J. TILDEN

1814–1886

"I STILL TRUST THE PEOPLE"
BURIED IN NEW LEBANON,
COLUMBIA COUNTY

.

$\mathcal{F}$or a man who was a winner most of his life, Samuel Tilden is probably most remembered for an election he lost. And it was a big one, the presidency of the United States. And he lost by a single vote. And there were no hanging chads at the time.

Tilden was born February 9, 1814, in New Lebanon, New York, and would become one of the state's most prominent "political lions." In 1867, as chairman of the New York State Democratic Party, he took on the notorious Tweed Ring in New York City and its onerous leader William "Boss" Tweed. Many thought that Tilden had embarked on a classic mission of political suicide. Tweed had virtually every city official and office holder in his well-lined pockets, and his nefarious influence was felt at every level of state government. Tilden was tenacious in his attacks on Tweed, and through deft legislative maneuverings and a crusade-like devotion to the dethroning of the corrupt leader, he was triumphant in reforming the face of New York City politics forever.

A former New York State assemblyman, Tilden was elected governor in 1875. He was a respected and influential leader in his party's reform movement. Tilden's popularity grew immensely during his term in office, and at the Democratic National Convention in St. Louis on July 27, 1876, he was nominated to be the party's national standard bearer. His Republican opponent was to be another governor, Rutherford B. Hayes of Ohio.

The Hayes-Tilden election of 1876 is still being studied today. One of the bitterest in history, the contest was fiercely fought from one end of the country to the other. On the morning after the election, all signs pointed to a Tilden victory. He held a margin over Hayes in the electoral count of 184–165. He was also ahead in the popular vote by over a quarter of a million votes. Still, the electoral votes in Florida, Louisiana, and South Carolina (and a lone vote in Oregon) were seen as unofficial and could sway the victory to the Republicans. Teams of supporters from both sides streamed into these contested states to shore up their candidate's votes. Threats, subtle and otherwise, were made. Bribes were offered. Payoffs were made. Scandals were threatened. All to keep the electors' votes in line. It was American politics at its worst.

Finally a commission was empowered to settle the dispute. The commission was to be equally divided between the two parties, but at the last moment a Hayes supporter was appointed to a swing seat. In a vote strictly along party lines, the commission decided by a vote of 8–7 that Governor Hayes was the winner of all the disputed electors, thereby giving the

Republicans the White House. Tilden continued to hold a 250,000 vote lead in the popular vote, even after the election was officially over.

Ignoring pleas to run again in 1880 and in 1884, Tilden retired from public life and spent his final years amassing a huge fortune from his varied business interests. He died on August 4, 1886.

Grave Location: Samuel J. Tilden is buried in one of the most magnificent crypts I have ever seen. His plot is in the center of the beautiful Cemetery of the Evergreens, 382 Cemetery Road, in his hometown of New Lebanon. Drive through the main gate and you will see his huge tomb on a rise straight ahead. Four white marble stairs lead up to his ten-ton marble sarcophagus. With its grand lion heads and intricate funereal carvings, it is stunning in its Victorian era beauty. Across the top are chiseled the words: "I STILL TRUST THE PEOPLE."

Author's Note: New Lebanon is truly in the heart of Shaker Country, and I recommend a visit to any of the popular Shaker sites near Tilden's grave. The Cemetery of the Evergreens is only minutes from the Shaker Museum at Old Chatham, New York, and the Shaker Village at Hancock, Massachusetts. New Lebanon was the original home to the United Society of Believers in Christ's Second Appearing (Shakers), and their museum has an ever changing program of exhibits, speakers, demonstrations and events. The North Family Site at Mount Lebanon Shaker Village was recently designated as one of only six sites in the United States on the World Monuments Watch List of 100 Endangered Sites because of its significance, its urgent need for preservation, and the viability of the plan to meet that need.

Factoid: Tilden was a lifelong bachelor and had no children. At the time of his death his estate was valued at over $6 million, and with no immediate family he bequeathed much of his fortune to the establishment of the first public library in New York City.

For More Information: National Park Service, "Samuel Tilden Biography," www.nps.gov/gate/learn/historyculture/samuel-tilden-biography.htm.

98

PRESIDENT MARTIN VAN BUREN

1782–1862

EIGHTH PRESIDENT
OF THE UNITED STATES
BURIED IN KINDERHOOK,
COLUMBIA COUNTY

*M*artin Van Buren was born December 5, 1782, in Kinderhook. He remained a presence there for all of his seventy-nine years. He occupied almost every major political position in the US government during a long career spanning a half century. He was elected a state senator of New York (1812), New York attorney general (1816), US senator from New York (1821 and 1827), governor of New York (1828), US secretary of state (1829), vice president under Andrew Jackson, and finally president (1837–1841). He held positions in the highest levels of government at a crucial time for our nation—a period of expansion and growth as well as a time of great turmoil and tumult.

His life was long and fruitful. He was born near the end of the American Revolutionary War and died during the Civil War. Although diminutive in stature (standing only five feet six inches tall), he was a towering figure on the national political scene and cut a wide swath through the halls of power both in Albany and in Washington.

While he was president, he purchased a thirty-six-room mansion in his hometown to use as a residence for the rest of his life. This home, Lindenwald, is today under the care of the National Park Service and is open for tours.

Van Buren died of pneumonia on July 24, 1862, at his home in Kinderhook.

Grave Location: Martin Van Buren is buried in the Kinderhook Reformed Church Cemetery on Albany Avenue just a few blocks from the small downtown business district. His tall obelisk can be seen from the highway. A New York State historical marker denotes the final resting place of the man known as Old Kinderhook. This small Columbia County village is proud of their most famous native son.

Author's Note: There are six US presidents born in New York State. Four are buried in Upstate New York, while two rest eternally Downstate (Theodore Roosevelt on Long Island and Ulysses S. Grant in New York

President Van Buren was known as Old Kinderhook. Many political supporters formed "OK" clubs in his honor. It is believed that the common expression of OK, meaning everything was fine, comes from the OK Clubs formed for our eighth president. Courtesy of the Metropolitan Museum of Art, David Hunter McAlpin Fund, 1956.

City). Most presidents are buried with great fanfare in grand tombs or in elaborate grave sites. Van Buren's final resting place is one of the most unassuming presidential graves of any former chief executive.

Factoid: President Van Buren has a couple of quirky notes in his factoid file. They are great for fans of presidential trivia. He was the first president born in the United States—that is, *after* the signing of the Declaration of Independence. He is also the only US president who was raised in a home where English was not the major language spoken. His family spoke only Dutch until he learned English as his second language when he attended a local public school in Kinderhook. He was also the first New Yorker to become president.

For More Information: National Park Service, "Martin Van Buren National Historic Site, Lindenwald," www.nps.gov/nr/travel/presidents /van_buren_lindenwald.html.

99

CAPTAIN WILLIAM VAN SCHAICK

1837–1927

"VINDICATED!"

BURIED IN TROY,

RENSSELAER COUNTY

One of the most tragic and forgotten disasters in American history is the fire aboard the steamboat *General Slocum*. This disaster claimed more lives than any other American event until terrorists struck the World Trade Center on September 11, 2001. And yet few have heard of it.

On June 14, 1904, more than 1,300 parishioners of St. Mark's Lutheran Church, a landmark on Sixth Street in New York's Lower East Side, gathered along the shores of the East River to board the *General Slocum*, a 235-foot-long paddle wheel steamboat for an afternoon outing to Locust Point, Long Island. The church had chartered the 265-ton boat for $350. Most of those on the outing were mothers and their school-age children celebrating the end of Sunday school for the year.

The throng filled every inch of the boat from stem to stern. Oompah bands played German favorites, and families in their proper Sunday best laughed and visited with friends and neighbors. The sky was blue, and the weather was perfect.

As the boat headed north up the East River, near Ninetieth Street, the first sign of trouble appeared. Smoke began billowing up from a corridor where apparently a fire had been festering in the boat's Lamp Room. People began inching away from the smoky area and waited for the crew to extinguish the fire. They waited and waited as the fire grew in intensity. The captain of the boat, William Van Schaick, was not notified for a full

eight minutes of the trouble below deck. By the time he was called to the scene, the blaze was out of control and panic had gripped the *Slocum*.

With orange flames chewing their way along the wooden decks, people began donning the more than three thousand life preservers. Tragically, the floatation devices had long lost their usefulness, and the buoyant cork inside them had disintegrated into dust. Those who had strapped on the lifesavers soon sank to the bottom of the river, weighed down by the heavy layers of finery and the thick boots and shoes they were wearing. Fire hoses were unrolled and manned by crew and passengers alike. The hoses, never having been used before, burst upon the first pulse of rushing water and were useless, having rotted with age. The lifeboats were fastened to the ship and could not be used. The passengers were doomed.

The *Slocum*, completely ablaze and shrouded in smoke, could clearly be seen by the bystanders along the shore. Those onlookers screamed for the ship to dock on the west shore of the river, the nearest point. Captain Van Schaick, however, realizing the potential for an even greater disaster should the shoreline oil storage tanks meet up with the flaming ship, proceeded up river for another mile. He headed for North Brother Island, through the treacherous currents of Hell's Gate. By the time the ship ground its way to shore, it was a charred ruin, listing badly, with burned bodies strewn everywhere. The final death toll was an astounding 1,021. The captain survived.

The *General Slocum* had passed an inspection just a month before the tragedy. Questions needed to be answered, and blame needed to be assigned. Captain Van Schaick became the lightning rod for the anger and grief of the thousands of family members looking for a scapegoat to punish. He and officials of the Knickerbocker Steamship Company, the parent organization, went on public trial. The captain was the only person convicted. He was found guilty of criminal negligence and manslaughter. He was sentenced to ten years in prison and was delivered to Sing Sing Prison in Upstate New York to serve out his term.

Van Schaick had a long career as a trusted sea captain and always felt that he had done his best to avert an even greater tragedy that fateful day. He truly believed that by making his decision to bypass the shoreline and try to reach North Brother Island he was acting to save as many lives as he could. An inquest was formed to study the case, which later ruled that it was the steamboat company's lack of inspection guidelines that had led to so many deaths. Van Schaick was vindicated after serving nearly half his sentence. He was pardoned by President William Howard Taft and released from prison.

Grave Location: William Van Schaick is buried in Oakwood Cemetery, located at 50 101st Street in Troy. His stone is very small, and can be found in the center of Section S1. "Uncle Sam" Wilson (chapter 100), Russell Sage (chapter 94), and other famous figures are interred in Troy's Oakwood Cemetery. Their graves are noted on the cemetery maps available at the main office.

When Van Schaick died on December 8, 1927, he was buried in an unmarked grave. In 1999, his grandniece erected a small stone over his final resting place in Oakwood Cemetery. It reads: "Captain William Henry Van Schaick, 1837–1927. VINDICATED!"

Author's Note: Many people are familiar with the Triangle Shirtwaist Fire of 1911, seven years after the *General Slocum* fire. In that tragedy, 146 young Irish immigrant girls died because greedy business owners had locked the doors of their high-rise sweatshop, thereby sealing their fate when fire broke out. Much speculation is offered as to why this fire, terrible as it was, is more embedded in our memory than the more calamitous *Slocum* fire.

One school of thought has it that the German victims of the boat fire grew less and less sympathetic as World War I approached in Europe. Others feel that the Irish girls who leapt to their deaths in the factory fire made for a more heartbreaking tale in that their deaths were caused by a direct act of greed by their bosses. As one *Slocum* survivor said, "The Triangle girls were overworked and oppressed. We were just on a family picnic." In any case, two similarities grew from dual disasters. Both spawned major overhauls in safety regulations in their respective fields. The factory fire brought on sweeping changes in workplace safety rules. The *Slocum* fire ushered in an age of stricter safety regulations in the steamship business.

An amazing outcome of the *General Slocum* fire was the immediate change it brought to the German neighborhoods of the Lower East Side. Once a thriving, productive community of more than eighty thousand nationals, the German population there was almost totally wiped out within one census period. For the surviving German families, fond memories of their community were all but eclipsed by hundreds of funerals, buildings draped in black bunting, lines of dozens of hearses, and an entire school emptied forever of its young students. Most moved out of this sad area, leaving it for the next wave of immigrants.

Factoid: A year after the *General Slocum* fire, a large memorial to the victims was unveiled at the Lutheran Cemetery in Middle Village, Queens. Many of the fire's victims are buried here. Little Adele Liebenow, just an infant in 1904 and the youngest survivor of the *Slocum* fire, had the honor of ceremoniously pulling the flag off the monument, revealing it to the large crowd assembled, which included many other survivors. On January 26, 2004, Adele died at the age of one hundred. At the time she was the last living person who was on the ship that fateful day.

For More Information: New York Public Library, "General Slocum Disaster of June 15, 1904," www.nypl.org/blog/2011/06/13/great-slocum -disaster-june-15-1904.

Oakwood Cemetery, Troy, www.oakwoodcemetery.org.

100

SAMUEL "UNCLE SAM" WILSON

1766–1854

THE REAL UNCLE SAM
BURIED IN TROY,
RENSSELAER COUNTY

*S*amuel Wilson is a man whose concocted image is as vivid to all Americans as perhaps any other personage. Regardless of what he actually looked like, we eternally envision him as a tall, lanky man with a wispy white beard. His sleeves are usually rolled up, and he is posed as if standing up for America. He is almost always dressed in his familiar red, white, and blue suit and tall top hat. Yes, Samuel Wilson *is* America!

Well, maybe.

The real Uncle Sam was born Samuel Wilson in Mason, New Hampshire. After serving as a drummer in the Revolutionary War, Sam and his brother Ebenezer *walked* west from New Hampshire to Troy, New York, where they went into the meatpacking business. By the time the next great war came along—the War of 1812—Sam Wilson was one of the leading military meat procurers in the Northeast. It has been retold over generations that Wilson would stamp his barrels of meat with "US" for United States. One time, a contingent of military contractors visited Wilson's meatpacking plant in Troy and, with tongue in cheek, asked a worker what the US stood for. Put on the spot, the worker replied, "Uncle Sam," his hard-working, honest, and reliable boss. The story stuck, and thus the legend of Uncle Sam was born.

It wasn't until one of America's foremost illustrators drew up the now iconic image of Uncle Sam that the myth really took off. James

Montgomery Flagg was the first to depict the familiar figure of Uncle Sam. Flagg placed this image on the cover of the popular *Leslie Weekly* magazine on July 6, 1916, to accompany a feature titled "What Are You Doing for Preparedness?"

This illustration became the well-known "I Want You" army recruitment poster, and between 1917 and 1919, four million posters were sold. Flagg called it "the most famous poster in the world." Later it was taken out of mothballs for World War II, and the poster again became extremely popular.

In a nation so steeped in symbolism, it is a rare treat to be able to actually go and visit the grave site of one who inspired such a symbol. While we know that there really was a Paul Revere and a Betsy Ross, it is also important to know that there was a real Uncle Sam and that he is honored with a memorial at his grave in Troy. And how do we separate the "real" from the "myth"? Well, let's let Congress sort it out for us.

On September 15, 1961, this notice was entered in the Congressional Record: "Resolved by the Senate and the House of Representatives that

This towering aluminum statue of Uncle Sam in Troy's Riverfront Park is just one of many to the city's patriotic icon. Statue by George Kratina.

the Congress of the United States unanimously salutes Uncle Sam Wilson, of Troy, New York, as the progenitor of the America's national symbol of 'Uncle Sam.'"

Grave Location: Samuel Wilson's grave is one of the most visited of any in Upstate New York. He is buried in Troy's Oakwood Cemetery, located on Oakwood Avenue directly across from Frear Park. Small roadside signs provide directions from the cemetery entrance to Wilson's grave. There you will find several historical markers and commemorations of Wilson and his legacy. For years a local Boy Scout troop has raised and lowered an American flag at his grave site. Visitors can stop at the cemetery office to get a map of the many famous people buried in this cemetery.

Author's Note: Troy was once the center for shirt collar production in the 1800s. It led the nation in manufacturing of shirts, detachable collars, shirtwaists, and shirt cuffs, which earned it the moniker Collar City.

More recently, Troy has adopted the more chamber-of-commerce-friendly nickname Birthplace of Uncle Sam. A casual ride around Troy will take you by a multitude of businesses that carry the name Uncle Sam in their title, from laundromats to coffee shops to florists.

Factoid: When James Montgomery Flagg presented an original "I Want You" poster to President Franklin D. Roosevelt, he remarked that he had been so broke when he drew the now-famous poster that he used himself as a model to save on modeling fees. FDR replied, "I congratulate you on your resourcefulness, Mr. Flagg. By saving on your modeling hire, your method suggests our Yankee forebears."

For More Information: Rensselaer County Historical Society, www .rchsonline.org.